Systematic
Planning
for
Educational
Change

William G. Cunningham

Old Dominion University

Systematic Planning for Educational Change

 Mayfield Publishing Company

This book
is dedicated to
Jerry, Margret, Gail,
Sandi, Mike & Kerri.

They help shape
all that I do.

Library of Congress Catalog Number: 81-84692
International Standard Book Number: 0-87484-551-3

Manufactured in the United States of America
Mayfield Publishing Company
1240 Villa Street, Mountain View, CA 94041

Sponsoring editor: Judith Ziajka
Manuscript editor: Kathleen MacDougall
Designer: Nancy Sears
Illustrator: Pat Rogondino
Cover designer: Paige Johnson
Compositor: Acme Type
Printer and binder: Bookcrafters

Contents

Part 3
The Future

Appendix A

Appendix B

Foreword

This book appears at a time when the concept of educational organization as linear systems, and related concepts of rational planning models, are rapidly becoming unfashionable. Studies of educational administrators reveal that, all too often, their behavior is characteristically reactive rather than proactive: they tend to initiate little but, instead, spend much of their time responding to problems and events brought to them by others. Indeed, they tend to spend much of their time dealing with rather mundane matters—presiding over meetings with relatively unimportant agendas and generally being engrossed with the minutiae of running their organizations—to the virtual exclusion of focusing on powerful leverage-points of action. In addition, a great deal of attention is being given to such characteristics of educational organizations as uncertain and ambiguous environments, nonrationality of organizational structures, and goals that are diffuse, unclear, overlapping, and often conflicting. Thus it is increasingly popular to describe educational organizations as loosely coupled systems, clans, and organized anarchies.

At the same time, however, a growing body of research literature suggests that effective schools tend to exhibit a cluster of specific organizational characteristics. These include effective leadership by the school administrators, clearly stated goals, definite standards of behavior and performance, high expectations for achievement and success, a climate that is not only orderly but supports productive, achievement-oriented behavior. In the jargon of the day we hear references to "the principal principle" to emphasize the newly understood importance of the leadership of the principal in developing schools that are not failures but, rather, are seen as effective. But exhorting a school administrator to be a more effective leader avails little. To improve their leadership behavior, school principals, superintendents of schools, and deans of colleges as well need guidance as to *what* behaviors are likely to strengthen their leadership—especially during the hard times that educators now face. This book should do much to meet the critical need to provide that kind of knowledge.

In this book, Professor Cunningham first describes and discusses important different contemporary perspectives for viewing and understanding planning. These include theoretical models, various approaches to the processes of planning, and the influence of important contextual realities. He then presents a wealth of well-organized material on a wide range of techniques and procedures for implementing planning in the practice of educational administration. The presentation is replete with numerous careful descriptions of illustrative examples taken from educational settings. The result is a state-of-the-art textbook well grounded in sound contemporary scholarship yet one that provides a great deal of specific information that can be used by educational administrator's confronting real problems in practice.

As one who has particular interest in a human resources management approach to educational administration, I am particularly impressed with one distinctive feature of this book. That is the care with which Professor Cunningham seeks to link processes and technologies with the human dimension of the organization. The literature on planning, goal-setting, and prioritizing typically stresses the technology that may be used; scant attention is often given to the human factors involved in the situation. Yet, as many practicing educational administrators will testify, human factors are frequently critical in the success or failure of rational planning systems. In this book, however, we find serious attention to issues and techniques such as the management of participative methods and the use of organization development. Surely now, when all organizations—including the corporate giants of the private sector—are awakening to a fresh understanding of the essential link between the management style used in dealing with people on the effectiveness of the organization, the focus on human factors is a significant feature in a book such as this.

Systematic Planning for Educational Change is an important and timely book that, I feel sure, will be welcomed as a useful contribution both by those who teach administration and by those who practice it.

ROBERT G. OWENS
Indiana University

Preface

We know what we are but not what we may be.

-SHAKESPEARE

Inherent in the administrator are many of the skills necessary for successful planning—personality, vision, intuition, and wisdom. However, there is a growing body of systematized knowledge about process, context, theory, structure, tools, and techniques of planning that will improve the administrator's chance of accomplishing his or her organizational and individual goals. Administrators who lack intuition and vision tend to become technicians; but those who lack systematized knowledge become dreamers. Both are likely to fail.

Educators have sometimes failed to reach their desired and eloquently stated purposes because they were unable to deal with the complexities of planning, making decisions, and implementing change itself. Although these failures affect everyone, the ultimate losers are usually the students.

The tools and techniques discussed in this book offer today's best answers to the problems of planning for and implementing educational change. The key technique is to use a balanced, systematic approach that recognizes the political, economic, behavioral, and structural realities of the educational change process—from the concept to the consequences for those affected by the plans. Although the book is grounded in theory and research, it is a practical text and provides many tools that administrators will be able to use immediately in their own school districts. The kinds of pitfalls and problems that arise in real life are discussed, and some of the best methods for avoiding and recovering from these problems are analyzed.

The book has been specifically designed to serve two major audiences. The first is the student of planning and change in educational organizations. This is not a well-disciplined field; although there is relatively strong agreement on the terrain that must be covered in planning courses, there is relatively little agreement on the focus. So, for example, course titles suggest a wide range of focuses—systems approach, application of administration theory, educational planning, planned change, planning and management technology, policy planning and analysis, organizational change, dynamics of planned change, management science and technology, and futurism and planning, to name a few. This book is comprehensive in that it covers the terrain and leaves open the possibility for idiosyncratic differences in emphasis.

Although most of the examples deal with public school administration, the concepts, tools, and techniques described in this book are appropriate for college and university, community college, adult and continuing education, and private school administration.

The second audience to which the book is directed is the professional administrator who needs to review and keep abreast of the latest developments. The book presents a number of tools—planning process, context, and theory; participation, group process, and communication in planning; management by objectives; function line-item budgeting, planned programmed budgeting, and zero-base budgeting; task planning, Gantt charting, and program evaluation review technique; committee, nominal group, and Delphi techniques; decision making and decision-tree analysis; organizational development and team building; computer and management information systems; and planning for the future—these all have the potential for greatly improving one's skills as an educational planner and agent for change. The book should help practicing administrators to sharpen their approaches to organizational planning and change efforts and to develop their professional administrative abilities. Ultimately the understanding and implementation of such skills should improve educational direction and culture, especially in turbulent times.

Balance and thoroughness have been prime objectives in the development of this book. Only those administrative tools and techniques that have received considerable attention and been credited with much success are included. The book quotes many of the experts in the field and aims for a balance of theory and practice.

The book is organized into three parts: one on theory with appropriate citations and references; the second on tools, techniques, and examples; and the third, a concluding chapter on future needs in education. The first part, "Process and Theory," places the process and context of planning and change efforts into perspective and presents the historical and theoretical background needed to evaluate the techniques described in the remainder of the book. The second part, "Tools and Techniques," develops the major component structures of the planning and change process. This part is the heart of an integrated system for planning and implementing change within educational organizations. The conclusion stimulates the reader to think about the future as part of the planning process. One is asked to stretch beyond what is to what could be. The usefulness of the second two sections is more in their analytical concepts—the way of thinking about planning and change—than in the formal structure of the tools and techniques described.

ACKNOWLEDGMENTS

For their insights into the administrative process, I wish to thank the many practitioners and scholars on whom this book is built; their work is cited throughout the book. I must also thank here some of the many people who have directly influenced my professional life. I want to thank Donald Walker, now at Indiana University of Pennsylvania, for giving my professional life direction and support; William G. Katzenmeyer, Duke University, for helping me put together an educational program that gave me the base I needed; and Willis D. Hawley, Vanderbilt University, who showed me how to begin putting my knowledge to work. I would like to thank Dennis Rich and John C. Watts, of Goodyear Tire and Rubber Company, for providing me with the challenges of difficult planning and administrative tasks, and support and assistance in their completion.

Special thanks should go to Robert G. Owens, Indiana University; John Hoyle, Texas A & M University; Bruce Cooper, Dartmouth College; Gilbert Hentschke, University of Rochester; and Dale Mann, Teacher's College, Columbia University, all of whom showed a relative stranger a great deal of encouragement regarding the initial development of this book.

I also owe a great debt of gratitude to John Kohl, Montana State University, Robert Larson, University of Vermont, and Perry Johnson, Virginia Polytechnic Institute and State University, who read the entire manuscript and provided valuable suggestions and feedback. Perry Johnson's knowledge of planning is extensive; he provided especially valuable input to this book and is the sole author of Chapter 4, "The Planning Context." Special input was provided by Robert H. MacDonald, Old Dominion University, on planning and group process; Joseph Mooney, Old Dominion University, on management by objectives; John M. Hoben, Plymouth-Canton Community Schools (Mich.), on a planning model; Nolan Estes, University of Texas–Austin, on computer information systems; Walter Gant, Yorktown Public Schools (Va.), for material on the Delphi technique; and Dwight Allen, Old Dominion University, and John

Hoyle, Texas A & M University, both of whom played a major role in the development of the chapter on educational futures.

Many secretaries were helpful in the preparation of this manuscript and its revisions. Particular thanks go to Sharon Kennedy, Chris Webster, Cindy Spear, Audrey Webster, Norma Russel, and Donna Wallace for their excellent help.

I would like to thank my father, Gerard J., and mother, Margaret M., and my sister, Gail Penn, for their continuing interest and support of my work. Last and most of all I would like to thank my wife, Sandi Lee, and our children, Michael S. and Kerri B., for the happiness and love we were always able to exchange even during this time-consuming effort. I hope you find the book worthy of the greatness of the people who have had such strong influences on me. Part of each is in this work.

W.G.C.

Part 1

Process and Theory

Process
Theory
Context

1

The Planning Process

In the battle of life it is not the critic that counts; not the man who points out how the strong man stumbled, or where the doer of a deed could have done better. The credit belongs to the man who is actually in the arena; whose face is marred by dust and sweat and blood; who strives valiantly; who errs and comes short again and again because there is no effort without error and shortcoming; who does actually strive to do the deeds; who knows the great enthusiasms, the great devotion, spends himself in a worthy cause; who at the best knows in the end the triumph of high achievement; and who at the worst, if he fails, at least fails while daring greatly, so that his place shall never be with those cold and timid souls who have tasted neither victory nor defeat.

—THEODORE ROOSEVELT

The most widely accepted description of the management process was propounded by Henri Fayol in the early 1900s. His five basic functions appear in most basic texts of management regardless of whether the books are directed toward educational, business, urban studies, or medical administration. Fayol's now famous and generally accepted functions of management are planning, organizing, commanding, coordinating, and controlling (Fayol, 1949).

Although there is much debate as to which of these functions is most important in determining managment success, there is much agreement that planning is the foundation upon which the other four functions rest. This is presented graphically in Figure 1-1. Administrators need the understanding and direction provided during the planning process if they are successfully to carry out the remaining four functions.

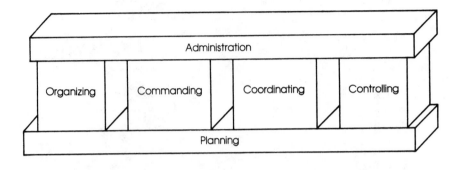

FIGURE 1-1
The Five Functions of the Administrator

As navigators soon learn, points of fixed reference such as "navigation by the stars," "the sun," or some other point is essential to purposeful and safe travel. Any helmsman heading to home port soon learns the devastating effects that wind and sea currents have if needed course adjustments are not made in reference to a fixed navigation point. This is equally true for administrators. Without a planned direction and policy limits for acceptable organizational behavior, the administrator has no reference points upon which to "fix" the course of organizational behavior. The organization begins to falter, pushed this way and that by haphazard events.

Planning provides the fixed points of reference upon which all the other dynamic elements of the administrative process can be founded. It is the mechanism by which a system adapts to and implements change. Planning establishes the basis for intelligent direction, cooperation, and adjustment. Knezevich states that "the dynamic environment confronting organizations, the need to identify and define emerging roles for the organization, and the need to relate organization to various environmental systems make the planning function critical as a matter of high priority" (Knezevich, 1975, p. 29).

PLANNING: A DEFINITION

The purpose of planning is to provide a bridge between useful knowledge and purposeful coordinated action. Planning is used to gain control of the future through current acts. By means of planning, administrators look ahead, anticipate events, prepare for contingencies, formulate direction, map out activities, and provide an orderly sequence for achieving goals.

Fayol (1949, p. 36) believed the most important instrument of planning was the "plan of operation," which contained the "object in view, the course of action to be followed, the various stages on the way, and the means to be used." Planning for Fayol was the act of foretelling or preparing for the future. Luther Gulick explained planning as "working out in broad outline the things that need to be done and the methods for doing them to accomplish the purpose set for the enterprise" (Gulick and Urwich, 1937, p. 21). Edward Banfield (1959, p. 17) presented a much narrower definition of planning as "the process by which he [or she—the administrator] selects a course of action [a set of means] for the attainment of his ends. It is 'good' planning if these means are likely to attain the ends or maximize the chances of their attainment."

Plans have been used to serve various purposes within organizations. They provide goals that sometimes serve to give direction. Some also provide a schedule that specifies the hierarchical process and the intermediate steps required to achieve an outcome. Planning creates a precedent in that it gives direction to and limits the freedom of decisions that must follow. In this way plans reduce a complex world to a somewhat simpler one.

Planning can be defined as selecting and relating knowledge, facts, images, and assumptions regarding the future for the purpose of visualization and formulation of desired outcomes to be achieved, sequential activities necessary to achieve those outcomes, and limits on acceptable behavior to be used in their accomplishment. Planning typically brings about some needed and agreed-upon changes that are designed to correct or improve in some fashion the existing situation. It is through planning that organizations justify their existence and through performance that they maintain their right to continue to operate.

THE BENEFITS OF PLANNING

Change is the rule, not the exception. It may be sudden and extensive, or it may be slow and almost imperceptible. However, things do not remain constant and changes often give rise to problems that confront administrators. By anticipating the future, administrators can prepare for needed changes and mitigate some outcomes that might be considered undesirable. Planning helps administrators to be better prepared to deal with both foreseen and unforeseen problems. Planning is a tool for adapting to an exciting new innovation, for resolving conflicts, improving old approaches, upgrading existing quality, improving communication, and achieving many other desired outcomes. However, planning is much more than any of these since it facilitates problem-solving capability.

Morphet, Jesser, and Ludha (1972, p. 31) suggest that while educational change is bound to happen, desirable educational change must be made to happen. They suggest that changes will occur with or without planning. However, by anticipating probable developments, administrators can prepare to facilitate needed changes and to avoid some that might be harmful. Appropriate planning procedures make it possible to identify maladjustments or deficiencies that are causing, or are likely to cause, educational problems, and thus enable those in decision-making roles to determine in advance what adjustments are necessary.

Planning promotes the use of measures of performance. Since it is quite clear that the public is increasingly demanding more accountability from schools, measurable results are of great value to educators. The planning process allows both for the establishment of predetermined and agreed-upon outcomes or results and for the development of measures to determine the success of the organization in achieving those results. Administrators can determine if deviations from the planned course of events demand a change in strategies or perhaps a change in goals or priorities. Some discrepancies require the modification of activities and operations or increased efforts, while others indicate an opportunity for success that was not originally seen. However, without knowledge of desired outcomes and measures of performance, administrators are likely to disregard the unexpected and to persist in the wrong course of action or to miss major opportunities. In fact, no plan at all is perhaps more disastrous than a poor plan. At least a poor plan might be corrected once its shortcomings are discovered when someone attempts to apply it.

Organizations are often forced by unforeseen events to move from one crisis to another, performing what is called reactive planning. In reactive planning the administrator solves one crisis after another in much the same way a fireman fights fires. Each crisis creates new direction, new activities come to the forefront, and others are usually ignored until they reach a crisis point. It is called reactive planning since the administrator is reacting only to internal and external information that deviates from the norm.

A school principal operating under this approach would allow abnormal activities to schedule his or her workday, workweek, and year. Louis Panush, in an article entitled "One Day in the Life of an Urban High School Principal," presents a poignant example of this approach to school administration. Panush spends his entire day dealing with one abnormal activity after another without any idea what his day is going to be like. Panush ends (1974, p. 49) by asking: "Just what role did I play today? What role do I play on many other similar days? What provisions are there for me, as for many, many other principals in large urban schools, to use our talents, educational background and know-how, thoughts and energies to do the job that principals are for?"

Most criticism of reactive planning is directed at the total organizational and individual frustration that results when only crisis and abnormal situations get the attention of administrators. When planning is reactive as opposed to proactive, the organization becomes drained and loses vitality, creativity, and often effectiveness.

This decrease in organizational satisfaction and effectiveness can be reduced through proactive planning. The number of crises decrease and the quality of the adjustments increase as proactive planning is improved. Without the benefit of a sound planning process, administrators must rely heavily on traditional methods (preserving what is working now), standard operating procedures (coordination by standardization), stability (changes create greater possibility of pressing problems), and short-term survival and maintenance. Such organizations try to maintain the status quo since the planning process does not provide the stability needed for innovation and adjustment. Organizational safety, security, and status seem to take precedence over the welfare of the client since the organization lacks the guidance and common understanding that established plans provide. Proactive planning does not allow the organization to control completely what will happen to it, but it does increase control, allow for refined and appropriate reactions, and provide the security for administrators to think more flexibly and to adapt better long-range solutions.

Planning also offers significant opportunities for developing and maintaining individual growth. Andreas Faludi has cogently argued this point. He states that human growth occurs through planning and its related consciousness:

> Nevertheless, even planning efforts that lead to no action may still result in human growth. This is because the rational planning process forces one to make assumptions explicit about one's self, one's environment, and how one relates to it, and it to one's self. In doing so, these thoughts become cast into an ordered argument, thereby improving awareness of the structure of what I shall term the action space, and the way its structure relates to preferences held. Ultimately, because in planning one must reflect on one's goals, it also increases awareness of one's self.
>
> Awareness thus results from deliberation made during the process. It is improved as a result of feedback concerning the effects of action on the environment. Overall, the result of engaging in rational planning is therefore learning, including self-learning, and hence an increase in the capacity to attain future growth. (Faludi, 1973b, pp. 49-50)

In general, planning compels the administrator to visualize the whole operation and enables those in the organization to see important relationships, gain a fuller understanding of tasks and activities, prepare for needed future activities, make needed adjustments, and appreciate the basis upon which organizational activities are supported.

THE PLANNING PROCESS

Planning is not an automatic process. Practitioners and scholars alike have spent much time developing models to stimulate effective planning (Bolan, 1969; Brieve, Johnston, and Young, 1973; Friedman, 1967; Howard and Brainard, 1975; McConnell, 1971; Naylor, 1977; Stuart, 1976). These independently developed models are amazingly similar. Although there is much disagreement regarding theoretical approaches to planning, there is significant agreement on the major steps of the planning process itself.

Robinson's 1972 compendium on planning shows that there is a good deal of agreement as to what the steps of the planning process should be. Harris (Robinson, ed., 1972, p. 9) states that "the well-established paradigm of the planning process" requires the establishment of purpose, the formulation of alternatives, the prediction of outcomes, the evaluation and selection of alternatives, and finally implementations. In his classic book *The Systems Approach*, W. C. Churchman states:

> We can discern the essential ingredients of a plan as the planner understands the term. A goal is set, a group of alternatives is created, each alternative is scanned as to whether it will or will not effectively lead to the goal, one of the alternatives is selected, the plan is implemented, and the decision maker checks to see how well the plan worked. The last piece of information will be needed to control the operation of the plan, as well as to plan better in the future. (Churchman, 1968, p. 147)

The link between knowledge and action develops best when the planning process is built directly into the management system. When plans are developed outside the management system as written documents—say, six-year plans—to be used for reference, they stimulate thinking about future desired outcomes but they seldom stimulate action (Larson, 1980). Administrative planners must have vision, intuition, and commonsense to determine where the organization is required to be and how it can best get there. But unless their visions are built into the job itself, the link between knowledge and action never develops. At best, such a planning system codifies good intentions. We all know people who have vision but no follow-through—we call them dreamers. We often hear them discussing "work in progress" that never seems to get completed and complaining about "the total inability to get anything accomplished in this school system!" Organizational planners who do not have an action-oriented planning process are condemned to ineffectiveness.

Vision, however derived, demands realization in some concrete form. Perhaps Bushnell (1969) makes the strongest case for more action-oriented planning systems:

What is needed is a more massive and coordinated approach to educational reform, where piecemeal efforts are linked together with considerable time and attention given to development of coordinated strategies for bringing about desired changes. To be successful, further innovations must not only be discussed in terms of what is to be changed but also in terms of how the change is to take place. Dewey, Kilpatrick and even such contemporaries as Conant have failed to achieve their often eloquently stated objectives because of their failure to cope with the complexity of the change process. Perhaps for the first time a new approach to arraying goals and strategy which can assist decision makers in analyzing choices open to them and preparing better ways for coping with the change process is now in the offing. (Bushnell, 1969, p. 46)

This new approach builds the planning process into the entire management system.

Figure 1-2 presents a model of an action-oriented planning system. Although the background needed for planning is unique to each organization and setting and is acquired only by working within the organization, the process for planning can be generalized. The planning model illustrated in Figure 1-2 is similar to one suggested by Russell Ackoff (1970, 1974), which is based on four planning stages: (1) *ends planning* or the process of determining goals, objectives, and policy; (2) *means planning* or the selection of methods of execution; (3) *resource planning* or the process by which we obtain the necessary resources (raw materials, money, manpower, etc.), and (4) *organizational planning* or the process by which we give shape to and improve mutual relations between people and groups. Ackoff classifies ends planning as a strategic concern and means, resource, and organizational planning as tactical or operational concerns.

The planning process developed in this book revolves around eight key questions:

1. Where are we?
2. Where do we want to go?
3. What resources will we commit to get there?
4. How do we get there?
5. When will it be done?
6. Who will be responsible?
7. What will be the impact on human resources?
8. What data will be needed to measure progress?

The answers to these eight questions have to be cast in a form that will stimulate purposeful activity. Such answers can appear as descriptions of needs, challenges, capabilities, and opportunities in the internal and external environ-

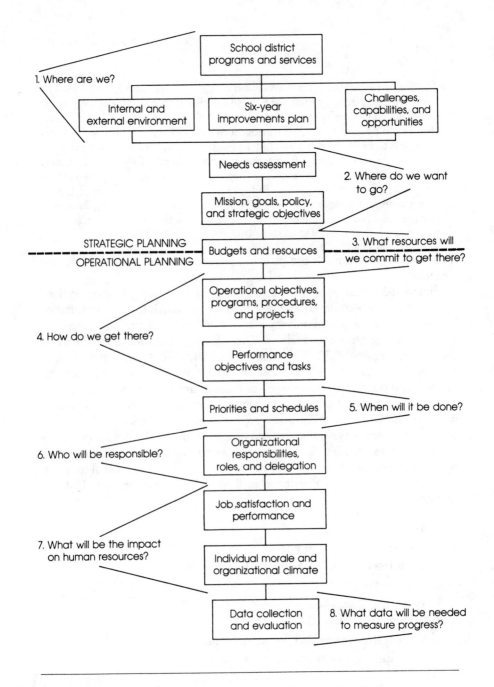

FIGURE 1-2

The Planning Process

Source: Plymouth-Canton Community Schools, Michigan. Reprinted with permission.

ment; as strategic budgetary, and operational plans; and as assessments of progress. The remainder of this book discusses the components of this planning process and the tools for refining it.

GUIDELINES FOR PLANNING

1. Plans are needed if organizations are to accomplish desired outcomes efficiently and effectively.

2. Plans reduce individual and organizational stress by providing direction and increasing control over present events. Employees should not be concerned about organizational direction on a daily basis but should be able to direct their creative talents toward the implementation and ultimate success of organizational activity.

3. In order to obtain staff commitment and coordination, all organizational planning requires a model that is widely known and well understood by the members of the organization.

4. Planning efforts must be divided into two types—strategic and operational. Strategic planning is required to provide long-term direction regarding all organizational activity and to ensure that the organization is doing the right things. Operational planning is required to ensure that resources are used correctly so that desired results are achieved in the best manner possible. Both strategic and operational planning have their own unique questions that must be answered if the organization is to operate properly.

2

Strategic and Operational Planning

The task of "deciding" pervades the entire administrative organization quite as much as the task of "doing." . . . A general theory of administration must include principles of organization that will insure correct decision-making, just as it must include principles that will insure effective action.

—HERBERT A. SIMON (1960)

The two major types of planning are strategic planning and operational planning. Strategic planning is seeing that the organization is doing the right thing; operational planning is ensuring that the organization is doing things right (see Figure 2-1). Strategic planning is defined as the process of deciding on objectives for the organization, on changes in those objectives, on the resources used to obtain objectives, and on the policies that are to govern the acquisition, use, and disposition of the resources. Strategic objectives are directed toward long-term survival, future resources, future potential, and flexibility and adaptability to changing conditions. Strategic objectives are future directed, usually are client oriented, and are directed at external needs. Strategic plans determine the character and direction of the organization and are often based on value systems.

Operational planning is the process by which administrators ensure that resources are obtained and used effectively and efficiently in the accomplishment of the strategic objectives. Operational planning focuses on present resources, operational problems, and stability. It is concerned with measurable, verifiable objectives. Operational objectives are usually program-, project-, and staff-oriented and are directed at required internal activity and outcomes. Operational plans are designed to obtain the desired ends with a minimal or efficient use of organizational and societal resources using methods that stay within policy constraints.

BOTTOM-UP PLANNING VERSUS TOP-DOWN PLANNING

For the planning process to work correctly, strategic plans must be developed and made final prior to developing and implementing operational plans. Operational plans should not be developed first with the intent of imposing strategic plans on top. Operational plans developed in this way reflect narrow interests and self-serving ventures, typically fail to elicit cooperation, and are often inconsistent. Higher-level administrators are then forced to refine and blend together operational plans into so-called strategic plans. This upward flow causes the top planning team to modify and refine operational plans rather than develop coordinated strategic plans.

Operational managers view the refinement, modification, and blending of operational plans as meddling into their affairs by top-level administrators. They often become discouraged as the plans that they spent some time developing and refining are cut up and changed for what they often see as arbitrary reasons. Planning that begins at lower levels—the bottom-up approach—usually results in frustration as lower-level administrators see their plans ignored or chopped up because plans do not meet the strategic goals top-level administrators see as important. This is a no-win situation since operational plans must be modified to eliminate fragmentation if a unified plan is to be achieved. Resource constraints can also force modifications in plans. Thus the whole planning effort ends up being viewed as a sham by operational personnel who come to have a lack of respect for the planning process and to see the central administration as autocratic and interferring.

Besides causing human relations problems, the bottom-up approach to strategic planning is not effective since top-level administrators who lack an understanding of day-to-day operations modify operational plans in ways that often make them very difficult to implement. The major objective is to consolidate and coordinate the plans received, and therefore central-office planners are neither aware of nor concerned with unique operational problems and constraints. Again, operational personnel who see their plans changed to meet strategic needs at the expense of operational needs begin to view the whole planning process skeptically. At the same time, top-level administrators lose confidence in the ability of lower-level managers to develop acceptable plans. There is a lack of commitment to the planning process that results in division,

STRATEGIC PLANNING

"Doing the Right Things"

Mission, goals, change, development

OPERATIONAL PLANNING

"Doing Things Right"

Operations, performance, results

FIGURE 2-1
Types of Planning

conflict, and an ineffective planning system. This results in a growing distrust between central-office staff and school-building staff—each blaming the other for organizational problems.

Table 2-1 highlights some of the differences in the perspective of principals, supervisors, department heads, and the superintendent, school board, and central-office management staff. Table 2-1 suggests that lower-level operational managers, concerned with day-to-day operations, do not have the background and perspective needed to develop strategic plans. Usually such managers focus most, if not all, of their attention on getting the work done correctly and keeping the organization on track. Such a focus is not conducive to the high-risk, flexible thinking needed for effective strategic planning. However, such managers are well prepared to develop operational objectives if given some

TABLE 2-1
Differences in Perspective

	OPERATIONAL PLANNING PRINCIPALS, SUPERVISORS, DEPARTMENT HEADS	STRATEGIC PLANNING SUPERINTENDENT, SCHOOL BOARD & CENTRAL OFFICE STAFF
Focus	Operating problems and realities	Longer-term survival and development
Objective	Present performance	Future school system success
Constraints	Present resources/ school environment	Future resources/desired system-wide environment
Rewards	Efficiency, stability	Development of future potential, flexibility
Information	Present teacher, parent, and student reaction/facts	Future community, state, and federal desires/values
Organization	Bureaucratic/stable	Entrepreneurial/flexible
Leadership	Conserve that which succeeded in the past	Inspire change for future needs
Problem solving	React, rely on past experience, standard operating procedures	Anticipate, find new approaches, creative ideas to meet future challenges
	Low risk	Higher risk

Source: Modified from Igor Ansoff et al., 1976, p. 12.

kind of strategic guidance. On the other hand, school board members, superintendents, assistant superintendents, and the like are usually not well prepared to make operational plans. Their day-to-day activities do not prepare them for operational considerations. They are concerned with long-term survival, future resources, meeting the needs of various interest groups, and developing creative ideas to meet future needs. They are aware of diverse value systems that work in the strategic environment. They are not aware of key operational problems, unique student–teacher–parent–community blends, school attitudes, facility and equipment constraints, work loads, and many other aspects of the operational environment.

People in the central office tend to overlook the pressing operational problems or imbalances in work loads with which day-to-day operational personnel are most familiar. For example, top-level administrators might modify an operational objective to state that all teachers of reading in K–7 will cover an average of one unit per week using the Ginn C360 series. This is an operational objective and should be established by teachers, supervisors, and principals under the guidance of some kind of strategic objective that refers to "coordination and pacing of the reading program throughout the school system." The explicit operational objective as developed by the central office might put undue pressure on both teachers and students to attempt the impossible. It may not be reasonable to expect teachers and students to cover a unit a week every week—and the supervisors, principals, and teachers are in the best position to know this. In addition, most school-level personnel want to have input into the specific performances they will be expected to implement and upon which they will be evaluated.

Although the superintendent and planning team do not have the details needed for operational planning, they are the only ones with the perspective to develop effective strategic plans. This makes it especially inappropriate for the strategic planning team to be forced into devoting its time and effort into blending methodologically uncoordinated and narrowly defined operational plans into a strategic system. Central-office managers usually focus most of their attention on the political, economic, and social forces acting upon the school system and on the search for maximum support of future efforts. Such work is not conducive to the type of thinking needed to plan day-to-day operational activity. However, such administrators are well prepared to develop strategic objectives needed to provide direction to all future operational activities. Central-office administrators, because they are disengaged from present operating problems and the daily routine, have the perspective required for effective strategic planning.

The logical conclusion is to split the planning function. The authority and responsibility for strategic planning and decision making is placed with top-level administrators. The strategic planning process, the first part of the planning function, serves as a guidance system for the second part, operational planning. The responsibility for the second part is placed with line administrators, who are concerned with how best to carry out operations and develop operational plans that implement strategic plans. Steiner found that:

> There is a trend in a number of large companies to break up the corporate planning staff into two groups—strategic planning and operational planning. . . . IBM, Xerox, and W. R. Grace, for example, found it advantageous some years ago to separate strategic and operational planning. General Electric recently went through a major top-level staff reorganization to separate the strategic from the day-to-day operational planning. All in all, it seems that this type of organizational shift will speed up and become more typical in companies in the future. (Steiner, 1970, p. 138)

The split of the planning process has continued throughout the 1970s and into the 1980s.

Although there is still considerable debate, both research and experience suggest that the planning process works best when it flows from top to bottom. Strategic plans developed at the top more appropriately meet the long-term survival and development needs of the organization, while operational plans that are coordinated and focused by strategic plans better meet the operational realities that school administrators and teachers must face on a daily basis.

> The need for coordination of planning at different levels is too obvious to require discussion. But what is not obvious is that a corporate [strategic] plan should not be an adjusted aggregation of plans prepared by divisions, departments, or other parts of the organization. Plans prepared by sub-units for aggregation at the top tend to be propaganda for a larger share of organizational resources. To be sure, effective corporate planning requires planning in every part of the organization, but it should be coordinated methodologically and conceptually from the top. (Ackoff, 1970, p. 46)

The top-down approach is less likely to be viewed cynically, since there is much less need to modify or change plans developed at the operational level. The top-down approach eliminates the need for major modifications due to incongruous goals and lack of perspective that often occurs when bottom-up plans are reviewed by top-level administrators. The review process still occurs, but because plans are coordinated, much less modification is required. This results in a quicker, more efficient planning process and one that is more believable for all involved. It is not easy in any form of organization to obtain the required coordination of planning efforts; however, coordination is best achieved when strategic plans, made at the top, are used to guide operational plans developed by subunits within the system.

Without a specific and defined strategic goal it is impossible to develop coordinated and consistent operational objectives. People will naturally gravitate to supporting and fighting for their own pet interests, which are often quite different from one another and sometimes even conflicting in nature. If unguided, fragmented operational plans are coordinated and consolidated at the top in order to develop the strategic plan, fragmentation, lack of coordination, general confusion, and often conflict will result at lower levels. Principals and teachers will become discouraged with the planning process when they find their conflicting conceptions being modified to fit into bottom-up strategic plans. The only other bottom-up alternative is asking all operational personnel to rework their plans in some way until they are consistent—often a discouraging and time-consuming endeavor. Thus, the best approach is first to develop strategic plans under the direction of top-level administrators and then to use these strategic plans to guide the efforts of operational personnel in the development of operational plans. This is known as the top-down approach to planning.

FINANCIAL RESOURCES

It is impossible to discuss planning without discussing budgeting, for the school budget is an expression of the school plan in fiscal terms. A good budget will present a proposed plan for a school district, the expenditures necessary to support such a plan, and the anticipated revenue to cover such expenditures. These three parts are often referred to, respectively, as the strategic plan, the expenditure plan, and the revenue plan.

The strategic plan, which includes strategic goals and objectives, is created through an ongoing process of administration and should be clearly defined prior to the beginning of the budgetary process. The expenditure and revenue plans provide input for ongoing operational planning. However, if the budget does not support the strategic plans, the linkage between operational and strategic planning will not develop. This usually greatly weakens the effectiveness and usefulness of the entire planning process.

Although it is traditionally thought of only in connection with controlling, budgeting is an important part of planning. Budgets tend to define in advance a set of fixed commitments and fixed expectations. Although budgets can be flexible, they cannot help but result in the specification of a framework within which the school will operate, evaluate its success, and alter its programs.

The school budget draws heavily on the strategic planning that has gone on within the school system. In fact, the budget is an aggregate of the strategic plan with an estimate of the receipts and expenditures necessary to finance the operational activities required to carry out the strategic plan. No amount of operational planning can make up for inadequate resources; however, good operational plans must take into account what resources are likely to be available and use them to the system's best advantage.

Strategic planning provides school systems with specific direction regarding future action. That direction is expressed in terms of mission, goals, strategic objectives, and policy related to desired long-range outcomes. Strategic planning provides coordination and direction for operational planning. However, the strategic plan does not by itself define the scope of operational activity. It is during the budgeting process that the scope of the following year's activity is defined.

The budget refines the broad strategic plan into more exacting specifications of required, or at least funded, action. Obviously the quantity and quality of programs suggested by a strategic plan can vary greatly; it is during the budgeting process that this quantity and quality is largely determined. In addition, because operational plans are either supported or constrained by decisions made during the budgeting process, general budgeting constraints should be developed before too much effort is expended on the development and refinement of operational plans. Just as responsibility expands or shrinks to fit authority, operational activity expands or shrinks to fit resources available. How successfully and how extensively a strategic objective will be accomplished is based on the level of financial commitment made to that strategic objective. Morphet, Johns, and Reller make this point quite clearly:

> Once the educational program is agreed upon, estimates can be prepared indicating the probable costs. The word "costs" is used deliberately, because there are different costs for different levels of quality in many components of the educational program. Therefore, several alternative budgets and sub-budgets should be prepared before the final budget is adopted. These alternative budgets will show the additional costs necessary to provide additional services or a higher quality of services. (Morphet, Johns, and Reller, 1977, pp. 467-477)

The moment of truth comes each year with the compilation, scrutiny, and eventual approval of the budget. Any strategic plans that have not been budgeted will seldom be started and, if started, are not very likely to succeed. Most operational objectives also stand or fall on the basis of financial commitment. Thus the budget adds the dimension of feasibility to the strategic plan. Feasibility is determined as allocations of resources are made among the various strategic objectives. The end result is the budget.

The strategic plan plus the budget are the guidance system upon which operational plans can be based. Wasted effort and staff discouragement develop if operational plans are found to be totally out of line with resources available for commitment to the achievement of a strategic objective. An example of this problem occurred when secondary school principals, departmental chairpersons for vocational education, and vocational education supervisors were asked to develop a comprehensive operational plan for a new strategic objective to "determine needs for, develop, and expand a system-wide program of adult and community education using innovative instructional methods, improved program delivery, and more effective operational and administrative systems so as to better meet the needs of the adult population over the next five years." The principals, chairpersons, and supervisors met to rough out an operational plan and to select a task force to develop a comprehensive plan to submit for budget approval.

The task force devoted approximately 200 manhours (much of it overtime) collecting data, formulating ideas, and developing a final operational plan including cost estimates. In addition to the time expended by the task force, there were a number of group meetings and a large amount of time expended by secretaries. The plan was rushed to meet budgetary time constraints so it would be available prior to budgetary consideration. But then, in examining financial resources available, the budget committee, with input from the city-wide financial staff, realized that all strategic plans could not be funded for the following two years and decided that the adult and continuing education program duplicated services already being offered in the community. For financial reasons, the task force's entire plan was scrapped after having only been given very cursory examination. Since the plan was never resurrected, all the effort and time devoted to it were wasted. This resulted in a great deal of animosity among those who participated in the project and a lack of confidence regarding the planning process in general and certain administrators in the school system in particular.

The real culprit, of course, was inappropriate sequencing of the planning process. The budget was not used to define the scope of activity required at the operational level. In fact, a very rough transition plan (from strategic to operational) with some refined cost estimates was all that was necessary to make budgetary decisions. The full operational plan was premature and developed on the basis of a strategic plan unsupported by any financial commitment.

Many similar examples can be found. For example, heavy commitments of operational manpower are often invested in plans for state mandates that later are not funded and therefore are impossible to implement. Hence, the importance of using both the strategic plan and the budget in the development of operational plans becomes more pressing during times of fiscal restraint and retrenchment.

Strategic objectives developed during the strategic planning process are refined during the budgeting process. In the previous section, careful distinction was made between strategic objectives and operational objectives; however, in actuality there is a fuzzy line between these two processes. The budgeting process fits somewhere between these two planning processes and becomes the point where strategic planning ends and operational planning begins. George S. Odiorne, author and consultant, has been involved in developing planning systems for both business and public organizations. Odiorne is an outspoken critic of planning systems that place detailed operational planning prior to strategic and budgetary planning:

> Timing is of the essence in goal-setting. Those objectives which are multi-year in character need to be stated before the budget allocations are decided, not after. Those of an operational character can be stated at the beginning of an operational period after the budget allocations and not before. The best planning in government will probably have two sets of objectives, one long-range set stated prior to budgeting or resource management, and a second or short-range set after the budget is decided. (Odiorne, 1976, p. 29)

It is only through the top-down sequence that the planning process can be both efficient and effective. To recapitulate, the flow begins with strategic planning, followed by budgeting, followed by operational planning and finally by task planning.

HUMAN RESOURCES

Another important aspect of the planning process is the impact that plans have on employee attitudes, job satisfaction, organizational climate, and, ultimately, individual performance. Effective planning must go beyond strategic, financial, and operational consideration if the carefully laid plans of the organization are ever to become a reality. Problems are often caused not by a lack of strategic, budgetary, or operational support but by a lack of commitment from those who are to carry out the plans.

Planning problems typically develop during implementation when individual and group conflicts begin to emerge within the organization. Strict control mechanisms such as close supervision can reduce such behavior problems slightly. However, there is reason to believe that such supervision has limited effectiveness (Argyris, 1978; Blake and Mouton, 1964, 1978a; Halprin, 1971; Hemphill and Coons, 1957; Lewin, 1948; Likert, 1967; McGregor, 1960). In addition, it is especially time consuming and expensive when used to control behavior. There is nothing more important to planning than committed people, and commitment does not usually increase with control. Chris Argyris states:

> I believe that any human organization—no matter what its goals—which intends to utilize people as components must, in its design, take into account the nature of the human personality. The more the individual is ignored, the greater the probability of dysfunctional consequences that will lead to expensive ineffi-

ciencies. I further believe that this proposition is especially true for any social system designated to facilitate human growth. (Argyris, 1967, p. 154)

Human personalities link all components of the organization and make the accomplishment of plans a reality. An adage explains this point: "Proper organization will allow common people to accomplish uncommon things." Clearly, planning must contribute significantly to the improved utilization of human resources and the ultimate release of human talent if it is to achieve its true purpose. More and more, the planning for and incorporating of human resources is an important part of the total planning process.

The quality of an organization—how it is structured, how it operates, how it gets things done—determines how well the organization does and how its people feel about their jobs. The manager's responsibility is to develop organizational conditions that most effectively meet both the needs of the organization (the plans) and the needs of the employees (Mills, 1978).

Administrators must consciously be aware that there will come a time when existing organizational structure and interpersonal relations will no longer suit the evolving goals, objectives, and financial resources of the organization. Resulting structural and interpersonal problems are often expressed in destructive ways when points of reference become outdated, authorities and responsibilities no longer seem to be clearly defined, relationships within units and between units become distorted and strained, and irrelevant activities and information seem to increase. Such difficulties manifest themselves as frictions between individuals within a department and between departments; as duplicated or neglected tasks; as confused lines of communication; in managers who see the organization and procedures as a hindrance to the achievement of objectives; and in supervisors who interact poorly with their subordinates—in short, in a general lack of coordination. Assuming that plans have been satisfactorily developed, such conditions warn of the need for adjustments within the work group, the individual, or both.

Efficiency is usually doomed if the individual and his or her work group remain static during the implementation of plans. The planning process must include a concerted effort to obtain real commitment. This requires some formal process by which the needs of the individual and the group are built into the planning process.

COMMUNICATION

Planning works best when it begins at the top and flows to the bottom. Communication works best when it is not one-directional but multi-directional, flowing up, down, and across. Rensis Likert (1967) calls this phenomenon the linking pin theory of organization. The linking pin theory describes an organization as composed of small groups linked by individuals called "linking pins"—members in one group and leaders in another. Through linking pins, multi-directional communication is supported by multiply overlapping group structure.

As was discussed in the section on planning sequence, the superintendent, assistant superintendent, and board members are in the best position to have the attitude and perspective needed for strategic planning. However, all too often, top administrators find that new strategies are frustrated because they cut across established operational values and attitudes within the organization. Unless operational administrators have an opportunity to be involved, to have input, and to see the broader perspective, there is little likelihood that strategic plans will be supported. Without broad participation and communication, the experience, ideas, and values of operating managers will not be utilized fully in strategic planning and so the stimulus to thinking that results from interactions between managers will never fully be realized. However, once input on strategic plans has been heard, debated, and digested, decisions must be made, and this is the responsibility of top-level administrators and board members.

It follows then that operational planning should be made by operational administrators with the support of top-level administrators and the advice of teachers. It is as important to have teachers involved in operational planning as it is to have operational administrators and principals involved in strategic planning. This top-down planning with multidirectional communication forges the link, in this case between plans and actions, that will result in the final conversion of useful knowledge to purposeful coordinated action.

Thus, a planning process in which plans flow from the top down does not mean that communication regarding the development of those plans has to flow downward from a central control. The top-down approach to the planning effort does not mean one-directional communication. In fact, the planning effort may be unsuccessful if all communication flows downward only. Planning will have a better chance of success if each administrative level charged with the authority and responsibility for making and deciding upon plans, establishes procedures by which those who are going to have to participate in the subsequent action required to carry out those plans have had an opportunity to express their own views and hear the views of others. Then when a decision is finally reached by top-level administrators, the entire organization will understand it, even though large groups within the organization may not necessarily agree or would have preferred a different decision. In this way, employees have an opportunity to air their views, to find out where their colleagues and associates stand and what they believe in, and, most important, to determine if decisions reached seem to be in the best interest of all involved. It is through multidirectional communication and top-down planning that all of these conditions can be met simultaneously.

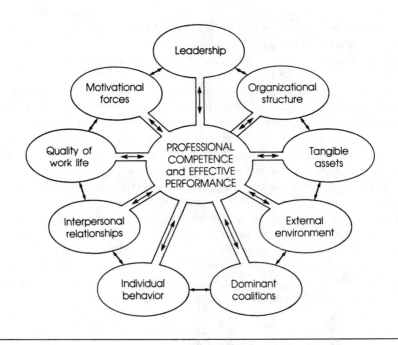

FIGURE 2-2

Factors Influencing Professional Competence
and Effective Performance

PROFESSIONAL COMPETENCE AND EFFECTIVE PERFORMANCE

Planning is the most important of all the administrative functions since it is the foundation upon which all others rest. The planning process is used to marshal all of the knowledge and wisdom within the organization into an effective plan of action. Figure 2-2 presents factors of effective organizational behavior. Effective plans and effective performance require that each of these factors be appropriately planned for and balanced with each other. The planning process provides the structure within which administrators can best utilize their knowledge and provide the direction, stability, and calming influence that are needed to guide the organization.

Planning is needed in both calm and stormy situations if the organization is to best serve its purpose. Educational administrators are faced with many difficult problems, such as decreased funding, inflation, mainstreaming, social promotion, falling test scores, weak curriculum, attendance problems, discipline problems, declining enrollments, integration, accountability, teacher militancy, teacher stress, teacher burnout, community control, and declining respect. In fact, some believe that the very foundation of the educational system is beginning to erode. There are good reasons to believe that schools of the future may not even resemble schools as we know them today. It is through the planning process that the transition to new futures is made. And it is good planning that allows this to happen with minimal effort and distress and with maximum results. Today's administrators must be better prepared than they have ever been before if they are to meet the growing challenges.

In this century society has become a knowledge society. Educational administrators must have a proven system of planning that will allow for the integration of useful knowledge and purposeful action. The dynamics and interdependencies of today's educational organization have increased so much that without a common starting point to hold the administrative functions on a stable course, administrators will become lost in the complexity and sheer number of variables with which they must deal. An ever-tightening economic picture, along with increased demand for accountability, adds further impetus to the requirement of applying defensible approaches to planning.

GUIDELINES FOR PLANNING

1. The planning process should flow from the top down, with central-office management and the school board responsible for strategic plans, and staff, school-building management, and classroom management responsible for operational plans. However, communications regarding the development of plans must be multi-directional, flowing up, down, and across.

2. The operational plans should not be made final until after resource commitments have been made. The budgeting process determines the scope of and commitment to strategic objectives and determines the level of operational activity possible.

3. Effective planning must go beyond strategic, financial, and operational considerations to obtain a commitment from those who are to carry out the plans. Of and by themselves, goals and objectives are seldom a good motivator of people unless they are part of a systematic planning process.

4. A systematic planning process marshals the knowledge and wisdom within the organization into an effective, coordinated, and supported guide to organizational action. A good plan and quality people will result in effective organizational competence and performance; the absence of either will result in organizational failure.

5. The case for basing decisions upon a systematic plan rests on the importance of challenging preconceived notions and providing common articulation and documentation. A systematic plan provides the administration with a clearer perception of the problems and opportunities faced. In this century our society has become a knowledge society and so educational administrators must have a set of shared perceptions that will allow for the integration of knowledge with action. An ever-tightening economic picture, along with increased demands for accountability, adds further impetus to the refinement of the educational planning process.

3

Planning Theory

Give a man some fish and he may live for days.
Teach a man to fish and he will live a lifetime.

Only in the last decade has formal planning in U.S. public education been considered a serious and professional endeavor requiring an academic specialization. Much has been learned in that time, especially in the technique and technology of planning, but even as the methodologies are being refined, the assumptions, both in terms of planning theory and the organizational values that support planning, are undergoing fundamental changes. However, such changes in planning theory have more of an influence on the perspective of the individual who is involved in planning than they do on the planning process itself.

Planning requires a more or less permanent structure in order for it to be made operational. This book examines many of the structural considerations needed to support the planning process. The comprehensiveness of the planning structure and the importance that is assigned to it are determined by one's assumptions about how planning should be carried out—that is, by one's theoretical approach to planning.

Planning theory helps to explain how the individual decision-maker selects a course of action. Planning theorists basically look at the questions of why a planner chooses one set of actions over another. Theories are then tested by following decision-makers through the planning process to see how well theories actually explain planning behavior.

THE RATIONAL-COMPREHENSIVE MODEL

Virtually all discussions of planning begin with the rational-comprehensive model. This model is not only the benchmark against which others are measured, it is also the clearest way to contrast what we do and don't know. At the core of the rational-comprehensive model is a set of methods designed to prepare information in such a way that decisions related to future outcomes and actions can be made through rational deliberations. Ideally, the rationality is achieved by: (1) clear establishment of an objectively defined set of goals; (2) the statement of all possible alternative modes of action to achieve those goals (alternatives are developed through a means–ends analysis); (3) the evaluation of alternative courses of action (a comprehensive analysis that includes all relevant factors); and (4) the selection of the alternative that optimizes the set of goals (the most appropriate means to a desired end).

In planning, a rational-comprehensive approach would require the planner to reconstruct the options, events, probabilities, and values that are believed to be related to the "final" selection of a particular action. The final plans, decided upon by the administrator, are the result of a conscious choice among alternatives. Advocates of this type of planning say that all conceivable courses of action must be identified and evaluated against all relevant ends. Faludi (1973b, p. 155) defines the rational-comprehensive model of planning as the approach "whereby the programmes put forward for evaluation cover the available action space and where the action space has itself been derived from an exhaustive definition of the problem to be solved." The crowning glory of the rational-comprehensive approach is that one "optimizes" the decisions available. The planner always selects a set of solutions that maximize the possible outcomes for the organization. The decision-maker makes a conscious effort to eliminate or at least minimize the number of alternatives available to, but unconsidered by, the organization.

It is not easy to trace the major influences on the concept of comprehensive rationality. Although some of the concepts were first suggested by early administrative and organizational scholars such as Taylor (1923), Weber (1947), and others, it was Herbert Simon who in 1947 first thoroughly articulated the rationality model and discussed its related problems (Simon, 1976). Martin Meyerson and Edward C. Banfield's (1955) case study of public housing in

Chicago found the realities of planning sadly deficient, when measured against Simon's model of pure rationality. James March and Simon collaborated in a monumental study of all that was then known about organizations and organizational behavior (March and Simon, 1959). The book dealt only in part with planning per se, but it was a significant part, much more sophisticated than Simon's 1947 venture, reflecting a decade of work by numerous contributors to the theory of planning and decision making.

March and Simon took a more moderate position than in the 1947 model; in their 1959 work they advocated "satisficing," rather than comprehensive rationality, as the principle of choice. To satisfice is to do "well enough," but not necessarily "as well as possible." The level of attainment that defines satisficing is one that the decision-maker is willing to settle for—it is the best available and therefore "well enough." March and Simon believed that "optimization" continued to be a desirable goal in principle but unattainable in the ordinary course of events. They state:

> The basic features of organization structure and function derive from the characteristics of human problem-solving processes and rational human choice. Because of the limits of human intellective capacities in comparison with the complexities of the problems that individuals and organizations face, rational behavior calls for simplified models that capture the main feature of a problem without capturing all its complexities. (March and Simon, 1959, p. 169)

They described this more moderate approach to planning as "bounded rationality."

March (1962, 1973, 1978) provides a very lucid discussion of decision making in organizations in his more recent work. He describes a model of decision making called "resolution"; it is one where the most participation and the largest investment of time and resources are spent in developing solutions to problems. It most closely resembles the comprehensive-rationalist approach except that "satisficing" replaces "optimizing," the problem situation itself is the source of possible actions and consequences, solutions are selected from possible actions, solutions deal with only parts of problems, and solutions are only loosely coupled together. Such solutions remain within the idea of bounded rationality but are predominantly analytical—the manager is trying to come up with the best solutions possible to the problems being faced. Examples of "resolution" decisions in education occur in the areas of integration, special education, and discipline, where possible actions have to be taken within the environments educators control.

In the resolution model of planning, preferences and actions are discovered more through chance events that enter the problem space for one reason or another than action being based on preferences that the planner has carefully evaluated and selected as being the best or optimal course of action. The goals of the school system become problematic in that administrators have choices that are limited by the problems the district is facing. The problems themselves bound the planning space and reduce the complexity of the decision-making process.

Such decision boundaries can be carried to extremes, where decision-makers actually encourage or create problems so as to reduce the possible problem space and to simplify the planning process. A superintendent might sense a developing uneasiness within the school environment and decide that the existing curricular and instructional strategy is outdated and ineffective and needs to be studied and completely updated or that existing evaluation procedures are faulty and need to be modified. This strategy might focus attention on a smaller, more manageable problem space. Everyone becomes concerned about the smaller, more manageable problem and loses sight of the bigger, more complex problem.

March also sees solutions being used to bound the problem space. Administrators look for (or create) problems to fit their solutions. March sees organizational planning as "a collection of choices looking for problems, issues and feelings looking for decision situations in which they might be aired, solutions looking for issues to which they might be the answer, and decision-makers looking for work" (Cohen and March, 1977, p. 81). People think up solutions and then try to find a problem that can be solved with the solution. March uses the term "choice opportunities" to describe this situation. He suggests that "choice opportunities," "solutions," and "problems" all churn around together during the planning and decision-making process. One is reminded of the opportunism displayed by many grant-seeking school districts as they search federal programs for problem areas to which they can apply their solutions and obtain funding.

March also talks about decisions being made by oversight. Oversight is depicted as a decision made by distraction, where in focusing on one problem something quite unexpected develops into a solution. Thus, oversight decisions occur when the organization, preoccupied with the wrestling among various choices and problems, falls into a solution that has much broader ramifications than the original choices and problems being addressed. Because of the distraction, an oversight decision may quickly be omitted, although of course it may not even be attached to a problem. Such choices often appear to just "happen." For example, some school districts have discovered middle schools, magnet schools, or futuristic schools where the problem receiving attention in the district was school desegregation. In actual practice, these solutions are only indirectly related to the original problem, and in fact address a broader, possibly more important problem issue—quality education for the masses.

THE DISJOINTED-INCREMENTALIST MODEL

It is only a short step to Charles Lindblom's (1959) famous description of the planning and decision-making process as a "science of muddling through." He suggested that comprehensive rationalism was a romanticized view that needed to be debunked. Basically, "muddling through" is the recognition that we have limited time, intelligence, and information and therefore are forced to work on only small segments of a problem at a time. The administrator must do a great deal of muddling and on the basis of his or her own and others' perceptions, visions, and experience must choose the correct moves at the strategic time. Muddling advocates argue that comprehensive rationalism does not compensate for the opportunity cost (for resources such as time, money, or man hours) used in planning that could be allocated to some other program or administrative effort.

Braybrooke and Lindblom (1963) and Lindblom (1965) both discuss the shortcomings of rational-comprehensive planning and outline an alternative model called disjointed incrementalism. At the core of the disjointed-incrementalist model of planning is the concept of continually building upon the current situation, step-by-step and by small degrees. Its supporters argue that it is the "art of the possible" as opposed to the "art of the ideal." These critics of rational-comprehensive planning consider it neither possible nor desirable to perform comprehensive evaluations during the planning process.

Faludi defines the disjointed-incrementalist model as "planning where the programmes considered by any one planning agency are limited to a few which deliberately do not exhaust the available action space, and where that action space is itself ill-defined" (1973b, p. 155). Lindblom argues that to plan rationally distracts decision-makers from more feasible approaches related to existing practice. The planning space is bounded by what is already being done. He does not suggest that rational choices should not be made, but only that the range of alternatives included and the range of ends considered should always be limited to increments from existing practice.

Disjointed incrementalism is based on these arguments: (1) values, goals, and the empirical analysis of needed action are not distinct from one another but are deeply intertwined; (2) since means and ends are not distinct, means–ends analysis is often inappropriate or limited; (3) the test of a "good" plan is one that is based on agreement on the appropriate means to an agreed-upon objective; (4) analysis is limited and normally subjective in that possible outcomes, potential alternatives, and many affected values tend to be neglected; and (5) the final proof of the effectiveness of planning is whether plans are accepted and/or implemented. This suggests that one should limit alternatives to a handful similar to present actions for which information is available, for which well-understood ends are clear, and for which one can obtain popular support.

In disjointed incrementalism, planning is always related to an existing base and only small changes are made to that base. Alternatives must be adjacent to the existing reality before they enter the problem space for consideration. A piecemeal or incremental approach is taken in solving the problem, which tends to decrease the likelihood the problem will ever be solved. (If you continue to take an increment from one point to another, you theoretically—and possibly actually—will never get there.) However, the planning space is reduced and much of the complexity is removed from the planning process. Comprehensive rationalists do not see this as planning but merely as fine tuning of an already functioning mechanism. Perhaps Dale Mann best puts this concept in perspective:

> The remedial orientation counsels that the purpose of policy is not to Achieve Goodness, or to Eradicate Evil, but merely to keep things together and hopefully improve them—some. Freud captured the remedial orientation when he said, "Much is won if we succeed in transforming hysterical misery to common unhappiness." The remedial decision maker sets modest expectations for his decisions. (Mann, 1978, p. 47)

Since this model of decision-making tends to preserve the core of the organization, it has for its friends and allies all who are benefitted by that organization. It is argued, however, that such systems put a heavy-to-impossible burden on proponents of substantial change. Such an approach to planning does not provide opportunity for significant changes; there are built-in resistances that help to hold down the size of incremental changes. In addition, such incremental decisions may stand in the way of problems that are not well addressed by the organizational base. The relation between problems and incremental changes is complicated. For this reason, new organizations sometimes come into existence to solve problems that existing organizations should have been able to deal with. For example, the recent push in education for voucher plans may be an attempt to induce or encourage larger incremental changes in schools.

In a sense, disjointed incrementalism is diametrically opposed to rational-comprehensive planning. Upon its appearance in the literature in 1965, Lindblom's model was widely criticized for its presumed lack of concern with structural considerations. This model was believed to preclude extensive change during a period when radical change may be needed. The organizational status quo tends to be protected because traditional alternatives are regarded as the ones to be relied upon in decision making. Some argue that a survival strategy is employed and a survival syndrome permeates the organization. The attitude these critics deplore may be summarized as "if we can do it and it gets us closer to what might seem desirable, then let's do it." Decisions are made on the basis of what is politically feasible rather than on what is ideal or most desirable.

OTHER MODELS

These two approaches to planning and decision making are of course not the only theories or organizational analyses that explain one's approach to the planning process. However, they are the most often mentioned and debated. It would be impossible to present all of the theories and debates regarding planning and decision making. (They extend from politics, through business and policy science, and into ethics.) However, a few of the basic premises of other decision theories can be discussed.

Some theories stress the enormous complexity of the planning and decision-making process, where planners must juggle many decisions, dealing with each intermittently while attempting to develop some integration among them. Others see the decision-making process as the alignment of competing interests. Some view planning as bounded or confined in scope to relatively "safe" issues. Safe issues are usually defined as those that will be acceptable to some person or group. Sometimes plans are developed by manipulating dominant values, attitudes, and thinking. Decisions can be based on "grooved thinking" or standard responses even to problems that diverge more and more from a standard set. Some argue for nondecision, or deciding not to decide. Nondecision allows events to happen; afterwards, they are described in some systematic fashion as a decision or plan. (This is *post factum* analysis rather than goal-oriented decision making.)

Each of these and many other modes of planning and decision making can be used to bound rationality during the planning process. The question of which are realistic or best suited to the planning process is the subject of major and unresolved debate; while not ignoring the debate, this book takes the stand that the more rational the planning process, the more desirable are its outcomes. This will provide structures for better preceiving and evaluating all such approaches in actual practice.

Any review of planning theory shows that the debate has not been focused or reduced but rather has been expanded. As a result, some have tried to develop a synthesis or eclectic approach. Amitai Etzioni has proposed a "mixed scanning" model as a synthesis of rationalist and incrementalist planning (Etzioni, 1967). Mixed scanning provides particular procedures for the detailed "rationalistic" examination of some sectors—which, unlike the exhaustive examination of the entire area, is feasible—with a truncated "incrementalist" review of other sectors. Other critics have suggested that the rationalistic approach is more appropriate for strategic planning (where the planner has greater freedom for change) and that the incrementalist approach should be used in operational planning (where existing practices are so important and where planning is moving from what exists to what is desired (as defined by the strategic plan).

Dror (1968) describes six types of rationality, one of which is the classical or "pure" rationality and four of which constitute "adjustments for reality" and technological improvements within the pure rational paradigm. The sixth rational model Dror terms the extrarational; he includes in it the hunch, the guess, the "feel" for what is the right decision. The extrarational is of interest here for even though Dror does not discuss its organizational implications, it is clear from his discussion that intuition plays an important part in many decisions. Predictive models of any sort under any conditions ultimately depend upon subjective judgments; the more uncertain and unstable the environment, the greater the necessity to rely on something other than the pure rational paradigm.

INTUITION AND THE PLANNING PROCESS

Without the clear vision or intuition that underlies many decisions, the rationalistic methods and tools are merely isolated bits and pieces. Some rationalistic planners may possess skills and techniques but have no vision as to what should be done for the good of the school system. Their lament often identifies them: "If only I knew what needed to be done in this school system!" On the other hand, if a planner is not knowledgeable about skills and techniques required to express his or her vision through clear and supported action, the realization of that vision will be very unlikely. The effective planner must have more than intuition about where the school system needs direct action; he or she must also have the skills and techniques with which to refine and ultimately achieve results. This point has most strongly been argued recently in the philosophy of science (Martin, 1972); it is suggested that intuition and science march hand in hand and that each intimately affects the other.

The narrow incrementalist who has very little to offer during planning other than random anecdotes and old war stories and the comprehensive rationalist who has borrowed theories and unrelated formulas both fall short in their planning responsibility. Responsibility for effective planning requires, in fact demands, that the administrator be a practitioner who is well steeped in planning knowledge and methodology. Without both practical vision and a knowledge base, the administrator is destined to an amateur performance at a time when effective school-system planning is most urgently needed. Dale Mann states:

> The task of an applied scientist is to mediate between two very demanding worlds, that of science or scholarship and that of practice or application. Anyone

who has tried to sustain first the creation and then the translation of valid, reliable scientific findings into terms that will make a difference in important problems of practice knows how hard it is to keep a firm footing on both ponies." (Mann, 1975b, p. 141)

All educational administrators have the responsibility to use planning tools and analytical concepts to more efficiently and effectively plan the future course of our nation's schools. The process of choice and commitment needs to be improved; however, such improvements will only come through the implementation and operation of a sound planning process. This point is made very well by Chin and Benne:

> Here change agents, initially focused on application of behavioral knowledge and the improvement of people technologies in school settings, must face the problems of using people technologies in planning, installing, and evaluating such changes in educational practice. . . . This line of reasoning suggests that, whether the focus of planned change is in the introduction of more effective thing technology or people technologies into institutionalized practice, processes of introducing such changes must be based on behavioral knowledge of change and must utilize people technologies based on such knowledge." (Chin and Benne, 1976, p. 23)

If I am to undergo an appendectomy, I would prefer that the scalpel to be used had been professionally prepared by a surgical instrument manufacturer instead of constructed in my doctor's tool shed. Yet this is what is being asked of school executives who are expected to plan future educational changes with no knowledge of the structure and tools of the planning process. Regardless of one's theoretical approach to planning, one must have a comprehensive understanding of the planning process itself and its tools.

How the decision-maker selects a course of action—how one starts to develop thought, the phrases one's thinking passes through, and the criteria used to evaluate thought—depends on the attitude of the decision-maker and his or her theory of planning. Some—comprehensive rationalists—have a preference for examining an entire analysis of desirable choices. Others—disjointed incrementalists—begin with an analysis of the existing (and probable) situations in order to determine what can be done best. The factors that determine a choice with regard to these dimensions are the picture the planner has of society, the organization, and the reality surrounding it, the type and scale of the problem, and the relative autonomy of the planner. It is one's own theory of planning that determines the ways plans are developed; but it is the planning process and structures that allow the plans to be developed and implemented in the soundest manner possible.

GUIDELINES FOR PLANNING

1. Rational-comprehensive planners make an exhaustive search of all information in an attempt to choose the best of all possible alternatives and outcomes. This approach represents an ideal for which most managers have neither the time nor the information.

2. Disjointed-incrementalist planners examine alternatives that one will surely be able to accomplish, seldom if ever deviating too far from what was done the week, month, or year before. This piecemeal approach limits the likelihood that any desirable solution will ever evolve or that any problems will ever be solved.

3. The rational-comprehensive model has the indisputable merit of focusing attention on some of the very patterns that distinguish modern school systems, particularly their rationality. On the other hand, the disjointed-incrementalist model has the merit of focusing attention on achievable and politically desirable outcomes, even within the rationally planned organization. It appears that each approach leads to some truth, but neither alone affords an adequate understanding of the complex organization and its approach to the planning process.

4. Perhaps the best approach is the more moderate one somewhere between comprehensive rationalism (which is based on theoretical ideals) and disjointed incrementalism (which is based on practical possibilities). Rational choices need to be made, but the range of alternatives included and ends considered will always need to be limited by such practical considerations as the importance of the decision and its impact, the time and information available, the number of unknowns involved, the degree to which changes can be made, and the possible actions that can be taken. These conditions often change with the situation and therefore the planner's approach also changes even though the process remains the same.

4

The Planning Context

Those who would influence schools and school districts need to take
account of the complexity and interrelatedness of controls
affecting these institutions. This means that such persons need
to be knowledgeable, politically astute, and personally persistent.

–CAMPBELL, CUNNINGHAM, NYSTRAND, and USDAN (1980)

An effective planning process requires recognition of the broad and complex
array of expected and unexpected decisions, events, attitudes, and the like that
affect local school district plans. It is not always clear where the "uncon-
trollables" might arise, how intense they might become, or what their ultimate
impact might be. However, we can identify and discuss various contexts in
which the planner might expect to work. The meaning of *context* here refers to
those influences over which the planner may have little control. From the
educational perspective, context consists of four broad, conceptually distinct,
but in reality highly interactive areas: the ideological, the governmental, the
structural, and the societal (see Figure 4–1).

THE IDEOLOGICAL CONTEXT

It is not possible for those who plan to avoid the knotty problem of the purpose of schools. This section deals with this question from two perspectives:
first, that of facing the reality of multiple and often competing or conflicting

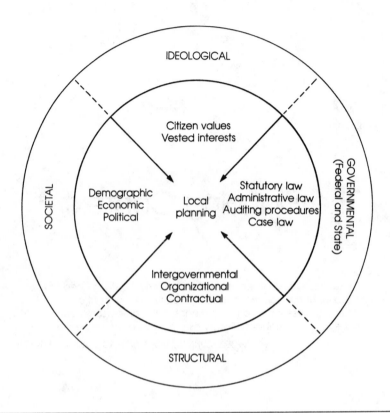

FIGURE 4-1
Planning Contexts for Education

goals; second, that of deciding from whose perspective goals might be formulated.

Multiple goals and values of citizens

The first thing for a planner to recognize is that in order to plan anything a particular value perspective is inevitably taken (Vicker, 1980). Plans for schools are never value-neutral, regardless of their technical aura. The fundamental question must then come down to, Whose values? Theoretically, the local board establishes policy, which in turn gives direction to the plans. But often board policy leaves room for interpretation, either because the board could not agree on a more narrow policy definition or because they saw potential community conflict if their intent were too well defined. In any case, the local board often does not give the direction needed when the planner turns to the specifics of planning.

Even where specific local goals are clear, there are often problems as federal and state program goals begin to merge with local options. This is discussed in some detail in the section on governmental context, but for now the point is to highlight the difficulties in trying to accommodate the disparate goals that have been established by three separate policy bodies (federal, state, and local) and their regulating and implementing agencies.

It is the planner's task, then, to integrate a profusion of goals, on the one hand, and to deal with often ambiguous or vaguely defined goals, on the other (Devons, 1968). Particularly in the case where goals are not clear, the planner must understand that the goal definition which any operative plan will clarify may cause considerable problems in the local community or disagreement among the staff people. An integrated multi-level program designed to teach children to read is a readily agreed-upon goal, for example, but the textbooks selected may stimulate cries of "humanism" and moral degeneracy from some portions of the community, may suit teachers in school A but not school B, or may suit teachers but not supervisors.

Essentially what the planner must deal with are normative feelings of what the schools are for—that is, beliefs about what is important for children to learn. This serves as an important value base for planning decisions. A lack of understanding or misunderstanding of what is believed to be important by those being served or those providing the services can wipe out the finest of plans in a single stroke (Young, 1966).

As the planning tasks become larger, more complex, and more substantive, it is all the more likely that one of two things will occur. Either someone or some group in the system will have to make judgments about what is best, or the focus of the planning effort will have to turn to the task of involving the various school publics in a process of goal setting. The latter takes time, is costly, may cause issues to be aroused in the community, and may not produce the consensus or the majority for the direction needed. Indeed, the process of involving the community in the setting of goals may well take a year or more and even then clear and precise goals may not have been developed. Still worse, the school community may become divided regarding what schools should be and what they should do. This sort of planning should therefore be regarded as potentially politically charged. The superintendent's review of such plans is advised.

If an expert professional judgment is made pertaining to those goals that affect the fundamentals of schooling, the experts are likely presuming to know what is in the public's interest. This may appear to the community as arrogant or elitist. The easiest or at least the most efficient position to take is that of professionalism, but this is a tenuous argument. It challenges, of course, the fundamental tenants of American democracy and lays bare the broader policy question of the role of the public—its feelings, thoughts, and values—and the role of experts in decision making. Whose values should be shaped into the plans? There is no single best answer, but the planner would be well advised from a political as well as an ethical standpoint to be aware of the dilemma and to take account of the issue as plans undergo development.

Multiple perspectives

We each are in some measure the product of our educational background and we each are influenced by the place we occupy in a bureaucracy. What the planner must understand is that there will likely be some conflict in the organization that is the product of how we have been taught to view educational issues—for example, from experience, from a scientific point of view, or from a legal perspective—and that these ways of knowing are very important to people. So important are they, in fact, that vested interests are built up around each perspective. That is, those who know about a problem from one (or more) perspective not only believe that this is the proper perspective, but form coalitions with those who believe similarly. As particular perspectives gain acceptance, the values that these perspectives carry suggest the questions that are to be asked. As those who see from this perspective are also those who can best answer the questions, their position in the scheme of things gains considerable credence, especially as they gain increased support for their views.

The planner, for example, may review the research on a reading program and after a careful match of variables and test results may make tentative decisions based on a school-system perspective. Teachers, however, may be convinced from experience that student self-concept is of long-run overriding importance in a reading program and so choose something other than the planner has recommended. Final decisions might be based on what the teachers feel most comfortable with. The outcomes of such decision negotiations may at times seem totally irrational, but this perception is likely to be a function of one's value system. In any case, tolerance of other perspectives—of what others see as crucial needs—is extremely important. Otherwise planners will rarely have an opportunity to succeed in their efforts. Plans will thus sit on the shelf, technically perfect but substantially vacuous.

THE GOVERNMENTAL CONTEXT

Aside from the ideology of schooling, which underlies all planning activity, there are several concrete and readily identifiable influences on the local school system. The place of government will be considered first, followed by a consideration of the governance structure of education and the effects of societal overrides.

This is not the place to review the history of the governance of education in the United States or to discuss the merits of current trends in governance. It is sufficient to point out that local school districts began with almost complete authority regarding decisions affecting local school programs. However, for nearly three decades, but particularly since 1965, the federal and state governments' role in developing policy that affects local school-district planning has been significant (Wise, 1979). State and federal governments have for centuries had the major legal responsibility for education, but it was not until the mid-1960s that state legislatures, state boards of education, and state courts began to exercise such direct control over local school-district matters. We will not review the specifics of this broad panoply of law affecting the local school district but only call attention to those legal constraints that constitute a part of the environment and are often overriding considerations to local planning efforts.

In the state and federal governments there are four primary foci with which the planner should be concerned. The first of these is the statutory law as enacted by Congress and the legislatures, the second the regulatory or administrative law established by the various state and federal agencies, the third the actual auditing procedures adopted, and the fourth the state and federal court cases handed down.

Statutory law

Statutory law regarding an issue is generally not of direct concern to the planner, as such law generally passes through administrative agencies before its effect is felt. There are two conditions, however, in which a review of the actual law or legislative process would be appropriate. The first is anticipatory in nature and consists of a review of pending legislation in any way affecting a program or project that is being contemplated by the local district. The actual review probably does not have to be the planner, for the state department of education undertakes such a review. (For information on federal legislation, the Council of Chief State School Officers or the National Association of State Boards of Education usually have day-to-day information on pending legislation, or, in the case of most states, the state liaison office in Washington, D.C., will do the necessary review.) The purpose of the review is simply that of having some assurance that a statute will not eclipse or seriously modify a local plan by restriction; or it may reveal, as happens with some regularity, that a bill which offers money for something the district wishes to do, carries with it some state or federal rules of procedure or criteria of substance.

The second condition under which state or federal law might be reviewed would be that of ascertaining intent. As school policymakers and administrators and indeed Congress and legislatures are aware, sometimes regulations coming down from governmental agencies misstate or overstate the intention of the legislative body. The effect is often to overstate the restrictions on local districts.

The planner must be aware of statutory law and state board policy that applies to teacher certification, required student hours in particular curricula, total number of school days required, requirements for special programs, student/teacher ratios, and the like. A copy of the state education code is readily available to every local school system and is in all states reasonably well indexed. A word of caution is in order, however, in that a variety of indexing words or phrases are used (those who index the code are not always familiar with how educators refer to issues) and that yearly code supplements are available and should be referred to. The planner might not personally carry out a challenge of or seek relief from an applicable statute, but it would be well within the province of planning to offer this as an alternative to the superintendent should the law seem to place roadblocks in the way of local program desires. If such efforts are not mounted, the statutes serve as future constraints that the planner must be aware of during the planning process.

Administrative law

Probably no area of legal constraint causes more problems than that of government regulation. The planner has little choice but to be aware of the broad parameters of administrative law that often dictate both the procedure for and content of local programs (Nevstadt, 1979; U.S. Government Accounting Office, 1979). If a state has statewide student competency exams in reading in the early grades, as many do, these examinations are developed largely or totally by those outside of the district but must, by administrative implementation of state law, be given to every child. These tests will almost certainly carry implications of certain methods by which reading must be taught and may well contain biases toward certain content. In practical terms this amounts to a very severe restriction on the reading programs that can be chosen locally. Test comparisons among schools and among school districts are highly politically charged issues that exert considerable pressure on local district planners to implement curricula which prepare all students to score well on these tests. The adoption of a program that did not at least in part enhance the specific skills called for by the tests would be an act of suicide for all school personnel.

There are numerous examples of even more direct regulation of local district operations in terms of both procedure and substance (Weatherly, 1979). The state and federal law relating to the education of the handicapped is one such body of law, the effects of which need no elaboration. The main point is that the planner must be aware of these prior to starting any major planning efforts. It is generally not a difficult procedure to learn of such potential restrictions, for the superintendent and upper-level administrators are made quite aware of the general regulations, and program officers in the school district (for example, the vocational education director) are provided federal and state information on more specific program requirements.

Auditing procedures

Neither the intent of Congress (McLaughlin, 1975) nor the immediate implications of the original federal regulations would have suggested just how the Elementary and Secondary Education Act—Title I—should be treated by the local planner (Stoner, 1978). The point is not to raise the question of who actually makes public policy, but to remind the reader that policymaking is not a neatly described or perfectly circumscribed process and that the real world calls for many perspectives to be taken into account.

With the advent of legislative oversight and program audit review has come the need to be particularly attentive to those who draw up the criteria and make the assessment and evaluation of programs. There are three powerful ways in which such information can be used: (1) to terminate programs outright or reduce (or increase) money available; (2) to feed back into the legislative process or into the courts to find the district out of legal compliance; and (3) for political purposes against a particular superintendent, district, or against schools generally. Any way you take it, when school programs call for an outside audit, the planner must be aware of the potential consequences. As in the case of administrative law, the necessary information for the planner is generally readily available through documentation provided to the district or through contacts at the state and federal offices of education.

State and federal court cases

The increase in formal litigation through the courts has gone hand in hand with the increase in statutory law (Lehne, 1978). Indeed, they are mutually reinforcing processes. The more that is litigated, the more the legislature feels compelled to either restrict or expand the law regulating schools. There is now a highly complex web of law, often conflicting, which speaks to almost every aspect of schooling (Kirp, 1980), from who is served free breakfast to who gets how much of what kind of instruction. Most school boards have one or more attorneys either on staff or on a retainer to help them interpret and remain in compliance with these laws. It would be advisable for the planner to turn to the attorney for advice if there is any reason to suspect that the program or project contemplated could precipitate a legal challenge through the courts regarding student rights, teacher rights, or any of the myriad of applicable case law.

To summarize the governmental context: the planner is faced with law developed and enforced from outside of the district that, as a general rule, must be incorporated into the planning activities of the district. Certainly if this law does not apply to individual cases, there is much to be taken into account when the planner considers comprehensive planning. Conflicts will arise among existing laws and between existing laws and local district wishes. For example, the "Title I teacher" will want the "Title I students" for a certain period of time to meet federal requirements, but the local teacher will want these same students to teach them the basics as required by state mandate or local board policy.

Furthermore, there will be problems of competing criteria for the planner. For example, mandated specifications of student/teacher ratios may run head-on into a local need to consider economic efficiencies; or two schools under court-ordered desegregation plans, each with one-half a class that must have a full-time teacher, may destroy abilities to develop efficiencies of size. Government does not often present totally irreconcilable law, but the planner who does not take the law into account would be considered naive at best and worthless at worst.

THE STRUCTURAL CONTEXT

There are a number of matters dealing with the way that education is organized that impinge on the planning done in a local school district. The considerations that follow are not to be taken as comprehensive. The planner should be aware of such considerations, however, for each in its own way can affect the planning that is done. Considered separately, these are the structures of intergovernmental arrangements, bureaucracy and the schooling organization, and employee contracts.

Intergovernmental arrangements

Anyone familiar with the structure of education in the United States is well aware that the governance patterns which we have did not result from a carefully planned scheme. For many decades towns and cities provided education as they saw fit. With the advent of heightened state and federal interest in education, new programs were added to serve particular aspects of curriculum, to serve a variety of special groups of students, and to solve a number of societal ills. As a rule, each new program was an "add-on" with its own structural mechanism for handing down regulations, reviewing and evaluating programs, and deciding questions of compliance (Meyer, 1979). The structure grew like topsy under the characterization of categorical programs and categorical funding.

What this has meant, in the case of federal law, is that each program has a distinct program head in the federal bureaucracy who is directly linked to a similar program head in a state bureaucracy. This person, in turn, is directly linked to someone in charge of program implementation in the local district and, not infrequently, a regional program director in the state. In the case of larger programs, there are separate departments even at the local level. Thus, for example, there is often a local director of Title I programs, of handicapped programs, of vocational education, and so on. Programs mandated by the state are quite similar in that there is often a "contact" person in each local district who is in charge of, for example, state testing.

The effect of this has been interlocking agreements among program officers at the local, the state, and generally the federal levels. The interest of the local program employees in local district planning is thus a secondary consideration, for the persons to whom the local program director is most accountable are the state and federal officers who review, evaluate, and fund (in full or in part) the local program effort. Even given the best of intentions, it is difficult for those in charge of such programs to plan outside of their state-federal mandates and equally as difficult to integrate their planning with other planning in the district. To put the matter bluntly, it is exceptionally difficult for the local planners to develop a truly comprehensive local plan that does any more than "take account" of these individual plans, for often the law and the funding prevent the very integration demanded of a comprehensive planning process.

Bureaucracy and the schooling organization

Every administrator with only a modicum of formal training is aware that the idea of bureaucracy was conceived a century ago as a way of making large organizations more efficient. The idea, originally applied to business and industry (Callahan, 1962), was adopted by educators not long after the turn of this century as a way to manage the increasingly large schooling organization. We will not debate the appropriateness of the structure of bureaucracy to the schools, but it is important to note that over the years two things have become clear about its use. The first of these is that it has taken on characteristics of rigidity, and the second is that there have been subtle but important adaptations in schools to allow for the professional nature of the education enterprise.

Rigidity is probably not caused by size and complexity alone, but certainly these are key ingredients. As the number of children seeking education grew and as school districts consolidated from a high of over 130,000 districts to a present level of 16,000, the size (in terms of pupils to be served) increased exponentially. The teaching and administrative arms of the bureaucracy grew proportionately, creating vast and sprawling organizations designed to teach children. The size was compounded by complexity caused not only by rapid growth but by the addition of new responsibilities and new programs that the schools were to carry out. The combination resulted in an organization that could not rely on loose interpersonal contacts as a way of governing itself but rather needed control from the top, with emphasis on the reliability of behavior throughout the organization. Rules were instituted and standard operating procedures gave appropriate direction to organizational activities (Allison, 1969). The routine became habitual and the organization seemed better adapted to the status quo than to the need for change.

The effects of this development are still much in evidence and constitute potential blocks for planning for change. This is not to make the case that the schools are unresponsive to change but only to point out that the structure is set up to reward repetitive, safe behavior rather than creative, new behavior (Argyris, 1973), which is often risky but nevertheless may be the subject of a planner's dreams. In short, the internal structure of the organization tends to favor things as they are, both because this is more comfortable for the incumbents and because change may well challenge the status, prestige, and power of an office. This is true, for example, though it often seems overlooked or misunderstood by planners, even when a change involves a minor matter such as the rerouting of information, for information in a bureaucracy is power—not only for making decisions but also for trading for other information (Devons, 1968). To be effective, the planner must carefully assess the effect of potential changes on the bureaucracy, being ready to do battle on some points and make trade-offs on others.

The second point, that of subtle adaptations, either took longer to evolve or was always there and just not noticed in any formal sense until quite recently. The bottom line is that much of the current research on school organizations suggests that accommodations have been made in practice to the fact that either school systems are too complex to govern from the top or that, regardless of size and complexity, schools are associations of professionals each of whom must be given considerable decision autonomy. The contemporary and evolving theory characterizes schools as loosely coupled systems (Weick, 1976; Weick, undated) with important decisions being made throughout the organization; even more important for the planner, the theory characterizes schools as organizations incapable of carrying out specific orders (or specific plans) from a central position in the hierarchy. The specific implications for planning seem to be the need to allow not only "teacher input" but teacher discretion in the rate, scope, and degree of implementation. In other words, it appears that for plans which require implementation at the instructional level, broad strategic objectives can be specified centrally but teachers must assist in the operational planning—a consideration which is discussed in Chapter 2. However, to expect uniform or smooth execution of a plan is unrealistic, not because teachers want to emasculate the plan but because there are always too many unforeseen variables in the dynamics of a classroom to be able to plan meticulously (Etzioni, 1967). Indeed, a teacher would be suspected of incompetency if he or she treated a plan as other than a guideline. In short, to state the extreme, do not expect to develop a plan, send it down the chain of command, and have it obeyed. This would seldom be possible or desirable. Bureaucratic theory suggests that this should work, but nothing in recent experience supports this view. If the parts of the organization are tied together strategically and the linkage of operational plans is encouraged, then this is probably the best a planner can do, given organizational realities.

Employee contracts

With the change in the broad governance structure of education have come changes in the ways in which employees look at management. As is the case with most widespread social and political movements, it is impossible to pinpoint either the cause (or causes) or the exact time that teachers became "militant." Certainly by the 1950s teachers were speaking out and creating concern, if not action, by boards of education. Teachers were voicing their view that they were undervalued and not in sufficient control of their own destiny. In 1960 in New York City a labor dispute resulted in a bargained agreement. Since that time teachers have made significant gains through bargaining as equals with the boards over wages, working conditions, and a variety of policy matters such as class size, extra duties, and curriculum.

Nor is collective bargaining the extent of teacher organization incursion on board power; political and legal action have become key weapons in the teacher arsenal. It is not uncommon to have large teacher lobbies in the state capital when the legislature meets, to have teachers actively supporting education-minded legislators and governors, and to be, in general, a highly sophisticated political force in the state. Teacher organizations have also successfully challenged local as well as state policy in the courts, thus using the judiciary to their advantage. The combined strength of teacher politics and legal challenges at the state and national level and collective bargaining agreements at the local level have changed the local district's position significantly.

What this comes to for the planner is that the more that matters of interest to the teacher are stipulated by law from outside the district or by contract law from within the district, the less latitude the planner has to make changes in the district. It is particularly poignant that the teachers have initiated law and legal interpretations, for this body of law will certainly be monitored for the compliance of teachers.

In summarizing the structural context, it should be reiterated that this discussion does not constitute a comprehensive overview of all potential problem areas; neither has it identified areas over which the planner must remain always inactive. The point in this discussion has not been to discourage the planner or to show the impossibility of local planning. The point is exactly the reverse; recognizing the limitations as well as the opportunities presented by governance, the local planner can be better attuned to the realities of the current policy structure.

THE SOCIETAL CONTEXT

Aside from the ideological, governmental, and structural context, there is the societal context. It is difficult to characterize but it cuts across all of the others. For matters of convenience, the societal context is discussed under the rubrics of the demographic environment, the economic environment, and the political environment of the school district. Each in itself and all together constitute an unseen hand that determines much of what a school district can do.

The demographic environment

The average daily attendance (ADA) or the average daily membership (ADM) are measures of the number of students in a district; either directly or indirectly these measures have much to do with the amount of money received by the schools. Overall district size makes some difference to a planner as larger districts generally can provide more resources for a planning effort and also provide more flexibility to attempt innovative programs and pilot projects. Of equal or greater importance to demography, however, is the rate of overall increase or decrease in enrollment. Under conditions of expansion, budgets generally grow, new schools are opened, new teachers are added, and new programs and new ways of operating can get caught up in the expansionist vigor. Under conditions of retrenchment, on the other hand, budgets tend to be reduced (adjusted for inflation and additional mandated programs), schools are closed, and flexibility is reduced. Planning may be needed even more to find creative and exciting alternatives to conditions generally viewed as adverse, but, ironically, usually the planning effort itself becomes more difficult to justify. In short, there is much for the planner to do in either expansion or retrenchment periods, but job expectancies will shift according to these conditions.

The make-up of the adult population in the school district jurisdiction is an important aspect of the demographic context. Education level and socioeconomic level are important factors in terms both of expectancies for the school (quality and scope of programs) and in the level of local support. When the education level is high, expectancies tend to be high; when the socioeconomic level is also high, the resource support is probably also high.

The converse of these factors is equally true. Of course most districts present a mixture in some proportion of the high and the low, but an astute planner can get some feel for the demographic context as we have used the term here and build expectancies accordingly. A confounding factor in this estimate, however, must be the level of state support. In those states that have greatly equalized spending per child in all districts and have more heavily mandated programs, these factors (excluding growth and decline) would be much reduced in significance.

A closely allied factor is the make-up of the student body. As long as there is at least a modicum of program flexibility at the local level, the kind of programs to be planned will greatly influence the planning operation. Where students aspire to blue collar jobs, vocational programs will be emphasized, and these will usually be of a relatively narrow band to reflect the job availability in the local area. This suggests that the planner should be interested in the local economy and should develop plans with potential employers and the local governmental planning office or regional industrial commission. It is not necessary to elaborate on how different the emphasis would be in a district in which the overwhelming number of students go on to college. Of course, most districts will present a mixture of the vocational and college-bound students. It will be incumbent on the planner to undertake a variety of tasks to assist the school district in properly preparing all the students.

The economic environment

Much of what needs to be pointed out regarding the economic environment has been discussed in the section on demographics. The total school budget is the key point of control for much of what goes on in a district. However, it is important to mention that the three major sources of revenue for most districts—federal, state, and local—each come into the district in different ways. Most of the federal monies are categorical in nature and the district must take the initiative in making applications and writing proposals to gain this money. In a district heavily financed by federal funds, therefore, an important job of the planner may well be to provide the orchestration of this process and even offer assistance in the planning of the proposals.

Some state money also comes to the district in this manner, but the amount is generally small. Instead, state money comes in as an index of wealth, student body make-up, tax effort, and a variety of other variables, most of which lie in the economic environment and generally beyond the control of the planner. It is important, nevertheless, for the planner to know something of this source of revenue for two reasons. First, planners are sometimes asked to project the future of the district over a five- or ten-year period. Projecting the state tax index, or the amount of money received from the state, is vital to the future of any district. Second, and this is closely tied to the first point, the amount of state aid remains an extremely important part of the general aid that a district can use to plan local programs. As this share becomes larger, the planner must become increasingly aware of restrictions placed on the use of this money.

Finally, though the local share of the total school budget has been declining nationally, localities still contribute approximately one-half of all revenues to the school districts. This ties in directly with the factors described above regarding local wealth and local expectations. Planners can be of immense benefit to a local school district by assisting in those programs that meet the needs as seen by the community. Districts with relatively low wealth can nevertheless be convinced to spend more for schools if they perceive that they are getting their money's worth. This is usually interpreted to mean getting what they value and thus the planner must be able to assess citizens' values, as discussed in the section on the ideological context for planning.

The political environment

The political environment in which a planner works is truly a blend of everything that has been discussed in this chapter. Politics as used here involves the general political milieu and includes overt expressions of what schools are really for, responsibility for what government does, and responsiveness to what people want. In a broad sense, politics also dictates the structural arrangements necessary for government to operate. The political environment of the local school is influenced by international events such as the Russian launching of Sputnik, which set off a wave of curricular reform, or by national movements such as the competency testing program, which spread from one state legislature to another in a furious wave of reform, or by local conditions or events that, for example, might touch off a need for a drug or alcohol abuse program or in-school day care for teenage mothers. Congress, state legislatures, school boards, political parties, and interest groups of every stripe and variety are all active in determining the broad political context. Religious and moral values as well as preferences associated with social class and even geographic region and locality must ultimately find expression through the formal political channels in order to be effective. Clearly, however, a planner does not have to wait for the formal expression of values, say through a statutory enactment, to take place before making accommodations for the shifting moods of the larger community.

Politics is thus the tempo that sets the rate and direction of change and, though generally not volatile (the late 1960s and early 1970s appear to have been an exception), is essentially beyond the planner's direct control. What can and should be done is to recognize shifts as they occur. It does not mean giving up idealism, but it does mean an awareness of the possible—"under the given conditions."

In summarizing the societal context of local school-district planning activity, we repeat the accepted position that there is not a great deal here that the planner can do other than recognize the conditions and plan accordingly. On the other hand, if so desired, planners can operate in a broader context, for as the following indicates, school-system planners do not have to rely on a Skinnerian response to conditions; that is, they do not necessarily have to react to every condition or be sensitive to every issue during the planning process.

TRANSLATION OF CONTEXT TO PLANNING ALTERNATIVES

Planning requires recognition of the broad and complex array of conditions outside of the school system itself. There is little that a planner can do to "plan" these conditions, for that would mean to control the outside environment; but alternative responses can be considered to provide some latitude to the planning process. These alternatives are seen as accepting, ignoring, negotiating, reconceiving, planning for contingencies, and expanding to policy or legislative planning.

The first and most obvious alternative is to accept all of the conditions as "givens." We list acceptance as an alternative because so often this stance is seen as the only course of action that can be taken rather than being seen as one possible alternative. The sensitivity of the planner is needed in judging when a condition should be treated in this manner and when another response would be appropriate. This, quite obviously, is akin to that motto which we see on the desks of many executives—that they be granted "the serenity to accept what must be accepted, the courage to change what can and should be changed, and the wisdom to know the difference."

Responsiveness is good, but not an unmitigated good. Overresponsiveness not only tears at the fabric of an organization, jerking this way and then that, but destroys the very idea of what planning is all about! One is reminded of the difficulties at the old Office of Education in Washington when they had a succession of new commissioners, four in five years, each with a new "priority." While it could be charged that a local district is sticking its collective head in the sand, or worse, that it is not being democratic in ignoring the planning context, it could be argued as well that responsiveness and responsibility are not always a matched pair and that to respond to every wind that blows is a weathervane existence and a defeat of planning. When to ignore is as difficult a choice as when to accept; the planner at least must recognize it as a choice.

Between the poles of accepting and ignoring lie the possibility of negotiating with the planning context. Where we cannot readily control a situation, where we either do not know what the relevant control variables are or we know them but cannot control their direction, it is possible to form a pact with others to at least stabilize the situation (Johnston, 1977). In the years of instability caused by the desegregation of schools, informal pacts were made between school districts and the protesting community to accept a given arrangement for a specified period of time, provided that additional desegregation law suits would not be filed during that interim. Nobody expected a final solution to be the result, but the district at least bought enough time to focus the agenda of the schools. It is not a "planning solution" by any means, but the outcome was to provide stabilized conditions under which planning could work.

Under conditions of extreme instability, it is possible to make adjustments in how planning is conceived. That is, instead of proceeding in a rationalistic fashion, with the future conceptualized and laid out, it may be necessary to proceed piecemeal, planning what can be planned, ready to retreat when it is necessary, and taking advantage of opportunities as they arise. Such piecemeal planning may only be needed periodically, since school districts are not always operating under conditions of extreme instability. This type of planning is seen as a temporary solution, temporary meaning two or three years if necessary. Second, such planning does not have to be totally devoid of planned objectives nor must it simply rely upon the conventional patterns of socialization for direction. The more apt analogy is that of a battle plan where units move forward, albeit on a broken front.

In a very different response, a planner has the option of moving ahead boldly flying under the colors of a normative banner. It may be seen as "crazy" or a "death wish," but it is sometimes also called leadership. This can be a risky venture in which, if all comes out well, the planner is a hero. If the plan smashes against rather than smashing through the "wall of reality," being discredited is the best a planner can expect. The risk can be in part minimized by the smart planner, however, by building support and providing contingency or back-up plans should the first line of attack fail. Contingency planning is, of course, a perfectly acceptable way of planning under any circumstances and may be augmented under these conditions by initiating sequential plans or deliberately offering different routes to the desired goal simultaneously, say in different schools or with different groups of children.

Finally, planning efforts can be expanded into the realm of policy and legislative planning. This involves scanning the federal and state law, as suggested earlier, not to look for constraints to be accepted, but to seek change in the law under which districts operate. This means the further politicization of schooling and involves writing and lobbying for and against legislative proposals. Efforts are needed at the appropriate level of government to support a favorable piece of legislation, to modify an undesirable law, or to delete a law altogether. This applies equally to statutory law, to state and local board policy, to administrative law, and to case law (through the appellate procedure of the courts). It is a view that puts a school district into the class of one of a number of competing interest groups. Educators generally do not like to think of their profession in this way, but as can be seen with the increased number of educator lobbyists in Washington, D.C., and in every state capital, this distaste is giving way to what is seen as making adaptation to the contemporary world. The planner can choose to help shape the planning context in this way rather than being shaped by the environment of which he or she is a part.

In conclusion, all of the contexts that we have discussed have been necessarily considered separately, but they are all part of an intricate tapestry, each thread providing color, design, and reinforcement to the others. They must be understood as the environmental conditions under which planners work. An effective planning process must enhance, redirect, or dampen these multiple influences so that they have the most positive possible impact on local education. Planners must recognize the need to shape each into the school systems' goals and objectives.

GUIDELINES FOR PLANNING

1. The planner needs to be aware of the influence of outside forces on local school-district plans.

2. Plans are never value-neutral, but are developed in the context of local citizens' values and federal and state program goals. The planner must expect to interpret these often ambiguous or poorly defined and articulated values and goals. There is no right way to arrive at a judgment or consensus about the ideology underlying plans.

3. Statutory law, both pending and enacted, administrative regulations, and case law must all be considered by the planner. In addition, the planner must be aware of the implications of legislative oversight and program audits.

4. The planner must take into account the rigidity and professionalization of the education bureaucracy, which tend to work against innovation and against imposition of planning from the top. The political power of teacher organizations will also affect the latitude the planner has at the local level.

5. The scocioeconomic make-up of the school district's population will affect the level and kind of support and expectations parents give the schools, as well as dictating the appropriate mix of vocational and academic programs.

6. The planner must understand the sources of revenue in order to make accurate projections and to assess the acceptability of plans to the populations which support them.

7. Planning is needed in periods of recession as well as expansion, though the planner will have a harder time justifying his or her work in times of declining enrollments and retrenchment.

8. Once the planner has understood all of the outside influences on his or her job, then the planner can "plan" his or her responses: whether to accept the outside conditions, to ignore them, to negotiate for some stabilized set of conditions or some temporary or piecemeal solutions, to develop alternative and contingency plans, or to map out a political lobbying effort to change the external conditions.

Part 2

Tools and Techniques

Mission, Goals, and Objectives
Resource Allocation
Planning Styles and Participation
Group Process
Task Planning and Coordinating
Decision Making
Organizational Development
Computer Information Systems

5

Putting Plans into Action Through Objectives

Results were given lip service, but activity was being rewarded.

–J. D. BATTEN (1966)

The concept of management through the use of objectives has existed since human beings first organized themselves into groups and will most likely continue to exist until they cease to be so organized. Objectives are used in management as an aid in documenting and communicating desired common outcomes to subordinates. Peter Drucker, in his *Practice of Management* (1954), formally publicized, refined, and extended this concept as well as coined the phrase "management by objectives" (MBO), which continues today to describe the use of objectives in management. In this work, Drucker explains why management by objective is so important:

> Each manager from the "big boss" down to the production foreman or the chief clerk, needs clearly spelled-out objectives. These objectives should lay out what performance the man's own managerial unit is supposed to produce. They should lay out what contribution he and his unit are expected to make to help other units obtain their objectives. Finally, they should spell out what contribution the manager can expect from other units toward the attainment of his own objectives. Right from the start, in other words, emphasis should be on teamwork and team results.

These objectives should always derive from the goals of the business enterprise. . . . Indeed, this must follow if we mean it when we say that the foreman is
"part of management." For it is the definition of a manager that in what he does
he takes responsibility for the whole—that, in cutting stone, he "builds the
cathedral." (Drucker, 1954, pp. 126-127)

Since its introduction, the concept of MBO has been pulled in many different directions depending on the writer's viewpoint, but in general it has been
supported by persons of diverse administrative beliefs. For instance, Douglas
McGregor (1957) thought of MBO as a tool for allowing employees to set objectives for which they would later be held responsible. He believed the major
reason that the evaluation and development of subordinates failed was that
superiors disliked making judgments about another person's worth. He likened
the superior's attitude to quality-control inspectors on assembly lines and con-
tended that the manager's revulsion was against being inhuman. To cope with
this problem, McGregor recommended that an individual should set his or her
own goals, checking them out with the supervisor; then the supervisor should
use these objectives as a counseling device in the appraisal process. Thus, the
supervisor would become one who helped the subordinate achieve his or her
own goals and objectives instead of a dehumanized inspector of products.

George S. Odiorne (1965) was the first to devote an entire book to the topic
of management by objective. Odiorne's major contribution was the translation
of the MBO concept into a comprehensive, workable system. He also
developed what has become the most frequently cited definition of MBO:

The system of management by objectives can be described as a process
whereby the superior and subordinate managers of an organization jointly identify its common goals, define each individual's major areas of responsibility in
terms of the results expected of him, and use these measures as guides for
operating the unit and assessing the contribution of each of its members.
(Odiorne, 1965, pp. 55-56)

Since Odiorne's 1965 book on the use and importance of objectives in management, many books have been written (Baldridge and Tierney, 1979; Bell,
1974; Carroll and Tosi, 1973; Dunn, 1975; Humble, 1970; Knezevich, 1973a;
Morrisey, 1970; Raia, 1974; Reddin, 1971). The earlier publications were exclusively by business writers; however, the latter ones (after 1973) include
works by educational writers. In addition to the books, there have been over
100 articles published in education, public administration, and business
journals.

Although administrators have often practiced some form of management
by objective, it began to receive more serious attention by business in the early
1960s. Its application quickly spread to government and its apparent success

encouraged management specialists in education to suggest it might help to solve some chronic administrative problems (for example, Bell, 1974; Lewis, 1976). Today, some form of MBO is practiced in business, government, and education; its premises are familiar to most administrators (Brady, 1976; Heyle, 1973; Newland, 1976). The impetus for this wide acceptance lies in the simplicity of the MBO premises:

1. The clearer the idea of what one wants to accomplish, the greater the chances of accomplishing it.
2. Real progress can only be measured in relation to goals and objectives.

In other words, if one knows where he or she is going, one will find it easier to get there, can get there faster, and will know when he or she arrives.

MBO FOR PLANNING OR SUPERVISING

Although there is agreement on the usefulness of MBO, there are two major schools of thought on how it should be implemented. The first school of thought, which follows the Drucker analysis, looks at MBO as an administrative planning tool. The second school of thought, which follows the McGregor emphasis, views MBO as a method of employee participation, development, and supervision. The Drucker school bases their implementation of MBO on the establishment of appropriate goals specifically related to educational planning; the rationale for adopting MBO is to analyze the organization's goals in light of the demands of its clients and the needs of a changing world. The McGregor school views the implementation of MBO as a way to provide participation, direction, and motivation to employees; their reasons include providing for improvement in supervision, staff development, and motivation.

Unfortunately, MBO often loses much of its overall usefulness when it is viewed only as a planning tool or a supervisory tool, for in fact if implemented correctly it will serve both purposes. MBO works best when it is used to develop strategic objectives, which focus on mission, planning, and change, and then links operational objectives, which focus more on operations, performance, and results. As discussed in Chapter 2, this becomes an overall management guidance and control system for both facets of administration—planning and supervision.

Management by objective is a systematic approach to management planning and supervision that establishes common goals and objectives that must be achieved and gives the authority and responsibility for achieving the objectives to those who must do the work. Objectives are needed to set guidelines for activity within the organization; they are a source of legitimacy that justifies the existence of the organization; they serve as standards to assess progress; and they provide orientation by depicting a future situation that the organization is trying to attain.

Strategic objectives provide direction and coordination but are somewhat intangible in relation to the allocation of effort and the measurement of performance. The operational objectives provide clear and measurable goals that make possible the allocation of efforts and the measurement of performance. The first provides guidance and a chance to plan for improvement in the school system and the second provides for meaningful activity and improvement of performance related to the repetitive systems and functions of the school.

If a framework of objectives has been worked out for the whole organization, there is less danger of misdirected effort. Top management can be assured that all employees are working toward common purposes that can be mutually consistent, appropriately challenging, and realistic in light of both internal and external opportunities and threats. It can be assured that people's potentials are being developed along lines that will increase the effectiveness of the organization.

Carroll and Tosi (1973, p. 16) summarized the research on MBO and stated that the "research supports the idea that MBO should result in higher levels of performance than those of management approaches that do not involve the establishment of performance goals, the provision of feedback relevant to performance as it relates to such goals and subordinate participation in the setting of such goals." Carroll and Tosi conclude that "the adoption of this approach can improve managerial performance, managerial attitudes and organizational planning." However, not all share this confidence in the impact that MBO will have on organizational success. Some suggest that its success depends on how well it is implemented. Jerry McCaffery, who has had a great deal of experience with the MBO concept, concludes that "like any tool, MBO may be used skillfully or ineptly. It may result in increased efficiency and effectiveness, organizational harmony and individual freedom, or it may result in cumbersome and costly procedures, ineffective outputs, and individual fear and frustration. It all depends" (McCaffery, 1976, p. 34).

THE MBO PROCESS

Management by objectives is, in some ways, like all the other systematic approaches to planning and management; it is more an attitude of the mind than a cookbook recipe or how-to-do-it approach. However, appropriate attitudes can be most effective when supported systematically. Although there are uniform approaches to management by objective, it is an idea or attitude of administration that should be implemented with a flexible, pragmatic approach; otherwise such efforts are likely to be self-defeating.

Drucker, in *The Practice of Management*, discussed the concept of and need for management by objective, but he did not offer a system for implementation. He concentrated on persuading management of the need for MBO by helping administrators develop the state of mind or attitude required to implement MBO. McGregor, in *The Human Side of Enterprise*, offered what might be viewed as a simplified or basic view of the MBO process. He described it as a four-step or four-phase process: (1) the clarification of the broad requirements of the job; (2) the establishment of specific "targets" for a limited time period; (3) the management process during the target period; and (4) appraisal of the results.

Odiorne, in *Management by Objectives*, expanded on McGregor's and Drucker's work and developed what he called the "stages of installation" of an MBO system. His system included three major stages along with sub-steps and some indispensable preliminaries, namely, to (1) secure top administrative backing; (2) clarify common goals (strategic objectives) before individual goals (operational objectives); (3) change the organizational structure in accordance with goals; (4) make sure MBO is a system for managing, not an addition to the manager's job; and (5) prepare managers to delegate activities over which they used to take personal control (this adds the teaching of subordinates to a manager's duties). Odiorne's (1965, pp. 68-79) stages and sub-steps of the MBO process are as follows:

I. Setting goals with subordinates
  (1) Identify the common goals of the whole organization for the coming period.
  (2) Clarify your working organizational chart.
  (3) Set objectives for the next budget year with each person individually.
  (4) During the year, check each subordinate's goals as promised milestones are reached.

II. Measuring results against goals
  (1) Near the end of the budgetary year, ask each subordinate to prepare a brief "statement of performance against plans" using his or her copy of performance objectives as a guide.
  (2) Set a date to go over this report in detail (search for causes of variances).
  (3) At this meeting, allow for free two-way communication.
  (4) Set the stage for establishing the subordinate's performance budget for the coming year.

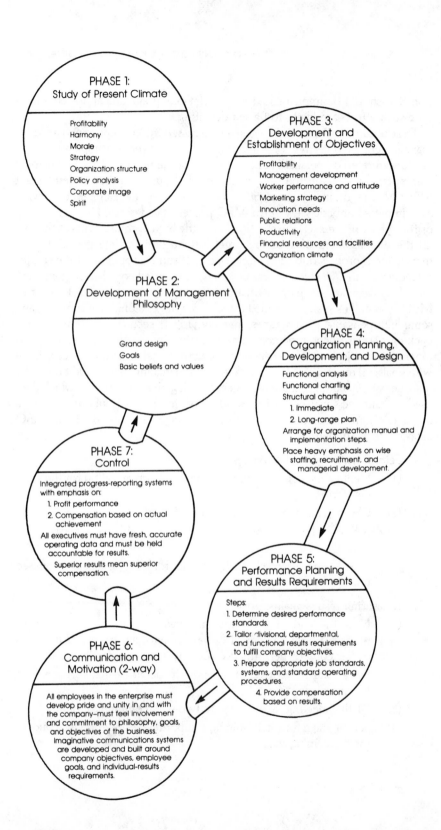

PHASE 1:
Study of Present Climate

Profitability
Harmony
Morale
Strategy
Organization structure
Policy analysis
Corporate image
Spirit

PHASE 3:
Development and
Establishment of Objectives

Profitability
Management development
Worker performance and attitude
Marketing strategy
Innovation needs
Public relations
Productivity
Financial resources and facilities
Organization climate

PHASE 2:
Development of Management
Philosophy

Grand design
Goals
Basic beliefs and values

PHASE 4:
Organization Planning,
Development, and Design

Functional analysis
Functional charting
Structural charting
1. Immediate
2. Long-range plan
Arrange for organization manual and
implementation steps.
Place heavy emphasis on wise
staffing, recruitment, and
managerial development.

PHASE 7:
Control

Integrated progress-reporting systems
with emphasis on:
1. Profit performance
2. Compensation based on actual
achievement
All executives must have fresh, accurate
operating data and must be held
accountable for results.
Superior results mean superior
compensation.

PHASE 5:
Performance Planning
and Results Requirements

Steps:
1. Determine desired performance
standards.
2. Tailor divisional, departmental,
and functional results requirements
to fulfill company objectives.
3. Prepare appropriate job standards,
systems, and standard operating
procedures.
4. Provide compensation
based on results.

PHASE 6:
Communication and
Motivation (2-way)

All employees in the enterprise must
develop pride and unity in and with
the company—must feel involvement
and commitment to philosophy, goals,
and objectives of the business.
Imaginative communications systems
are developed and built around
company objectives, employee
goals, and individual-results
requirements.

III. Reviewing organizational performance and defining goals for the coming year.

A broader approach is presented in J. D. Batten's *Beyond Management by Objectives* (see Figure 5-1). Batten's seven-phase program illustrates the sequence, the flow, and, most important, the dynamics of the on-going process. Batten believed that this system might go beyond what had traditionally become known as MBO.

Drucker did not agree that such a planning emphasis was beyond what was envisioned as the MBO process. In a 1974 article discussing management of service institutions, Drucker (1974, pp. 158-159) describes six steps that emphasize the planning function and are examples of what managers and leaders of service institutions must do:

1. They need to define "what is our business and what should it be."
2. They need to derive clear objectives and goals from their definition of function and mission.
3. They then have to think through priorities of concentration that enable them to select targets; to set standards of accomplishment and performance (that is, to define the minimum acceptable results); to set deadlines; to go to work on results; and to make someone accountable for results.
4. They need to define measurements of performance.
5. They need to use these measurements to feed back on their efforts, that is, to build self-control from results into their system.
6. They need an organized audit of objectives and results, so as to identify those objectives that no longer serve a purpose or have proven unattainable.

In regard to step 6, Drucker believed that the assessing and abandoning of low-performance activities, which waste energy and money in service institutions, would be the most painful but also the most salutary innovation.

MBO IN EDUCATION AND THE PUBLIC SECTOR

Stephen J. Knezevich (1973a) was commissioned by the U.S. Office of Education to develop an idealized model of the MBO process (see Figure 5-2). The process starts with the identification of organizational goals; this leads to setting division objectives and then individual objectives consistent with the goals. At

---

FIGURE 5-1

A Seven Phase Description of the MBO Process

Source: J. D. Batton, *Beyond Management by Objectives: A Management Classic*, reprinted by permission of the publisher. ©1980 by AMACOM, a division of American Management Associations, p. 54. All rights reserved.

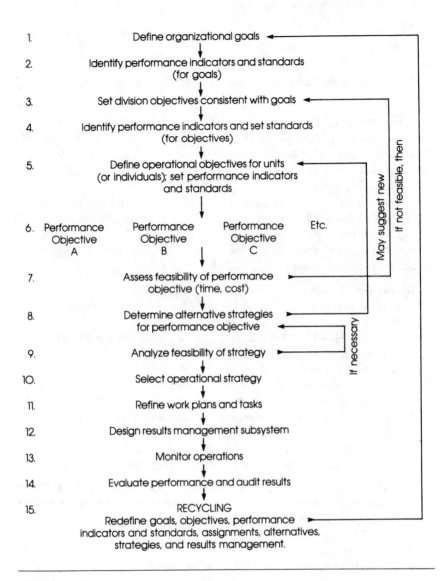

1. Define organizational goals

2. Identify performance indicators and standards (for goals)

3. Set division objectives consistent with goals

4. Identify performance indicators and set standards (for objectives)

5. Define operational objectives for units (or individuals); set performance indicators and standards

6. Performance Objective A   Performance Objective B   Performance Objective C   Etc.

7. Assess feasibility of performance objective (time, cost)

8. Determine alternative strategies for performance objective

9. Analyze feasibility of strategy

10. Select operational strategy

11. Refine work plans and tasks

12. Design results management subsystem

13. Monitor operations

14. Evaluate performance and audit results

15. RECYCLING
Redefine goals, objectives, performance indicators and standards, assignments, alternatives, strategies, and results management.

May suggest new

If not feasible, then

If necessary

FIGURE 5-2

A Fifteen-Step MBO Model

Source: Stephen J. Knezevich, *Management by Objectives and Results.* American Association of School Administrators, Washington, DC, 1973, p. 27.

step 7 there is an assessment of the feasibility of the performance objective, calling for a recycling back to step 3 if no performance objectives are found feasible in terms of time, money, or other constraints. This recycling back is described as the reactive process. The model continues with the identification of alternative strategies, leading to development of work plans and tasks at step

11. The resulting management phase covers steps 12 to 14 and includes monitoring to make sure the organization stays on target as well as evaluating and auditing the actual results. The refining and self-correcting mechanism is built in with the recycling phase noted at step 15, which begins the process all over again.

A system very similar to the one described by Knezevich was successfully implemented in the Bloomfield Hills, Mich., public schools. Figure 5-3 presents the basic hierarchy that was used in developing the objectives to be achieved as well as choosing the performance indicators and alternative strategies to be implemented. Notice that the state's standards of quality become the highest level input—the strategic objective—for the local school system. At the lower level, established performance criteria are used in supervision to provide for self-measurement and self-improvement of performance. A somewhat similar but less elaborate system is being tried in Virginia.

In both Michigan and Virginia, problems have developed relating to the reactive process between the federal and state and the local systems. Federal and state objectives were firmed up before the reactive process with the locality had occurred. Recent studies (Campbell, Cunningham, Nystrand and Usdan, 1980) suggest that state and federal planning is seldom successful if there is not local participation, motivation, commitment, and a sense of local ownership. Local development and installation of federal and state programs must be viewed as a continuing process of policy-making, during which various interested groups press for their varied visions. Success is increased the more these varied visions can be molded into the local plans.

The MBO approach was implemented in the Department of Health, Education, and Welfare in 1969 when Secretary Robert Finch placed a high emphasis on its development and implementation. Since that time it has received mixed reviews but there tends to be satisfaction with the system's results (see for example, the January/February 1976 *Public Administration Review* symposium on "Management by Objective in the Public Sector"). That MBO is continuing to be refined, has not disappeared (or, as some prefer to describe, evaporated), and is spreading to other agencies such as the Office of Management and Budget are all signs of its vitality and success.

Basic reactions to the implementation of MBO have been cautiously optimistic. Changes such as MBO do not always get a fair hearing because of resistance rooted in suspicion and distrust, especially from inside the bureaucracy. If people can get away with hiding what they do, they will resist changes that require exposure, especially if they are unsure of the motives of those asking for the exposure.

Chester A. Newland, who is very familiar with the federal approach to MBO, states that there is no single source of activity that makes the MBO process successful or more accepted in the federal government. However, he

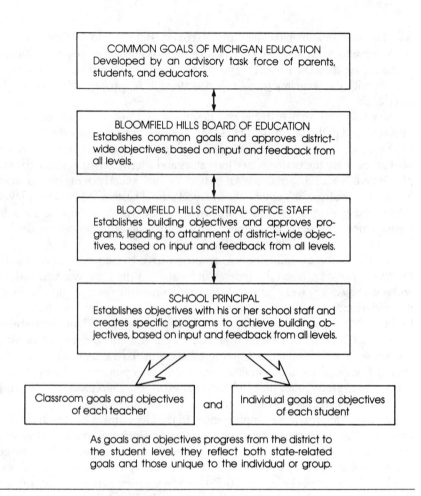

FIGURE 5-3
Chart of Bloomfield Hills' MBO System

lists several key elements of the federal MBO process and some basic concepts of administration that underlie its initial success:

1. Setting of goals, objectives, and priorities in terms of results to be accomplished in a given time.
2. Developing plans for accomplishment of results.
3. Allocating resources (manpower, money, plant and equipment, and information), in terms of established goals, objectives, and priorities.

4. Involving people in implementation of plans, with emphasis on communication for responsiveness and on broad sharing in authoritative goals and objectives.
5. Tracking or monitoring of progress toward goals and objectives with specific intermediate milestones.
6. Evaluating results in terms of effectiveness (including quality), efficiency, and economy. (Newland, 1974, p. 358)

PLANNING AND THE TOOLS OF MBO

Strategic planning

Goals, objectives, and policies constitute the semipermanent framework within which most administrators operate. Anthony (1965) describes the development of this framework as strategic planning. Such plans are called strategic because they have an enduring effect that is difficult to reverse. For instance, a decision to regroup grade levels to allow for a middle school program or a set of alternative schools is a much more difficult objective to change in midstream than are altering a bus route, rescheduling classes, or adding or eliminating a course or even a program. Strategic planning has much longer range implications than does operational planning. However, *short* and *long* are relative terms and so are *strategic* and *operational planning.*

Goals are statements of educational purpose—ends for which a design is made. They should provide a rule of choice among future possibilities. Future choices are made in order to maximize (roughly) the goals. Thus, goals help organizational members to make later decisions on what can and should be done and what cannot and should not be done. Goals, far from being the simple expression of the highest values of society, develop from inherently controversial issues.

The realization of goals becomes possible through strategic objectives. *Strategic objectives* have a definite scope and suggest direction to the efforts of those within the organization; therefore they must be stated clearly and concisely. Such objectives are a prerequisite to the determining of any course of action and should be clearly defined and understood by all members of an organization. If the planning system is to be consistent, the strategic objectives must always be directed toward the ultimate achievement of goals. Objectives should be capable of attainment and measurement and, once decided upon and implemented, should not be changed conspicuously. They provide scope and long-range direction to the efforts of administrators involved in operational planning. Continuous changes cause inefficiency and loss of confidence in leadership and direction.

Policies are statements or understandings that limit the course of action to be followed by administrators in obtaining objectives and, ultimately, in achieving goals. They are defined as verbal, written, or implied overall guides setting up boundaries that supply the general limits on acceptable organizational action. Policy narrows what can be defined as acceptable alternatives to be used in accomplishing objectives. Policies are the mechanisms by which top-level administrators can delegate operational planning to lower-level administrators since they furnish constraints on the alternatives that may be considered in order to obtain objectives.

The Watergate activities during the 1972 presidential election provide a classic example of operational activities, based on the goal of re-electing Richard M. Nixon, which were clearly out of line with what might be considered acceptable policy. Policy limits the operational behaviors that can be considered in accomplishing objectives and goals. To consider an example closer to home, a policy might suggest that a teacher cannot use excessive force that might physically or psychologically harm a student. Such a policy eliminates the possibility of taping the mouths of verbally disrupting students or tying physically disruptive students to their chairs.

The set of goals, objectives, and policies becomes the *strategic plan* for the organization; it constitutes the framework within which most operational administrators will function. Whether one approaches this effort as a comprehensive rationalist, disjointed incrementalist, or from somewhere in between, the results provide the strategic plan. The heart of the strategic plan is the definition and establishment of proper goals and objectives. In this connection, the first job of the administrator is to decide the purpose of the organization. Many related questions will naturally follow. For what purposes does the organization have the social, human service, and expert resources? What is the appropriate role for the organization? Does the organization have the power needed to achieve its purpose? Can the organization be changed to meet new purposes? These and similar questions must be answered in order to determine organizational goals and objectives.

Nothing may seem simpler or more obvious than to know what an organization should be doing. An automobile manufacturer fabricates automobiles, a hospital provides health care, and a school system educates people. However, when educators have failed to provide clear direction related to purposes, frustration and program failure have resulted. Peter Drucker has said that "sooner or later even the most successful answer to the question 'What is our business?' becomes obsolete" (Drucker, 1974, p. 157).

Typically, purposes and goals change as new goals are added. Institutions that try to attain simultaneously a great many different goals confuse their own members and the outside public on whose support they depend. Also, no organization has the abundance of truly effective resources to accomplish all that might be desired of them. A lack of clear purpose causes people and money to be allocated to activities that are no longer productive or appropriate.

Dwight Allen (1978) suggests that schools have too many obsolete offerings for children and need to set specific and courageous goals for the abandonment of outmoded programs. He suggests the development of courses in computer skills to replace courses in trigonometry and geometry. Others have questioned the school's role in racial integration, family life education, values clarification, law and order education, and drivers' training. It has recently been suggested that the school of the 1980s will be expected to assume a great portion of the role more traditionally played by the family, especially in relation to child development. Preschool programs for children below the age of five are typical examples. These are crucially important strategic considerations that will have a profound influence on the purpose of schools and the future of society.

Operational planning

The next part of the MBO process is the translation of goals, strategic objectives, and policies into specific operational plans. The operational plans give specific detail as to how the work must be done to complete the task, which is part of the procedure and, when coordinated with the completion of other tasks, results in the achievement of school-system objectives and goals. The specific operational plans provide the detailed procedures and budgets for the functioning of each individual school and department or unit.

Operational planning is defined as the process by which lower-level administrators assure that resources are obtained and used effectively and efficiently in the accomplishment of strategic objectives. It is concerned with the procedures and methods of completing work. Procedures should be complementary and lead cumulatively to the accomplishment of desired goals. Most principals and teachers spend most of their planning time on operational planning.

A *procedure* is a series of related tasks that make up the chronological sequence of work to be accomplished. It is a general statement of the work believed necessary in order to remain within policy constraints and to accomplish strategic objectives and goals. Normally, a procedure includes a statement describing each task, when it will take place, and by whom it will be performed. Whereas a policy requires interpretation for its use, a procedure is usually very specific and requires little interpretation. The procedure, or task plan as they are often called, is the result of determining the manner of work performance of a task, giving adequate consideration to the objectives, policies, procedures, facilities available, and total expenditures of time, money, and effort.

Before final approval, the entire results of the task-planning effort should pass through the central administration where calculations of total costs and benefits as well as the relationships with strategic plans and other operational plans are checked for task assignments. If the operating plans are not financially and functionally sound, they are revised and adjusted accordingly. Central office administrators should point out deficiencies, provide guidance, and emphasize the important aspects of task plans in relation to overall strategic plans.

As is true in all forms of planning, as conditions change, so must methods, procedures, policies, objectives, and goals. They cannot be chiseled in stone for they are influenced by occurrences and are in fact themselves often outside the administrators' control. As Peter Drucker (1974, p. 163) states, objectives "are not fate, they are direction. They are not commands; they are commitments. They do not determine the future; they are means to mobilize the resources and energies of the business for the making of the future."

SETTING OBJECTIVES

There have been a number of excellent books (Armstrong, 1968; Burkhart, 1974; Instructional Objectives Exchange, 1972; Krathwohl et al., 1964; Mager, 1962; Steles and Bernardi, 1969) devoted solely to the topic of writing objectives. Knowledge about objective writing is important since "management by any kind of objectives and results" is only slightly better than having no objectives at all. It is slightly better since with poor objectives at least it is possible to realize that they were wrong or were written poorly. With none at all, the administrator has no, or at least little, idea what went wrong. However, poorly stated objectives, formulated through questionable procedures, although better than no objectives, may hamper, if not doom, the operation of a potentially powerful MBO system.

The MBO process requires the derivation of specific objectives from general ones so that objectives at all levels within the organization are appropriate, well stated, and linked together. Operational objectives are often broken into objectives for the organizational unit and performance objectives for the individual; strategic objectives usually provide direction for the entire organization.

Objectives should be clear, unambiguous, measurable, reasonably attainable, of high priority, challenging, and have a deadline and a specific assignment of accountability. They must remain within the authority and responsibility of the organizational unit or subordinate involved. Such objectives should be achievable within the time span suggested and should be sufficiently measurable to check progress at specific intervals within the time span. They can be of the reoccurring type that continue year after year, or they can be appropriate for one academic year or only part of a year.

Objectives should be used to establish outcomes or results (product) and/or specify activities (process). The process or activities to be implemented can be stated as an objective, but those activities must be clearly paired with the purpose or result for which they are carried out. Emphasis on results is needed to ensure that the existence of the activity or people doing certain work (teaching in classrooms, completing reports, attending meetings, working on programs) never distracts or confuses employees as to individual and unit purpose. Ultimately all administrators must measure results, not effort. Alan Harrington's warning is appropriate here: "Watch out when a man's work becomes more important than its objectives—when he disappears into his duties."

Objectives, regardless of their level, have certain components that are necessary in their formulation. These components are usually classified under five major descriptive dimensions:

1. Who—institutional, departmental and/or individual dimension
2. Behavior/process—activities and/or results dimension (Note: activities should be tied in some way to desired final results)
3. Measurement—qualitative and quantitative dimension
4. Time and prerequisites—the amount of time and prerequisites needed
5. Proficiency—specified level of performance

If the objective misses any of the above-mentioned dimensions, it must be reformulated. The following strategic, operational (unit), and performance objectives provide an example of this classification model:

STRATEGIC OBJECTIVE

1. The school system
2. will improve the academic performance of nonspecial education students failing a course
3. as measured on the basic competency test
4. given at the conclusion of the 9th grade academic year
5. as evidenced by a 95 percent pass rate among nonspecial education students.

OPERATIONAL OBJECTIVE (UNIT)

1. All junior high schools in Norfolk school district
2. will develop a "school-within-a-school"
3. to provide intensified small-group instruction for academically slow students not classified as special education

4. through daily class bells (periods)
5. of less than 16 students receiving intensified individualized instruction in the area of study they failed.

PERFORMANCE OBJECTIVE (PRINCIPAL)

1. The junior high principal
2. will identify, recruit, and schedule
3. teachers to teach
4. during the academic year
5. all five of the intensified basic skills classes in reading, math, language arts, science, and social studies.

PERFORMANCE OBJECTIVE (TEACHER)

1. The intensified basic skills math teacher
2. will develop individualized math units for student remediation and intense individualized instruction
3. which will be used by academically slow students (failing a math course) during intensified small-group instruction
4. in 'school-within-a-school" class periods
5. to improve the performance of 80 percent of such students to a level where they can pass the average math course and the minimum 9th grade competency test.

Notice that all five components appear in the objective regardless of its level or purpose.

There are a number of additional ground rules to assist the administrator in setting operational objectives. Although a given objective may not satisfy all the various criteria, the objective should be consciously checked against each to enhance its validity and usefulness. Charles H. Granger (1972, p. 65) suggests some of the criteria to be applied when developing objectives:

1. Is it, generally speaking, a guide to action?
2. Is it explicit enough to suggest certain types of action?
3. Is it suggestive of tools to measure and control effectiveness?
4. Is it ambitious enough to be challenging?
5. Does it suggest cognizance of external and internal constraints?
6. Does it relate to both the broader and more specific objectives at higher and/or lower levels of the organization?
7. Possibly most important, does it suggest desired performance or results?

While objectives should be stated in qualifiable terms, sometimes objectives cannot and should not be reduced to specific measurement. Objectives may be verbal descriptions of the ideal conditions that would exist if the goal were attained. This condition exists in the example of an operational objective presented above. Odiorne (1976, p. 29) suggests a rule of rigor that can be applied: "Measure that which is measurable, describe that which is describable, and eliminate that which is neither." He suggests that objectives require criteria, but not all criteria will be measurable.

As in other areas of public administration, it is argued that many of the most important outcomes of education cannot be measured. This is a major point of contention in applying the MBO process:

> It is commonly argued that public service institutions aim at intangible results, which defy measurement. This would simply mean that public service institutions are incapable of producing results. Unless results can be appraised objectively, there will be no results. There will only be activity, that is costs. To produce results it is necessary to know what results are actually being achieved. (Drucker, 1976, p. 16)

Although outcomes may be intangible and difficult if not impossible to quantify, there are many indicators that allow one to determine if the ideal and intangible conditions desired have been achieved. Performance can be measured, or at least judged; however, the indicators may describe rather than measure performance. For example, "mass literacy" as a strategic objective is totally intangible. However, the linking of operational objectives—such as "Each elementary school teacher in the Shaker Heights school district is responsible to see that 90 percent or more of his or her students are reading at or above grade level as measured on the SRA reading test that is administered in May of each year"—is easily measured. This and other similarly linked operational objectives become not only measures of operational accomplishment but indicators of accomplishment of the strategic objective. Thus, although strategic objectives may be intangible, the operational objectives required to accomplish them provide for clear and measurable outcomes that serve as indicators of strategic success. This makes possible both the allocation of effort and the measurement of performance—hence, a management guidance system. This system provides for the management and measurement of operational effort as well as indicates success regarding strategic outcomes.

In this context, strategic objectives and their resulting measurement become important and risky decisions since they provide direction and serve as criteria of performance and will be used to appraise and make judgments regarding the success of the organization. They determine where efforts will be spent and how activities will be evaluated. The implications of "mass literacy" as a strategic objective are great. The tangible operational objectives it suggests are severely restricted by this single strategic objective and its indicators of success. For instance, unless otherwise stated, stimulation of the more gifted students will automatically be postponed or given secondary status since the gifted students in a teacher's classroom will develop basic learning skills with much less effort than the average and less intellectually gifted student. In fact, much money has been spent in the United States to provide remedial work to bring low student achievement up to minimum levels. Schools also have worked especially hard with students who are unable or unwilling to learn in order to force them to attain basic learning skills. Such operational activity is the result of strategic objectives related to "mass literacy."

Indicators of successful achievement of this objective would include attendance figures, performance on competency tests, functional literacy statistics, standard of living, poverty level, people overtrained for nonskilled work, and so on. It could not be measured by performance on college entrance exams, opinions of student preparation by undergraduate college faculty, general leadership effectiveness, engineering, legal or medical advances, and the like. This second set of indicators would be related to the strategic objective of "full, cognitive, affective, and psychomotor growth." This strategic objective suggests programs of stimulation as well as remediation.

In addition to providing direction to operational efforts and a means to begin judging performance, strategic objectives also establish what Drucker (1976) calls "priorities, posteriorities, and candidates for abandonment." No institution is capable of doing many things, at least of doing many things well. Institutions must concentrate and set priorities. Strategic objectives are the result of risky decisions about what activities should be given priority, what activities should be given secondary status or postponed, and what activities should be abandoned. (This process can be greatly aided through the application of zero-base budgeting, which is discussed in Chapter 6.) Strategic objectives of abandonment and schedules to attain these objectives are just as essential a part of the MBO process; however, they are unpopular, disagreeable, and difficult to obtain.

For example, the 1975 Public Law 94-142 set up a number of strategic objectives related to school systems providing for special education in the "least restrictive environment deemed feasible." This strategic objective proved to be a very painful and disagreeable one for many special-education educators, who still believed in and wanted to maintain and expand the concept of centralized learning centers for special-education students. The strategic objectives related to Public Law 94-142 deemed necessary the reduction and/or elimination of learning centers and the use of specialists in regular schools. School systems that successfully implemented the law typically established objectives for the reduction and abandonment of the learning center concept. Though there was resistance, it was essential to the success of achieving "least restrictive environments." With declines in enrollments and in public and financial support, school systems are going to need to establish objectives that will bring about reductions in buildings, staff, and services. Although objectives affecting "candidates for abandonment" are difficult to establish, they greatly reduce the time period over which the organization must expend energy, often agonizingly, to adjust to hard times.

This leads to a final problem in the development of objectives. To be part of an MBO system, an objective must be operational; that is, capable of being converted into specific performance, into work, and into work assignments. This is a very important distinction, since the terms in which objectives are sometimes stated can best be described as oversimplified deceptions. As Drucker has often said, "If objectives are only good intentions, they are worthless." A major difficulty in implementing MBO programs has resulted from this inability to state clear operational objectives. Generally speaking, the broader and vaguer the objective, the more agreement with it, but the less practical use that can be made of it. Objectives must be precise enough for community and organizational personnel to know whether they have been attained and yet general enough to develop some level of agreement as to their desirability.

THE REVIEW PROCESS

Once the objectives have been set, the administrator can plan the needed task activities and take proper action to see that the objectives are met. The administrator must determine if what is being done in fact leads toward the objectives. Drucker's original conception of the MBO process stressed "measurement" and "control." He stated that administrators

> must be able to measure performance and results against the goal. It should indeed be an invariable practice to supply managers with clear and common measurements in all key areas of a business. These measurements need not be rigidly quantitative; nor need they be exact. But, they have to be clear, simple and rational. They have to be relevant and direct attention and efforts where they should go. They have to be reliable—at least to the point where their margin of error is acknowledged and understood. And they have to be, so to speak, self-announcing, understandable without complicated interpretation or philosophical discussion. (Drucker, 1954, p. 131)

The review process is usually made up of intermediate reviews of progress to date and a final review of objective accomplishment. The intermediate review serves many purposes; however, its primary purpose is to determine if organizational units and subordinates are progressing satsifactorily toward the completion of operational objectives and, ultimately, strategic objectives. If not, some corrective action may be needed.

A second function of the intermediate review is to provide information related to performance. Personnel evaluation is an old and persistent concern in all organizations. The MBO process addresses the supervision of subordinates through the identification and establishment of individual performance objectives. The supervisor monitors the performance objectives, providing opportunities for development in these areas, and then discusses the results of progress being made.

As long as the supervisory function has a future orientation—emphasizing present performance and future expectations, it is consistent with the MBO process. It is only when it has a historical orientation—documenting past behavior and past results against historical standards—that it becomes inconsistent and possibly destructive to the MBO process. Drucker and especially McGregor were concerned with the use of control to dominate and manipulate one person by another (McGregor's theory X). The nondomination or positive approach is necessary if management by objectives is to work:

> The means (for achieving goals) are used for joint problem identification and solution rather than for punishment or blame. When a performance begins to move in an undesired direction, it is not the time for heads to roll. It is the time for managers and subordinates to meet together, (a) to determine the reasons for the changes, and (b) to develop solutions to the problems that have come up. Thus, the system takes on an "early warning" function of surfacing problems, beginning the resolution process before those problems reach the crisis state. (Commonn and Nadler, 1976, p. 69)

A third purpose of intermediate review is program evaluation. Today these evaluations are most often used for new programs that are supported by state, federal, or foundation funds. However, the same principles are applied during the implementation of an effective intermediate review process. Examination of Guba and Stufflebeam's (1970) content, input, process, and product model (CIPP) of evaluation shows how this system fits neatly into the MBO process (CIPP is just one of many effective models; see Worthen and Sanders, 1973). Examination of Figure 5-4 reveals that the Guba and Stufflebeam content and input evaluation model is a needs assessment and resource inventory and is effective for providing information needed for developing strategic objectives. The process and product evaluation determines if planned activities have achieved desired results and accomplished operational objectives. In this way, the evaluation provides an excellent indicator of performance and a useful source of information for making future decisions.

	STRATEGIC PLANNING		OPERATIONAL PLANNING	
	Context Evaluation	Input Evaluation	Process Evaluation	Product Evaluation
Objective	To define the operating context, to identify and assess needs and opportunities in the context, and to diagnose problems underlying the needs and opportunities.	To identify and assess system capabilities, available input strategies, and designs for implementing the strategies.	To identify or predict, in process, defects in the procedural design or its implementation, to provide information for the preprogrammed decisions, and to maintain a record of procedural events and activities.	To relate outcome information to objectives and to context, input, and process information.
Method	By describing the context; by comparing actual and intended inputs and outputs; by comparing probable and possible system performance; and by analyzing possible causes of discrepancies between actualities and intentions.	By describing and analyzing available human and material resources, solution strategies, and procedural designs for relevance, feasibility and economy in the course of action to be taken.	By monitoring the activity's potential procedural barriers and remaining alert to unanticipated ones, by obtaining specified information for programmed decisions, and describing the actual process.	By defining operationally and measuring criteria associated with the objectives, by comparing these measurements with predetermined standards or comparative bases, and by interpreting the outcomes in terms of recorded context, input, and process information.
Relation to Decision Making in the Change Process	For deciding upon the setting to be served, the goals associated with meeting needs or using opportunities, and the objectives associated with solving problems, i.e., for planning needed changes.	For selecting sources of support, solution strategies, and procedural designs, i.e., for structuring change activities.	For implementing and refining the program design and procedure, i.e., for effecting process control.	For deciding to continue, terminate, modify, or refocus a change activity, and for linking the activity to other major phases of the change process, i.e., for recycling change activities.

FIGURE 5-4

The CIPP Model of Evaluation

Source: Adapted from Daniel L. Stufflebeam, "Education Evaluation and Design," in Blaine R. Worthen and James R. Sanders (ed.), *Education Evaluation: Theory and Practice*. Worthington, Ohio: Charles A. Jones Publishing Co., 1973, p. 139.

The final review typically involves assessment of which of the operational objectives were successfully accomplished, how well they were achieved, the reasons for any failures, and how well the successful accomplishment of operational objectives contributed to the strategic objectives. This is the application of MBO to the accountability process. Again, it is important to stress the team approach and to look to the future in order to minimize defensiveness. Remember, the impact of certain activities may be small even though the efforts of those involved in implementing them were high. This is often a bitter pill to swallow and it is natural for some individuals to focus on the activity, to become defensive, or to subvert the system. Such psychological cover-ups must be strongly resisted if the organization is to be effective. But they must be handled correctly and carefully if the individual, unit, or organization is to remain intact and to "get on track" and begin accomplishing objectives. This is where many of the behavioral aspects of administration come into play.

In conclusion, control is a form of feedback that allows the administrator to move from diagnosis to prognosis and finally proactive activity. This usually eliminates much crisis and thus avoids reactive approaches to administration. Measurement helps provide direction to effort and vision. The proactive approach to administration is certainly not an easy one, but it usually provides better results than any other approach. Drucker states:

> Do the deviations from the planned course of events demand a change in strategies, or perhaps a change in goals or priorities? Are they such that they indicate opportunities that were not seen originally, opportunities that indicate the need to increase efforts and to run with success? These are questions the administrator in the public service agency rarely asks. Unless he builds into the structure of objectives and strategies the organized feedback that will force these questions to his attention, he is likely to disregard the unexpected and to persist in the wrong course of action or to miss major opportunities.

> Organized feedback leading to systematic review and continuous revision of objectives, roles, priorities, and allocation of resources must therefore be built into the administrative process. To enable the administrator to do so is a result, and an important result, of management by objectives. If it is not obtained, management by objectives has not been properly applied. (Drucker, 1976, p. 17)

MBO—A FACE-TO-FACE SYSTEM

The most important single reason for the failure of MBO has been the tendency to treat it as a paperwork system rather than a face-to-face management system (Odiorne, 1976). Where there is no face-to-face dialogue, most MBO systems will break down. The use of memoranda to eliminate person-to-person "interfaces" is seldom successful even though memoranda are an essential part of the system for verifying and following-up on decisions and agreements. Rodney H. Brady summarizes the importance of personal interface:

> MBO is perhaps better perceived as a muscle than merely a tool. The more it is used, the stronger and more necessary it becomes. However, if MBO is merely a management system on paper and is not allowed to be exercised as an integral part of running an organization, it will atrophy and become useless. (Brady, 1976, p. 74)

Organized feedback and individual participation in the MBO process go a long way toward developing an efficient and effective organization that serves the needs of its clients as well as its employees. Evaluation helps to provide meaningful direction to participative effort and helps organizations to discover ways of optimizing outcomes. The MBO process depends on the completeness and accuracy of the information upon which it is based and the creativity, knowledge, and expertise of those who interpret and shape that information into a meaningful plan for future efforts. The MBO process provides a tool by which administrators can select and relate knowledge, facts, results, and assumptions regarding present and future programs for the purpose of visualization and formulation of desired outcomes and purposeful activities.

GUIDELINES FOR PLANNING

1. Under a planned guidance and control system all members of the organization receive basic directions, plus the authority and freedom needed to operate to the best of their professional ability. All participants travel in the same direction, working toward mutually understood objectives, thus reducing confusion, misunderstanding, and wasted effort. Workable criteria are established against known objectives to evaluate and objectively measure performance of people and programs.

2. The school division's operational guidance and control system evolves from the planning effort and is made up of mission statements, goals, strategic objectives, policies, operational objectives, budgets, procedures, and finally, work methods (teacher plans and the like). This list begins with the more general strategic plans, which are used to provide direction and coordination for the more specific and measurable operational objectives that follow. The entire system allows for the delegation of authority and responsibility, which makes possible the efficient allocation of resources and the measurement of performance.

3. Although such guidance and control systems are discussed in the Bible and have probably existed since humans first organized themselves, they have most recently been described as systems of management by objectives (or, MBO).

4. There have been two major schools of thought regarding how objectives should be used. The first takes a very narrow view, seeing objectives more as a tool for supervision and control. The second, which encompasses the

first, sees objectives as a tool for planning, supervising and controlling school-system activity. The second has gained the greatest level of support since MBO systems often lose much of their usefulness if they do not incorporate and coordinate strategic objectives such that they are closely linked to the operational objectives. However, models of the MBO process seem to fluctuate between the extremes of these two schools of thought.

5. Objectives should be clear, unambiguous, explicit, measurable, reasonably attainable, of high priority, challenging, achievable within a deadline, and have a specific assignment of accountability. Objectives should tell (1) who is responsible for the work; (2) the activities and/or results that are expected; (3) how they will be measured; (4) the time span provided and the needed prerequisites; and (5) the level of proficiency desired.

6. MBO systems typically serve two major control functions. The first is to provide general information to managers regarding whether the organization is on track and progressing satisfactorily toward the achievement of objectives. The second is for use in the supervision of subordinates to establish expectations regarding individual performance and to identify target areas that need more intensive development efforts in order to ensure success.

6

Fiscal Planning

The schools of the future will eliminate uneconomic procedures so that available funds can go further. . . . Expenditures will be applied to the more functional and important type of learning. Relatively unimportant school activities must qualify after honest appraisal of their value.

–J. LLOYD TRUMP (1979)

The budget provides that moment of truth when the administrator learns which plans will be accepted, modified, or rejected. It becomes the basis of all future operational planning efforts by adding the dimension of future reality to strategic plans. Future reality is determined as allocations of resources are made among various levels of activities needed to accomplish strategic objectives.

Budgeting is done in order to ensure that required resources will be available at the right time and in the right amount to be able to complete proposed actions and accomplish planned objectives. Budgeting forces management to examine in detail both the general economic situation of which the school system is a part and the economic interrelationships among all the school system's various activities. In this sense, the adopted budget specifies the financial limits within which the planned actions of the school system must be conducted. Thus, plans and budgets together provide a picture of what is intended and expected and the means by which the objectives are achieved.

This makes the budget a very powerful tool in the planning process. As administrators soon learn, plans are seldom successful unless they are financially supported by the budget. In fact, the surest way to determine how effective a school system's planning efforts have been is to determine how well they are funded. If the budget does not support the plan, the system has little chance of accomplishing it—the planning effort becomes a paper system lacking both subordinates' respect and effort.

A HISTORICAL PERSPECTIVE

Budgetary practices became common in business and industry before local boards of education accepted them generally. Business, between 1907 and 1926, was interested in the use of the budget as a fiscal control device. The budget became a disciplined way to handle expenditures and was concerned mainly with accuracy and control. Such fiscal control and responsibility were the primary needs of the time.

Although planning and policy considerations were slightly more important in governmental budgeting activities, the major concern of public budgeting was also centered on regulating governmental activities. By the 1930s the line-item budget, characterized by expenditures listed in broad categories, became firmly entrenched (there was greater concern with the spending process than the planning process). The Depression only further added to the concern for greater control.

It was in this environment that the school budgeting process began to develop and take shape. Prior to 1920, budgetary practices in local school systems were relatively undeveloped and nonstandard. John W. Twente's (1922) study of 363 city school systems showed wide divergence in budgetary practices. Gradually the various states enacted laws that established guidelines for all districts in the receiving and disbursing of school funds and in the preparation of the budget. The methodologies were somewhat similar to those developed in the federal government and in business.

In 1949, the Hoover Commission recommended that "the whole budgetary concept of the federal government should be refashioned by the adoption of a budget based upon functions, activities, and projects: This we designated a 'performance budget.'" Performance budgeting was used with little success during the 1950s; it was a purely mechanical innovation that made the budget neither more understandable nor more useful in planning and decision making. However, the idea of placing greater emphasis on the planning function of the budgetary process lost little momentum as a result of the failures of performance budgeting.

The introduction of PPBS

Robert S. McNamara brought a new concept of budgeting, called planned programming budgeting systems (PPBS), to the Department of Defense in 1961. On August 25, 1965, President Lyndon Johnson announced at a news conference: "This morning I have just concluded a breakfast meeting with the cabinet and with the heads of federal agencies, and I am asking each of them to immediately begin to introduce a very new and very revolutionary system of planning and programming and budgeting throughout the vast federal government, so that through the tools of modern management the full promise of the finer life can be brought to every American at the lowest possible cost." By 1967, efforts were made to spread PPBS to state and local levels as well. It was also introduced as a pilot program in a number of school districts across the nation during this same time. The basic ingredients of the PPBS system are budgetary planning with emphasis on outputs, program activities, and accomplishments, planning for and attaching resources to programs rather than to line items.

The federal PPBS program was officially closed down in 1971, six years after it was initiated. Many states and localities, including California and New York, have also abandoned the system. There is much debate regarding the impact that PPBS has had on actual budgeting practices. There are few, however, who would argue that it did not increase awareness of the importance of the planning function in the budgetary process. An ex-budget official at the General Accounting Office, Harry Havens, concludes:

> The formal structure of PPBS is now dead; the analytical concept is still very
> much alive. In fact, the analytical concept was always more important than
> the formal structure. The primary value of the structure was to force the use
> of the analytical concept. (Havens, 1976, p. 43)

Jerry McCafferey stated that by 1976, many believed that although program budgeting had had its day, it was not totally gone. Expertise remains, as do some of the fundamental concepts. He stated: "Some agencies still use many of the information gathering and presenting techniques, even though underneath it all remains the line-item building block process" (McCafferey, 1976, p. 36). Richard Rose states:

> The PPBS program of OMB was officially closed down in 1971, six years after
> it was initiated, but the program analysis that it was meant to stimulate has not
> ceased. Whether judged by the number of planning and evaluation units, program
> analysis, or actual analysis done within federal agencies, there has been a substan-
> tial jump from the zero-base year of 1965. It can be argued that the concepts of

PPBS have prospered more following evaporation into the Washington climate than when it was a high Executive Office priority. (Rose, 1977, p. 68)

There remains a residual impact of PPBS on existing federal planning and budgeting processes. Legislatures and high-level administrators are now more inclined to specify strategic objectives; program managers are now more likely to justify budget requests in terms of those objectives.

Similar findings exist at the state and local level. In 1971, the Association of School Business Officials found that 387 of the 1,377 school districts responding to their questionnaire claimed to be installing PPBS or actively considering implementation. By 1974, Stephen J. Knezevich had identified about 500 school districts claiming to operate in the PPBS mode.

Possibly the most extensive research regarding PPBS was the "State-Local Finances Project" begun in 1969 through George Washington University (Mushkin, 1969). The project included the pilot implementation and evaluation of PPBS in five states, five counties, and five cities. The final reports of the 5-5-5 project had some traces of optimism but made no claims of success. By 1970, two states (California and New York) and its associated counties and cities had abandoned PPBS and the 5-5-5 program.

In 1975, Michael Kirst published a complete analysis of the rise and fall of PPBS in California. Although many had believed that local resistance to PPBS was caused by the high degree of technical expertise required, Kirst found just the opposite. There seemed to be strong agreement on the technical and analytical aspects. However, when the advisory commission broadened its purview to include objectives and the linking of budget to objectives, strong opposition from forces on the left and the right began to mobilize. The PPBS commission was not supported by any major political or institutional leader. Once the vocal opposition coalesced, the support for PPBS proved to be very shallow. It appears that legislators want public school accountability, but only if the particular planning and analysis techniques used do not provoke organized opposition beyond professional educators (Kirst, 1975).

The end results of most studies of the demise of PPBS are not clear. Although many argue that the formal structure is dead, there seems to be a belief that the analytical concepts and some of the PPBS budgeting approach is very much alive. Thus, PPBS today is as much a mode of thinking as it is a process.

Zero-base budgeting

The most recent concern regarding the use of the budgetry process in public and service-oriented organizations is that it perpetuates ineffective, unnecessary, and/or outdated objectives and related activities. Cyert and March

(1965, p. 34) were probably the first to identify this problem: "Past budgets become precedents for present situations; a budget becomes a precedent for future budgets; an allocation of functions becomes a precedent for future allocations. Through all the well-known mechanisms, the coalition agreements of today are institutionalized into semipermanent arrangements." Drucker (1974) expanded on this concern:

> Finally, being budget-based makes it even more difficult to abandon the wrong things, the old, the obsolete. . . . The temptation is great, therefore, to respond to lack of results by redoubling efforts. The temptation is great to double the budget, precisely because there is no performance. . . . (Drucker, 1974, pp. 145-146)

This budgeting concern has fostered a new concept of budgeting called zero-base budgeting (ZBB). Since 1970, zero-base budgeting has become a popular phrase if not yet an established management planning and budgeting tool. The planning functions of the budget were more important in the 1950s and 1960s since the United States was then in a fairly strong growth period. This is why PPBS seemed so important. Now that we are faced with a slowing period and possibly a decline, there is greater concern in looking at the effectiveness of programs and the potential for cutbacks and stabilization. There is now greater concern for managing costs and eliminating fringes. The fixed costs that were easy to justify on the way up quickly become an impossible burden to maintain and justify when growth slows or stops—and just that much more difficult to reduce when facilities are in place and staff and service functions have made themselves seemingly indispensable.

Zero-base budgeting is a term and technique introduced by Peter Pyhrr (1970) to deal with just these problems. Zero-base budgeting is based on a "ground-up" approach in which all programs and activities, whether old or new, must be rejustified in the budgeting process each year. As with most management techniques, the concept is not entirely new. In 1964, the U.S. Department of Agriculture began a "ground-up" approach to budgeting in which each agency had to justify its program from zero rather than the previous year's level of expenditure. But by 1968 the concept already had developed some critics. Wildavsky and Hamman (1968) pointed out that zero-base budgeting vastly overestimates a person's limited ability to calculate and grossly underestimates the importance of political and technological constraints. Pyhrr recognizes these problems and believes that with appropriate design modifications to meet the unique existing structure and budget formats as well as with process efficiencies, these problems can be greatly reduced. Others have suggested that zero-base budgeting might be applied selectively to those areas about which management is most concerned.

Pyhrr has been given credit for developing the technique of zero-base budgeting in 1969 while working at Texas Instruments. Despite its critics, the technique has spread to at least a hundred companies, such as Xerox, Magnavox, Southern California Edison, and to many governmental units, including Georgia when Jimmy Carter became governor there. Along with this growing interest in zero-base budgeting, there has also been an increasing number of articles published on the subject. Since Peter Pyhrr's 1973 book, there have been at least thirty articles, two books, and parts of other books analyzing the subject, and it has been a topic on the agenda of many administrative symposiums.

Budgeting as a plan and a control

Historical analysis suggests it is difficult, if not impossible, to separate the budget process into elements and/or techniques of planning and control. Anthony (1965, p. 11) states: "The cycle starts with the preparation and approval of a budget, which clearly is a planning activity. But the budget is also used as a basis for control; indeed many contend that the budgetary preparation activity is a principal means of achieving control." In fact, because they are separated in time, the conflict between budgetary planning, management, and control is reduced considerably. Plans are formulated, tried out, and checked; their results influence new plans, which are put into operation and tested again; and so forth in a continuing chain reaction.

A recent study by Fremont J. Lyden of eighty-eight cities further supports this point. In trying to determine if these cities used budgeting more for control, management, or planning, he found the following:

> In conclusion, it is clear that both Schick's initial typology of budget-making purposes and Axelrod's later criticisms of it are of value in understanding the government budget process. Schick provides an overall conceptual framework to interpret the meaning of the different structures of budgeting and the varied nature of budgeting as a policy-making process. At the same time, Axelrod correctly points out the sterility of simply categorizing the constantly changing process of budgeting into appropriately labeled boxes and the futility of charting the movement forward and backward from one stage to another.
>
> Each municipality's budget process includes aspects of all three decision-making systems. The meaning of reform is a particular emphasis given to control, management, and planning vis-à-vis each other. But these are supplemental thrusts, not conflicting ones. Each provides additional roles, information, skills, and evaluative criteria to the annual cycle of budgeting. Each recognizes different problems, expectations, and objectives which emerge and recede in importance in different cities at different times. Control, management, and planning each play their own distinctive part in the complete web of governmental budgeting. One

does not operate at the expense of the other two, but exists side by side with the others in a continuing and fluid relationship. It is not necessary to reject the old in order to try something new. (Lyden, 1975, p. 628)

FORMATS OF THE THREE MAJOR TYPES OF BUDGETS

The budget is used to plan for cash receipts and expenditures. In education we use what is sometimes called an appropriation budget. A fixed amount is set, in some relation to plans and needs, and increases in expenditures over this amount can be made only with the authorization of supplemental appropriations. Not infrequently there is considerable incentive to spend to the limit of the appropriation in order that it not be reduced in the following year.

The budget is also used to plan for debt repayment and efficient use of cash. For instance, as interest rates increase, so does the opportunity cost associated with cash balances in the general fund. The magnitude of this opportunity cost can be minimized by investing excess cash balances at a positive rate of interest, or in the case of cash deficiencies, to plan to hold off expenditures or speed the inflow of cash, thereby reducing the traumatic effect on the entire system.

Figure 6-1 provides a diagram of the cash-flow system in school districts. Clearly, the flow of funds in public school systems is enormously complex. The budget is an attempt to predict the flow into and out of the general fund during some future span of time. Cash is the lifeblood of the school system. Revenues that are part of the general-fund cash balance and are not earmarked for special programs or projects are disbursed for wages and salaries, utility bills, supplies, and so forth to accomplish planned objectives. One of the purposes of the budget is to discover whether at any time there will be insufficient funds on hand to cover needed expenditures. If cash shortages are not recognized in the budget, the school system may either have to go back to the city council or the taxpayer to request more funds or to reduce expenditures (personnel, material, and so on); both of these alternatives are politically (if not sometimes ethically) undesirable.

The budget usually covers one academic year and includes receipts and expenditures for both the previous fiscal year and the current fiscal year, and estimates for the following fiscal year. The budget might project receipts and disbursements on a monthly, quarterly, or half-yearly basis. The detail required depends upon the amount of information necessary. If the reservoir of cash is ample and the flow into and out of the reservoir relatively constant, estimates on a yearly or half-yearly period may be adequate. Should cash be scarce and

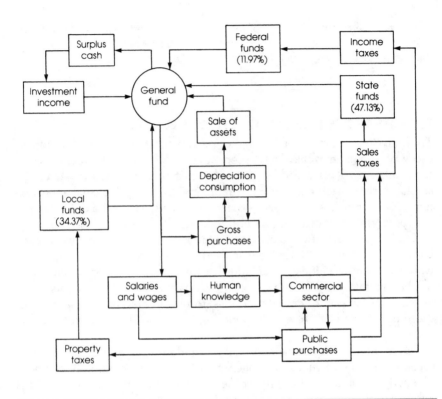

FIGURE 6-1
Typical Cash-Flow in School Districts

Source: Modified from D. Stuart Bancroft, "Financial Management of a Public School District,"
Management Accounting, July 1977, p. 25.

differences in rates of inflow and outflow from the general fund be considerable, it may be necessary to break down the annual budget estimates to
quarters or months.

Methods for estimating revenues from all possible sources are usually complex and require economic and financial experts as well as the assistance of
those responsible for collecting revenues. These estimates are usually updated
on a monthly or quarterly basis. The sources are varied and, as shown in Figure
6-1, come from revenues from local, state, and federal taxes and from the sales
of property. Other sources of funds include rebates, rents, tuitions, and insurance adjustments. Capital expenditures are covered by sale of bonds and
other forms of loans. Some revenues, such as property taxes, may produce

relatively stable and predictable amounts from year to year while other revenues may fluctuate greatly. Revenue projection is a topic beyond the scope of this book and usually is provided for and updated by a school system's financial experts. There are many texts that discuss sources of revenues and methods of estimating revenues for budgetary purposes (see, for example, Benson, 1968; Johns and Morphet, 1969; McLoone, Lupco, and Mushkin, 1967).

There are three major budget formats used to plan for the flow of funds into and out of the general cash fund: (1) line-item (function–object) budgets; (2) program budgets; and (3) zero-base budgets. The plan for classifying expenses is often the same in all three systems; however, the organization of these expenses is entirely different.

These three types of budgets are not incompatible and each can provide useful and needed information for planning, control, and management. Adherence to one does not preclude using some techniques of another approach. Instead, the three budget-making approaches can be complimentary, or one can become more important depending on organizational needs and situations (Lyden, 1975, pp. 625-628). If a sophisticated enough computer system is used for financial records and the data are properly organized, the computer can prepare cost and budget information in all three formats.

Line-item budgets

An object budget is a listing of the objects of expense, such as salaries, supplies, equipment, services, insurance, travel, professional improvements, postage, maintenance, utilities, fringe benefits, rents, debt reduction, and so forth, without regard to their function. A function classification lists estimates of expenditures in terms of the purpose for which they are made—administration, instruction, health services, pupil transportation, food service, operation, fixed charges, summer school, adult education, and so on. Today's general line-item budget has evolved from a combination of these two types.

Because of the wide variety of classification systems used to account for school expenditures and revenues and the consequent difficulties involved in securing comparable data concerning the financial operation of school systems, the United States Office of Education in 1957 issued a handbook, *Financial Accounting for Local and State School Systems*, which was updated in 1966 and again in 1973. The handbook provides recommendations regarding expenditure and revenue accounts to be used in budgeting and accounting. For the most part, state requirements and local school budgets have followed the basic recommendations made by the U.S. Office of Education. Table 6-1 presents a summary by functional category for a line-item budget that relies heavily on standard line-item categories. An example of object detail for one functional category—(Instruction, the third line on Table 6-1)—appears in Appendix A.

TABLE 6-1
Virginia Beach City School Board Estimate of Expenditures, 1980-81

CODE NUMBER	ITEM OF EXPENDITURE	EXPENDITURES 1978-79	BUDGET 1979-80	BUDGET 1980-81	INCREASE/DECREASE (%)	BUDGET, 1980-81 FIRST HALF	SECOND HALF
	Regular Day School						
12010	Administration	$ 637,412.07	$ 827,745.00	$ 869,202.00	+ 41,457 (4.7%)	430,101.00	439,101.00
12011	Research, Planning & Develop	236,899.95	290,997.00	189,315.00	− 101,682 (−53.7%)	69,600.20	119,714.80
12020	Instruction	34,690,158.81	38,492,066.00	42,396,024.00	+3,903,958 (9.2%)	21,567,732.56	20,878,291.46
12022	Other Instructional Costs	4,472,618.44	4,908,742.00	6,555,767.00	+1,647,025 (25%)	3,462,780.00	3,092,987.00
12030	Attendance and Health	668,447.72	804,066.00	917,900.00	+ 113,834 (12.4%)	326,692.38	591,207.67
12040	Pupil Transportation	2,638,991.63	2,797,019.00	3,392,980.00	+ 595,961 (17.5%)	2,735,321.00	657,659.00
12060	Operation of School Plant	3,469,812.46	4,050,425.00	4,466,605.00	+ 416,180 (9.3%)	1,633,482.61	2,833,122.40
12061	Maintenance of School Plant	2,529,911.17	2,501,136.00	3,087,943.00	+ 586,807 (19%)	1,432,721.65	1,655,221.40
12070	Fixed Charges	2,536,059.78	3,085,300.00	3,838,200.00	+ 752,900 (19.6%)	1,855,542.39	1,982,657.60
12090	Capital Outlay	706,980.10	483,948.00	748,950.00	+ 265,002 (35%)	400,888.47	348,061.53
	TOTAL REGULAR DAY SCHOOL	$52,587,292.13	$58,241,444.00	$66,462,886.00		$34,177,582.78	$32,942,327.22
	Special Programs						
12081	Summer School	$ 161,448.66	$ 262,525.00	$ 259,806.00	− 2,719 (−1%)	71,367.00	188,439.00
12082	General Adult Education	26,400.85	39,386.00	94,951.00	+ 55,565 (58.5%)	27,477.87	67,473.13
12083	Basic Adult Education	54,268.93	54,381.00	101,080.00	+ 46,699 (46%)	45,535.29	55,544.11
12084	Vocational Adult Education	115,656.63	121,254.00	201,187.00	+ 79,933 (39.7%)	100,340.36	101,846.64
	TOTAL SPECIAL PROGRAMS	$ 357,775.07	$ 477,546.00	$ 657,024.00			
	GRAND TOTAL	$52,945,067.20	$58,718,990.00	$67,119,910.00			

NUMBER	ITEM OF REVENUE	RECEIPTS 1978-79	BUDGET 1979-80	BUDGET 1980-81	INCREASE/DECREASE (%)	BUDGET, 1980-81 FIRST HALF	SECOND HALF
1.	State	$23,995,247.00	$26,849,140.00	$28,397,403.00	+1,188,237 (4.0%)	14,198,701.50	14,198,701.50
2.	Federal	6,772,474.00	4,993,000.00	6,530,013.00	+1,357,000 (21%)	3,265,006.50	3,265,006.50
3.	City	25,361,035.00	26,876,850.00	32,192,498.00	+4,955,618 (15.5%)	16,713,874.78	15,478,623.22
	TOTAL	$56,128,756.00	$58,718,990.00	$67,119,910.00		$34,177,582.78	$32,942,327.22

Source: Modified version used by permission of the Virginia Beach City School Board with personal acknowledgment to Dr. E. E. Brickell, Superintendent of Schools, and H. S. Abernathy, Director of the Budget.

Line-item budgeting and planning

Debate about the effectiveness of the line-item budget most often centers on the method by which new budget estimates are generated or planned (James, 1964). Budget estimates are typically made from one year (1979–80) to the next (1980–81) by adding a percentage increment of the previous year's budget (1970–80). This budgetary planning process is called the incremental procedure, or theory, of budgeting. Department heads take a fixed percentage increase of the previous year's appropriations; then the budget director, superintendent, and school board arrive at a final figure by taking a fixed percentage cut (or addition) in the department's requests. This is the basis of stability in the appropriations process (Wildavsky, 1974). Stephen J. Knezevich states:

> Educational goals were related only indirectly to utilization of resources. More often past practices were perpetuated with minor modifications. The typical procedure was to record expenditure for a given budget classification for one or two previous years, enter the request for the future year, and note additional amounts requested. Little effort was directed toward justification of increases on grounds other than vague allusions to "need." (Khezevich, 1973c, p. 67)

Such a budgeting approach may circumvent the planning process rather than complement and refine it. Many believe that incremental procedures perpetuate activities that may no longer be needed and ignore other activities that have been planned for. Taking last year's estimates for granted as the base and modifying them by a given increment for the future period might be an easy and stable way to estimate future needs, but it may also be wasteful, extravagant, and a trap to perpetuate obsolete expenditures. It may also defeat the overall planning process:

> Incremental decisions occur when, for example, last year's programs are regarded as a base, most activities are allowed to grow by some fixed percent, and whatever resources are left over, if any, are then assigned to new or changed programs. The incremental technique concentrates the decision-maker's attention on the new or changed programs. Whether last year's programs deserve to be continued is a question that ordinarily does not get much attention. (Mann, 1975a, p. 86)

The literature criticizing the use of line-item budgets for planning purposes is so broad and diverse that no attempt will be made to review it. For those interested, most books and articles on PPBS and ZBB set up the line-item budget as a strawman and attack it as part of the presentation of their own methods. But the line-item budget has shown that it is capable of weathering a great deal of attack. It has remained the most prominent budgeting system in education.

Recently, however, studies suggest that strategic objections must support functions and objects of expense or they will wither and die. Therefore, line-item budgets do indirectly support planning activities. Studies by Sharkansky (1968), Lyden (1975), and LeLoup and Moreland (1978) tend to suggest that line-item budgets do support strategic planning as well as promote financial control and management. They have found that line-item budgets are based on strategic plans even when the incremental approach to budget planning is used. Programs that did not gain support during the planning process tended to wither and decrease in appropriations. They may die a slower death with line-item budgeting, but they do die eventually. LeLoup and Moreland concluded:

> The strategy of moderation . . . may be desirable for agencies seeking certainty, stability and high support of their initial requests, but it will not lead to agency growth and may in fact lead to agency decline. To obtain substantial, "nonincremental" increases in programs and budgets, an agency must attain a position of political strength (with support inside and outside of government) to justify a large increase. "Don't come in too high" is poor advice for an agency wishing to receive more money; "come in as high as you can justify" would appear to be better advice based on the results of this study. (LeLoup and Moreland, 1978, p. 239)

Recent research suggests that budgeted expenditures must be part of a supported strategic plan if they are to receive appropriate fiscal support during the budgeting process. Budgeting based solely on standard increments in the absence of budgeting linked to planning seems to have had its day. The long-run consequence of incremental budgeting without planning is no longer tolerated in a society demanding greater accountability.

The program budget

The distinction between the line-item budget and the program budget (PPBS) is important. The major difference between the two approaches is that whereas the program budget displays costs on a program-by-program basis, the function–object budget shows costs by type of item purchased. Typically, the function–object budget deals primarily with organizational responsibility and the various elements of expense. It does not say anything about the need for the "objects" of expense, their use, or their relative efficiency in delivering performance as measured against the planned objectives.

A program budget, on the other hand, provides a method for determining the costs of program goals and objectives. A program budget represents the appropriation of a fixed sum of money to achieve a specific objective or set of objectives. Program budgeting relates the output-oriented programs required to achieve the objectives of an organization to specific resources that are then stated in terms of budget dollars. Program budgets are not increased incrementally but require management to decide how much to spend on a program to achieve a set of objectives. This form of analysis typically involves a comparison of alternative courses of action in terms of both cost and effectiveness, with ultimate approval being based on a set of cost-effective programs to achieve the planned objectives.

The analysis in PPBS generally consists of an attempt to minimize the dollar appropriation required to meet school-system objectives or, conversely, to maximize the output of a set of programs subject to the overall projected constraint from estimated receipts. The overall framework for this analysis is management's objectives, since the rest of the process boils down to measuring the extent to which the objectives are being met by selected alternative approaches. With conventional line-item budgets, the administrator does not always know what programs are being cut back due to budget cuts—the cut may be backed through each line-item. With PPBS, the administrator may select an optimal or best alternative (the most expensive) in one program and a less desirable alternative (less expensive) in another program based on the priority of the programs' objectives. Budget decisions are based on explicit statements of objectives and by a formal weighing of the costs and benefits of alternatives that might be selected to achieve objectives.

PROGRAM BUDGETING STRUCTURE

Probably the most important single task that must be accomplished in moving to PPBS is the development of a program budgeting structure. The task of adding program structure to the traditional line-item budget requires the identification and definition of programs that are required to achieve the school system's objectives. After this has been accomplished, much of the budgeting procedures are simply a matter of budgeting and accounting technology.

Harry J. Hartley (1968, p. 165) suggests one of many possible program structures based upon grade-level and subject-matter organization. His general program areas are:

Code	Program Category
001	Early childhood education (pre-K and K)
050	Primary grades education (grades 1–3; includes Reading, English, etc.)
150	Intermediate grades education (4–6)
250	Social sciences and humanities (7–12)
300	Mathematics and science (7–12)
350	Creative arts (7–12 or K–12)

400	Physical and health education (7–12 or K–12)
450	Business, vocational, homemaking education (7–12)
500	Pupil personnel services (K–12)
550	Special education (K–12)
600	Adult education and community services
650	Administration and general support services

The typical line-item classifications would be used under each of the program areas. Of course, this is only one of the many possible classification schemes.

These various components of program budgeting are probably best represented by Richard W. Hostrop's "cubular" concept. Figure 6-2 presents a modification of this cube. The cube presents the basic structure of program accounts used in PPBS. The basic three levels of the hierarchical ordering are program, function, and object over an extended time.

Alioto and Jungherr (1971) give the account code format for teacher supervision in the traditional function–object format as:

Fund	Function	Object
General	Instruction	Supervisors
A	12020	150

By adding two to four digits to the standard function–object code format, provision can be made for coding the various programs contained in the PPBS structure. A program code—for example, "050"—to represent primary grades education could be added to the existing function–object code as follows:

Fund	Program	Function	Object
General	Primary Grades Education (1-3)	Instruction	Supervisors
A	050	12020	150

This code embraces both the district's program structure and the function–object reporting requirements. The part of the code reading A-12020-150 meets legal and traditional financial reporting requirements for instructional supervision. The complete code, A-050-12020-150, provides the cost of supervision in primary grades education. Table 6-2 presents a summary of a semi-annual report of expenditures comparing budget estimates for a special education program. Instructional services and other functional categories can also be accumulated across all programs and reported in a line-item format, exactly the same as described in the previous section (see Table 6-1), if so desired.

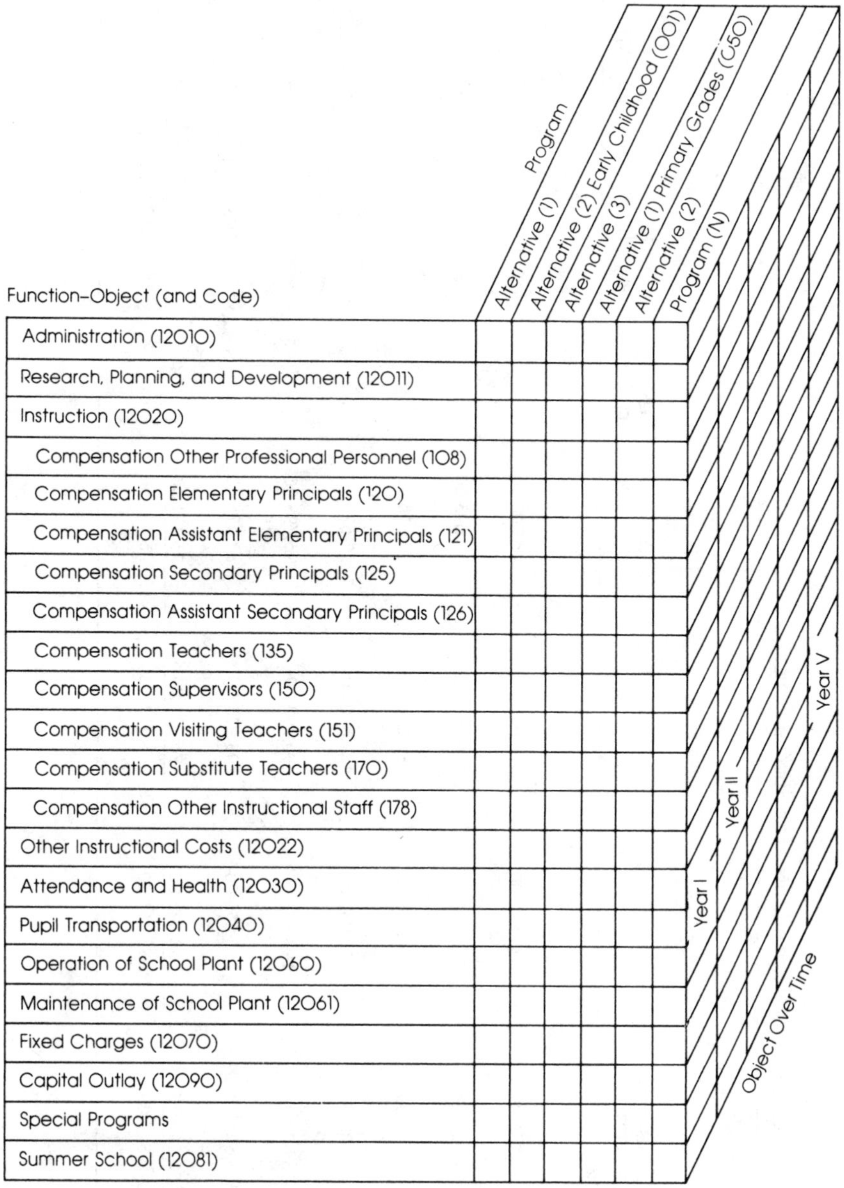

FIGURE 6-2

Cubular Concept of Program Budgeting

Source: From Richard W. Hostrop, *Managing Education for Results* (Palm Springs, CA.: ETC Publications), 1975. Used with permission.

TABLE 6-2

Program Budget Financial Statement for Expenditures for Special Education

PROGRAM: SPECIAL EDUCATION (550)

Cost Category	ACTUAL 1979-80 CONDITION	RECOMMENDED 1980-81 CONDITION	FIRST HALF 1980-81 ACTUAL EXPENDITURE	YEAR TO DATE FIRST HALF 1980-81 BUDGETED EXPENDITURE	UNDER BUDGET	OVER BUDGET	(%) PERCENT YEAR TO DATE
Administration (12010)	$ 1,263,765.00	$ 1,825,892.00	$ 1,378,050.72	$ 1,246,000.00		(−)132,050.72	.75
Instructional Services (12020)	20,091,815.00	22,713,386.00	11,356,693.00	11,356,693.00			.50
Other Instructional Services (12022)	522,852.00	574,313.00	287,156.50	287,156.50			.50
Attendance & Health Services (12030)	563,505.00	817,082.00	487,670.00	487,670.00			.50
Public Transportation Services (12040)	133,676.00	193,596.00	96,798.00	96,798.00			.50
Plant Operation Services (12060)	353,524.00	375,350.00	205,925.00	187,675.00		(−)18,250.00	.58
Plant Maintenance Services (12061)	150,440.00	152,842.00	76,421.00	76,421.00			.50
	$23,079,577.00	$26,652,461.00	$13,888,713.22 (102%)	$13,738,413.50		150,300.72	.52

PROBLEM AREAS WITH PPBS

Programs are typically organized around broad themes of organizational purpose. Because these programs are concerned with outputs and objectives, they tend to cut across functional responsibilities and traditional budgetary line items. With PPBS, expenses are analyzed and segregated into those that relate directly to programs and those that make up general administration and overhead. The difficulty is in determining what outputs of what particular organizational elements support similar objectives and how they should be clustered into programs. This difficulty is further compounded by such decisions as whether fixed overhead expenses should also be allocated to the programs. For instance, overhead costs might be allocated to programs in proportion to their salary costs.

Further, there is inevitable overlap due to the fact that some specific outputs serve multiple purposes or objectives (for example, improved services for the speech- and hearing-impaired); this is a situation that, despite obvious advantages, does little to simplify the development of program structure. However, a spin-off benefit of defining program structure is the identification of inconsistencies and duplications that will need to be resolved and eliminated. "As a result of organizing the district's activities into a program structure, the Portland, Maine, School District discovered many inconsistencies and unnecessary duplications in existing programs" (Alioto and Jungherr, 1971, p. 46).

Other developmental problems can occur when designing program budgeting procedures. Program structure sometimes suggests certain organizational problems. A program structure may not always follow the school district's established organizational hierarchy. Therefore, it may not be clear who should prepare the budget for a program when more than one unit shares the responsibility and funding for that program. Budgeting approaches can vary greatly—a small central group may prepare the budget with input from the administrators involved; program personnel at operational levels may prepare budgets that are then consolidated by a management team; or operating personnel who are involved in the same program may jointly develop the initial budget requests. The organizational structure for budget preparation depends upon the efficiency of working relationships and the need for coordination and motivation.

Zero-base budgeting: Simplifying decisions in hard times

The key difference between line-item incremental approaches to budgeting and zero-base budgeting is that ZBB does not build upon a base of the previous year's budget but begins at a decreased expenditure level or base zero. However, it is not this characteristic that is usually given credit as the true benefit of zero-base budgeting, but the fact that functions or programs can be ranked as to desirability and marginal activities can be identified.

As with most tools of administration, zero-base budgeting is more an attitude woven into a structured analytical process. Peter A. Pyhrr states that

> zero-base budgeting in its correct context refers to a general management tool that companies can use to improve planning, budgeting, and operational decision making. With it, managers can reassess their operations from the ground up and justify every dollar spent in terms of current corporate goals. Instead of staying within the same budgetary structure year after year, they can make major reallocations of resources from one year to the next. (Pyhrr, 1976, p. 5)

ZBB allows for the rankings of activities and increments, as well as the identification of activities, new or old, that the organization can no longer afford.

In zero-base budgeting, theoretically there are no givens. It suggests that one starts with the basic premise that the budget for next year is zero and that every expenditure, old and new, must be justified on the basis of its costs and benefits in relation to the strategic plans. Everyone would wipe the financial slate clean at the beginning of each fiscal year and start afresh. This, of course, suggests that there is no past; that experience and previous work is useless beyond the year; and that one is free to do as one pleases from one year to the next. As any administrator knows, this simply is not true and such a characterization is absurd. In the Department of Agriculture, there was resistance to implementing ZBB on practical grounds, because it seemed unrealistic, if not ridiculous, to some agency heads. In fact, the past serves as both a guide and a constraint upon the future. However, it is not necessary to start at point zero in the zero-base budgeting process.

Zero-base budgeting requires that educational administrators determine the minimum or basic requirements (increments) for running their activities. Any costs above the base increment are identified as added increments that must be justified. Next, each of the base and added increments receives a priority ranking followed by a hierarchical review with continual consolidated re-ranking. If increments cannot be justified, they must be eliminated—with a cost saving to the school system. The ranking process operates so as to focus attention on those increments on the margin—just above or just below the projected funding level for the following fiscal year.

DETERMINING INCREMENTS: BUILDING UPON MINIMUM REQUIREMENTS

The heart of zero-base budgeting is a ranking process in which management determines a priority for each program or decision package in the overall context as they view it. The ranking process is possibly best described by using a type of graphical representation that was first used by Paul J. Stonich (1977, pp.

31-32). Figure 6-3 summarizes how ZBB works. For simplicity of illustration, suppose a school district's language arts program was divided into three decision units: (1) primary, (2) secondary, and (3) special education. Further assume that each "decision unit" is broken down into four increments, or decision packages.

One package, the "base package," represents a minimum level of activity, and other packages identify extended higher-level activity or cost-level increments. Managers must establish a minimum level of effort (which must be below the current level of operation), then identify additional levels or increments as separate decision packages. After the appropriate base alternative is selected, incremental analysis begins. This requires the administrator to identify additional levels of effort and funding to perform that operation. If appropriate, these incremental levels may bring the operation up to or above its current level.

The highest-priority needs constitute the base package; this represents the bare minimum. The base package must include those functions and costs that are required by law or represent inescapable obligations. It typically defines the minimum level of activity below which effort ceases to serve any useful purpose. Setting this priority requires the operational administrator to determine the most important service needs provided by his or her unit.

Additional increments of service and cost are then developed; each successive increment contains those services that are next in order of priority. A decision package is defined as one incremental level in a decision unit. Typically, it takes the minimum level, plus one or two increments, to bring the operation up to current levels. However, even at the current level of effort, managers may change their method of operation and make operating improvements, so that the current level of effort may be maintained at reduced cost.

There are other methods used to determine increments under zero-base budgeting. One is to determine the minimum requirement for each decision package under standard or normal operating conditions. All costs over the norm would be identified as increments of that activity. In this case, the base or normal decision package might be excluded from review and only the increments would be considered. This procedure is somewhat similar to the traditional incremental analysis used for line-item budgeting, except for the number of increments and the method used to rank them in importance.

Another method for determining increments requires the submission of three decision packages for each activity budgeted. The base increment would be less than 100 percent of the current funding level; the current increment would include the additional activities required for a continuance of last year's programs including increased costs; and the new or improved increment would

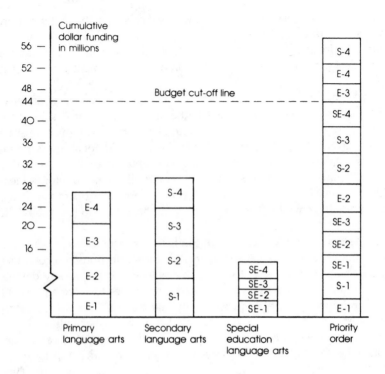

FIGURE 6-3

Graphical Representation of the Ranking of
Decision Packages for a Language Arts Program

Source: From Paul J. Stonich, *Zero-Base Planning and Budgeting*, 1977, pp. 31-32. Reprinted
with permission of the author.

include the required increases for an expansion of program objectives. A
similar method sets three increments, one based on the same-dollar amount,
and additions based on the same-performance amount and the recommended
amount. Yet another method is to establish a ceiling and prepare various
packages for funding efforts up to that ceiling. The ceiling is usually stated in
terms of the current fiscal year and is based on estimated funds available for the
next fiscal year. This level is the maximum that would be approved by top
management, so packages could only be developed to the ceiling level. The
base package might be stated as 80 percent of the budgeted, same-dollar incre-

ment; then a 20 percent increase to 100 percent; and finally the ceiling increment, a 15 percent increase, to 115 percent of currently budgeted funds.

The operating manager responsible for the decision unit normally oversees
the incremental analysis of that unit, since he or she is the person who is most
knowledgeable about the unit's operation and who will be responsible for implementation. This is the most important step in the ZBB process. Pyhrr states:

> The identification and evaluation of different levels of effort probably repre-
> sent the two most difficult aspects of the zero-base analysis, yet they are key
> elements of the process. If only one level of effort were analyzed (probably
> reflecting the funding level desired by the manager), and the request from the
> manager for funds exceeded funding available, management would have no
> choice but to do one of four things: It could fund the activity at the requested
> level, thus reducing profits; eliminate the program; make arbitrary reductions; or
> recycle the budgetary process. (Pyhrr, 1976, p. 8)

Referring back to Figure 6-3, we can see that each manager identified one base
increment representing minimum activity (E-1, S-1, and SE-1) and then
specified additional increments to bring the activity first up to current levels of
effort and finally to increase the level of effort expended on language arts.

RANKING PROCESS: PRIORITIES AND CANDIDATES FOR ABANDONMENT

All the time and effort spent developing viable decision packages will mean
little or nothing if an adequate review procedure has not been established. In
fact, one underlying assumption of ZBB is that the ranking process for the
forthcoming fiscal year will operate so as to focus attention on what are called
marginal packages—decision packages just above and just below the funding
level for the projected fiscal year. The ranking process also allows for the activities of one decision unit to be funded in full, for only the minimum level of
another unit to be funded, and perhaps nothing to be funded in the third unit.
This results in the identification of functions and duties that have lost their effectiveness—functions that have been placed at a low priority or eliminated.
The ranking process aids administrators in allocating resources away from outdated functions and makes those resources available to more effective functions. It provides a basis for cost reductions or additions as revenues fall or rise.

This is done by listing all the increments identified in order of decreasing
benefit to the school system. This ranking procedure establishes priorities
among the operational increments or activities described in the decision
packages. The cost and benefits of each increment are the formal criteria used
for the rankings. The give and take of the political process is vital in determin-

ing the priorities. Once the ranking has been completed, management can set the budget amount based on forecast revenues, and packages can be accepted up to this spending level.

In the language arts example, the analysis and ranking of the twelve increments was provided by a panel of principals and teachers, as well as by the assistant superintendent for instruction and the language arts staff; results in the priority order are shown in Figure 6-3. The first three increments ranked were E-1, S-1, and SE-1. However, SE-2 and SE-3 took priority over E-2 and S-2, thus indicating that funding up through the third increment of special education took precedence over the second level of either primary or secondary language arts programs. The special education increments had to be favored since money had been specifically earmarked for this program. The maximum spending resource level was estimated to be $44 million, which served as a cutoff point in the ranking process. The marginal increments that would require close examination are S-3, SE-4, E-3, and E-4. If the rankings of the marginal increments were still believed to be appropriate, then the increments would be cut off at SE-4; E-3, E-4, and S-4 would not be funded. The decisions made in the ranking process are then translated into budgets used to monitor performance.

One problem in zero-base budgeting is the time required to complete the review process. Ranking the many decision packages at each level can be very time-consuming and frustrating. Pyhrr (1976, pp. 10-11) has suggested some methods by which the difficulty and time in ranking decision packages can be reduced. He suggests that one should not concentrate on ranking packages that are regarded as "high priorities" or as "requirements" and that are well within the expenditure guidelines (other than to ensure that all cost-reduction opportunities and operating improvements have been explored and followed through). For example, do not spend too much time worrying about whether the package rated fourth is more important than the package rated fifth, but only assure that packages rated fourth and fifth are more important than the package rated fifteenth, and that the fifteenth package is more important than the package rated twenty-fifth, and so on. Managers should concentrate their efforts on the marginal increments and the levels of effort required to achieve objectives. Pyhrr states:

> With the decision packages ranked in order of priority, management can continually revise budgets by revising the cutoff level on any or all rankings—that is, it can fund package Nos. 1 through 55 but not package Nos. 56 through 75. This assures that the highest-priority decision packages have been funded. Of course, this means that some of the new high-priority programs have been funded by eliminating or reducing lower-priority, on-going programs. (Pyhrr, 1976, p. 10)

ALLOCATING RESOURCES ACCORDINGLY

Once the allocation decisions have been made, detailed budgets are prepared. These are done at the budget units when the approved decision packages are returned. This is mostly a mechanical function using the rankings and information previously accepted in the ranking process. The group of funded increments constitute the upcoming year's budget. The final budget is assembled by taking the base increment and adding on all other approved increments to show the total allocation for that budget item. An example of combined packages appears in Table 6-3; it lists the allocations for the transporting of pupils in the Greece (New York) central school district.

As can be seen in Table 6-3, the base increment appears under the "Reduced" column, the base plus the first increment appears under the "Current" column (more money is required to maintain current effort), and the third increment is added to the first two to get the "Improved" column. The total increments recommended as a result of the ranking process appear under the "Administration Recommendation" column.

The final format for a ZBB, although prepared in a vastly different fashion, can be made to look very similar to the end product of the more traditional line-item or PPBS approach. It all depends on the desired budget format and how the information is abstracted and accumulated. This process is typically simplified by placing the needed identifying digits, as previously discussed for program budgeting, in a well-coded chart of accounts that can be used to describe components of each increment.

PERFORMANCE AUDITS AND THE SUNSET CONCEPT

Recently, two related developments—performance auditing and the sunset concept—have incorporated much of the ZBB philosophy and process but limited the commitment of man-hours required. Performance audits do not have to be performed annually and are done when top management believes an audit or review is necessary. Like ZBB, performance audits require each manager to analyze, or to cooperate in analyzing, his or her operation, including the efficiency and effectiveness of each program.

The sunset concept has been popularized in Colorado, where it was approved by a senate bill in 1977. This concept states that the sun will set on given activities every three to seven years—that is, the activity will automatically be abolished on a given date. For the activity to be resurrected, it must pass the same type of scrutiny it would be subjected to in a zero-base system. The initial results in Colorado with the sunset concept seem to be more impressive than those in Georgia with the ZBB process. However, only time and experience will decide the usefulness of any budgeting system in any given era of history.

TABLE 6-3

Budget Resource Requirements, Greece Central School District

TRANSPORTATION OF PUPILS—REGULAR
A1-4-320-0-00-2-000

| | 1980-81 ADMINISTRATION RECOMMENDATION | | 1980-81 DECISION PACKAGE AND ALTERNATIVES LEVEL OF SERVICE | | | | | | 1979-80 CURRENTLY APPROVED | |
| | | | CURRENT | | IMPROVED | | REDUCED | | | |
	BUDGET	STAFF	BUDGET	STAFF	BUDGET	STAFF	BUDGET	STAFF	BUDGET	STAFF
000 Unallocated										
150 Salary Regular	$ 417,650	75.0	$ 417,650	75.0	$ 437,650	75.0	$ 342,061	65.0	$ 367,956	62.0
151 Salary Overtime	20,500		43,000		46,800		20,500		20,500	
152 Salary Substitutes	19,200		17,500		19,200		15,120		15,898	
154 Salary Summer	4,000		4,000		4,800		3,500		3,000	
230 Equipment	16,500		4,500		16,500		4,000		3,924	
301 Supplies	17,500		20,000		22,000		17,500		23,086	
310 Gasoline	87,208		86,802		87,208		73,604		67,553	
311 Oil, Lab., and Antifreeze	5,240		5,240		5,240		4,420		4,054	
312 Tires	9,000		9,000		9,600		8,450		9,000	
332 Repair Parts	35,000		35,000		35,000		33,250		29,406	
400 Contracted Services	3,000		2,750		3,000		2,625		2,500	
451 Contract Transportation, Private	190,000		150,000		190,000		106,000		286,191	
473 Equipment Repair	14,960		14,960		15,200		14,280		14,018	
481 Workshops (Tournaments)	3,600		4,500		5,500		3,600		2,000	
500 BOCES	31,000		31,000		31,000		31,000		31,536	
000 Fringe Benefit Charge	122,642		122,414		122,642		112,879		122,607	
710 Insurance Premiums	21,000		21,000		26,000		18,627		11,020	
Total	$1,018,000		$ 989,316		$1,076,740		$ 811,416		$1,044,249	
Net Difference					+87,424		−177,900		+54,933	

Source: Modified from Greece Central School District. *1979-80 Budget Manual: Zero-Base Budgeting* (Greece. N.Y., 1979: mimeographed).

GUIDELINES FOR PLANNING

1. School budgets express the school's plan in fiscal terms—the expenditures necessary to support the plan. The budget stimulates refinement of operational plans when it supports the strategic plans upon which they are based. However, if the budget does not support the strategic plan, there is little likelihood that strategy objectives can be achieved no matter how much operational planning occurs. No amount of operational planning can make up for inadequate resources. In this way, the budget adds the dimension of future reality or feasibility to strategic and operational planning efforts.

2. The budget is a projection of the flow of funds—the lifeblood of plans—through the organization. The budget presents the planned receipt and disbursement of funds that will be needed in order to achieve strategic and operational objectives. The success of the entire planning process is determined by how well plans are supported by the budget, since the feasibility of plans is determined as the allocation of resources is being made.

3. The traditional line-item budget is a better tool for fiscal control than it is for fiscal planning. Fiscal resources are tightly controlled by each line item within the budget while expenditure estimates are typically made from one year to the next by adding a percent increment of the previous year's budget. Since the impact of incremental increases is not carefully examined, this approach causes programs that are no longer needed or supported to die a much slower death than other budgeting processes. The reverse is true during periods of expansion.

4. A program budget is most effective as a planning tool during periods of program and organizational expansion since it displays costs on a program-by-program basis rather than on a function–object basis of expense. The budget is not increased incrementally but on the basis of fiscal commitments needed to achieve various alternative program objectives.

5. Zero-base budgeting is an effective planning tool during periods of decline and retrenchment since it does not build upon existing operational activity but upon a minimum level below which effort ceases to serve any useful purpose. This base increment, as well as increments needed to bring the base up to an expanded level of services, receives a priority ranking and a hierarchical review, the sum total of which determines which base packages and increments will not be funded. The ranking process focuses attention on base packages and increments at the margin—just above or below the projected funding level for the following fiscal year.

6. No matter which of the three major budgeting processes is used, the final format of the budget can be placed in the traditional line-item form. The line-item format can be achieved by developing an effective coding system and using the computer.

7

Participation in the Planning Process

No one is wrong. At most someone is uninformed. If I think a man is wrong, either I am unaware of something, or he is. So unless I want to play a superiority game, I had best find out what he is looking at.

–HUGH PRATHER (1976)

Some Eastern philosophies see groups as being non-goal oriented. In such a situation, listening to, experiencing, and being with other persons is seen as the end in itself. Such a group is characterized by a choiceless or desireless awareness. However, most groups exist for the purpose of accomplishing specific ends, and it is the achievement of this purpose or end that most planning efforts aim for. Up to this point we have discussed the context and process of planning. The planning system comes to life when members of the group become involved in the planning process.

As discussed in Chapter 2, planning works best when it begins at the top and flows down and the communication required to develop plans flows up, down, and across. Board members, superintendents, and assistant superintendents need to develop strategic plans (mission, goals, strategic objectives, and policy) using the input and perspective provided by interested parties such as supervisors, directors, principals, teachers, parents, students, and others. In this way, a much broader range of expertise, experience, ideas, and values is brought to bear on strategic issues, and greater understanding and commitment will develop regarding final plans even though all may not agree or have their preferred decision accepted.

When interested participants have a legitimate opportunity to air their views, to find out where others stand and what they believe in, and, most important, to determine if the final decisions reached best meet the needs of all interested parties, they will better understand the decisions and will be more supportive and committed. It follows that operational planning should be the responsibility of operational administrators, with the involvement of top-level administrators, teachers, parents, coordinators, and students. Those who must do the work should play a major role in determining operational plans. As the adage suggests, "Keep decisions as close as possible to the scene of action."

How to establish an appropriate balance of participation in planning and decision making has been debated and discussed for the last century. In fact, concern for this problem can be traced back to Aristotle and Machiavelli. Most agree that resolution of the debate is crucial not only to planning and decision making but to all phases of effective management and leadership. In fact, the pattern of participation established during the planning process most often creates a precedence for the type of participation that will exist in all other phases of the organization's operation. At one extreme we find an apparent willingness to assign the planning and decision-making function to the very imaginative or powerful or to a very small select group of individuals; and, at the other extreme, to assign such responsibilities to all members within the organization regardless of ability, knowledge, or power. Probably the best approach is a more moderate one lying somewhere along this continuum. The decision regarding the level of participation in planning is a difficult one but all planners are forced to confront it.

A HISTORICAL PERSPECTIVE

Kurt Lewin, Ronald Lippett, and Ralph White's 1939 study of autocratic, democratic, and laissez-faire leadership styles was a forerunner in the research on this topic. Their work in the 1930s and 1940s established the study of group process as related to planning, decision making, and leadership in general as a new and exciting area of inquiry for psychologists, sociologists, educators, and other social scientists.

In discussing the results of their studies, Lewin related the impact of group participation on children:

> On the whole, I think there is ample proof that the difference in behavior in autocratic, democratic, and laissez-faire situations is not a result of individual differences. There have been few experiences for me as impressive as seeing the

expression on children's faces change during the first day of autocracy. The friendly, open, and co-operative group, full of life, became within a short half-hour a rather apathetic looking gathering without initiative. The change from autocracy to democracy seemed to take somewhat more time than from democracy to autocracy. Autocracy is imposed upon the individual. Democracy he has to learn. (Lewin, 1948, p. 409)

The findings of Lewin and his co-workers were supported by a number of investigators. Coch and French (1948), for example, explored the reasons underlying resistance to changing methods of manufacturing textiles in a Virginia factory with 600 employees. They found that "change can be accomplished by the use of group meetings in which management effectively communicates the need for change and stimulates group participation in planning the changes."

French and Lewin (1950) suggested that democratic values of participation have a positive impact in changing basic beliefs, making individuals more responsive to technical change, increasing productivity, and contributing to more positive employee attitudes. Victor Vroom (1964) found that high participation combined with high need for independence results in the most favorable attitude toward work, and low participation with high need for independence is associated with the least job satisfaction. Vroom (1965), after a comprehensive review of the research, concluded that "there is considerable evidence to support the notion that job satisfaction increases with participation."

McGregor refined and further developed these concepts in his book *The Human Side of Enterprise* (1960). He compared his theory X view of tight human direction and control with what he called theory Y integration of individuals and organization—the creation of conditions such that the members of the organization can achieve their own goals best by directing their efforts toward the success of the enterprise. McGregor pointed out that objectives by themselves seldom become long-term motivators of people. Instead, planning and administrative systems that depended on exhorting employees to work diligently and obediently in order to protect their professional positions and standard of living failed to use human resources in the most efficient way. McGregor believed that in unilateral planning and its resulting supervision the requirements of the organization were given priority automatically and almost without question. The objectives of the organization are not necessarily best achieved by such unilateral administration, because this form of management by direction and control does not ensure the most efficient plan or the commitment that would make available the full resources of those involved. People will exercise self-direction and self-control in the achievement of organizational objectives to the degree that they are committed and believe in those objectives.

Douglas McGregor presented a comprehensive discussion of the importance of participation in establishing objectives. A central principle of theory Y management and integration was "the creation of conditions such that the members of the organization can achieve their own goals best by directing their efforts toward the success of the enterprise." In theory X management, which McGregor condemns, the individual's personal goals are ignored on the assumption that salary and position should provide enough reward and satisfaction. If the individual resists management directives in an attempt to satisfy his or her needs within the organization, the individual's future could be jeopardized because of a "selfish" attitude and the fact that the individual does not measure up to "management potential." Theory Y suggests that the organization will suffer when it ignores the individual's personal needs and objectives.

Edward C. Schleh (1961) introduced the idea of management by results, incorporating McGregor's premise that self-control was essential for effective management. Schleh saw goal and objective setting as basically the job of the superior but he added the important idea of consulting with subordinates. He cautioned that "individuals may lose sight of the central purpose of the enterprise if only activities which are required of them are specified" (Schleh, 1961, p. 52).

Chase's study (1952) of 1,800 teachers in 216 school systems indicated that participation in decision making produces positive effects. Teachers who reported opportunity to participate regularly and actively in setting objectives and making policies were much more likely to be enthusiastic about their school system than those who reported limited opportunities to participate. Bridges (1964) found that teachers preferred principals who involved them in decision making; this was true regardless of whether the teachers had a high or low need for independence. Teachers' satisfaction with work was directly related to the extent to which they participated in decision making and the establishment of objectives. Similar results occurred in the studies of Lawrence and Smith (1955), Levine and Butler (1951), Maier (1950), Mann and Baumgartel (1954), and Wickert and McFarland (1967), all of whom found positive results when democratic or participative management styles were used.

RECENT RESEARCH

The Ohio State studies

A concerted research program in the area of leadership in planning and other areas of administration was conducted at Ohio State University in the late 1940s and early 1950s under the direction of Carrol Shartle (Fleishman, 1961).

Roughly what was found is that most leaders' behaviors could be classified into one of two dimensions—initiating structure (characterized by individuals who organize and define group activity and their own relations to the group, define the roles they expect each member to assume, assign tasks, establish ways of getting things done, and push for the achievement of goals) and consideration (characterized by an individual who shows mutual trust and respect, good rapport, and multi-directional communication directed toward maintaining good interpersonal relations, allowing subordinates more participation in decision making, encouraging high morale and job satisfaction).

Researchers began to investigate the relationship of these two dimensions to productivity and employee satisfaction. Halprin (1971) developed a four-quadrant model based on the dimensions of consideration and initiating structure and found that administrators that were high in both dimensions were more effective leaders. Conversely, leaders who are perceived as being effective in planning and other management functions tend to be high in both consideration and initiating structure.

Edwin Fleishman (1973), one of the original social scientists involved in the Ohio State studies, reviewed the twenty-year history of these studies and concluded that "the preponderance of findings...seem to indicate that the high-structure–high-consideration pattern optimizes more different effectiveness criteria, whereas the low-consideration–low-structure pattern most often appears the least desirable."

University of Michigan studies—participative leadership

Another series of studies originated with Rensis Likert at the University of Michigan Social Research Center. Likert (1967) studied managerial systems and identified administrative clusters or factors that included structures, controls, and leadership styles as well as attitudes, motivations, and perceptions of subordinates. From his continuing study he was able to identify four types of management systems or leadership styles. They were exploitative-authoritative (system 1); benevolent–authoritative (system 2); consultative (system 3); and participative (system 4). The ideal state for organizations was identified by Likert as system 4. By ideal, Likert meant as measured by organizational performance or effectiveness defined both in humanistic terms—maximum employee satisfaction and morale—and in the traditional criteria of performance—maximum output and efficiency.

Specifically, system 4 appeared to be consistently associated (in every type of organization Likert studied) with the most effective performance; system 1 had the least effective performance; system 2 was more effective than system 1, but less effective than system 3; and so forth. Likert suggested that system 4 is more complex than the usual management system and requires learning effective leadership and problem-solving skills, but it produces human organizations that are about 20 to 40 percent more productive than systems 1 and 2. Likert's research has been supported by practical implementation of system 4 participative leadership styles at General Motors Corporation (Mills, 1978).

The central concepts of system 4 participative leadership are supportive relationships, multiple overlapping group structures, group problem-solving through collaboration, high performance goals, and adequate levels of technical competence. In a word, it is based on subordinate participation and communication. System 4 harnesses human motivation in ways that yield positive cooperation rather than fearful antagonism on the part of the people in the organization; by contrast, systems 1 and 2 tend to develop less favorable attitudes, more hostile attitudes, or more submissive attitudes. System 4 doesn't use economic motivation alone to accomplish goals; it also uses what Maslow calls the higher needs of self-actualization as well as a sense of personal worth and importance, and it combines these kinds of motivational forces to help achieve higher levels of accomplishment, satisfaction, and a sense of personal worth, which in turn yield higher levels of physical and mental health. System 4 emphasizes that the structure of the organization ought to be looked at as a series of face-to-face groups, each of which is effective at planning, establishing objectives, and solving problems. The groups work toward finding solutions that are going to yield results favorable to the groups within the organization as well as to the interests of those persons served by the organization.

The managerial grid

Theorists Blake and Mouton (1964, 1978a, 1978b) developed a concept of leadership style that they labeled the "managerial grid." Figure 7-1 presents a graphical representation of the managerial grid along with what Blake and Mouton identified as the five most important differences among administrative leadership styles. In the grid, the degree of concern for production is expressed horizontally and the concern for people vertically. Proponents of the grid say that team-builder leadership, in which there is strong concern for both production and people, is the most broadly effective style of leadership. Research described in *The New Managerial Grid* (1978a) tends to support this contention and concludes that the team-builder leadership style is the one most positively associated with productivity and corporate profitability, with career success and satisfaction, and with physical and mental health.

The team builder is defined by many facets and beliefs:

1. Shared participation in objective setting, decision making, and problem solving is basic to growth, development, contribution, and commitment.
2. Informed choice is the soundest basis for organizational interaction.

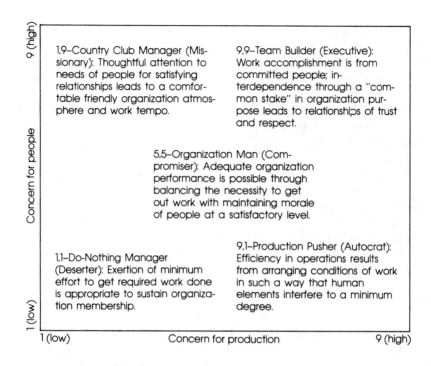

FIGURE 7-1
Administrative Grid

Source: Adapted from The Managerial Grid figure from *The New Managerial Grid*, by Robert R. Blake and Jane Srygley Mouton. Houston: Gulf Publishing Company, Copyright © 1978, page 11. Reproduced by permission.

3. Mutual trust, understanding, and respect undergrid effective human relationships in all organizations.

4. Open communication and participation support mutual understanding and trust.

5. Activities carried out within a framework of mutually understood goals and objectives integrate personal with organizational goals.

Blake and Mouton (1978a) presented over thirty studies that argued the benefits and effectiveness of the team-building participative approach to management and leadership. They argued that the team-building approach brings all concerns out and avoids crises. It also helps subordinates to learn and develop the competencies essential for effective participation and more in-formed action. They argued that participation should add to creativity and ver-satility of leadership and an understanding of final decisions. Objectives cannot be communicated more clearly than when all have participated in their development.

The team-builder approach does not assume that everyone will be of one mind. It suggests bringing subordinates together to face the contradictory character of their recommendations and help people to work together to develop organizational plans and decisions. Shared points of view and areas of disagreement, previously unrecognized, begin to emerge. Areas of similarity and differences are pared down, collaboration occurs, and decisions and agreements are made that are essential for coordinated, communicated, and understood effort. Mutual respect is maintained throughout with confidence that the solution ultimately reached, although not necessarily the one preferred by all involved, is more likely to be valid, has at least recognized most con-cerns, and will be easier to understand and implement.

The parallel organization

Stein and Kanter (1980) suggest that a form of parallel structure in organiza-tions is emerging; this new dimension allows organizations to do more things well than ever before. The "parallel" organization is one that attempts to in-stitutionalize a set of externally and internally responsive, participatory, problem-solving structures alongside the conventional organization that carries out routine tasks. Thus a needed management structure is added to the one that already exists. This parallel structure provides a means for planning and manag-ing change as well as a source of flexibility and responsiveness. More impor-tant, it provides a source of opportunity and power for individuals above and beyond the limited structures in traditional bureaucratic/autocratic organiza-tions. Such opportunity and power is critical to a high quality of work life and responsiveness to environmental needs.

People who work in organizations that develop such parallel organizations are highly motivated to perform; as a result, they develop and use their skills and knowledge productively (Stein and Kanter, 1980). They are more effective performers; they tend to support and empower one another and are more strongly committed to the school system and its goals; they raise their aspira-tions and are strongly engaged in their work; and they form political alliances and use active forms of protest to improve performance and provide an up-ward orientation.

Conversely, those organizations that do not practice these solutions exhibit increased stress, causing employees to withdraw, to devalue their skills, lower their aspirations, disengage from their work, and form protective peer groups that resist passively. A sense of powerlessness and a "what's the use" attitude develops. Employees become petty tyrants resisting needed change and innovation. They lower performance, they tend to withdraw support and fight with one another over power, and they prevent one another from acquiring skills and confidence. Such conditions lead to petty domination and little leadership and result in a focus on means, not ends, and in measuring performance by adherence to routine, not by accomplishment. This lack of involvement and participation ultimately results in decreased organizational performance.

Other research on participation

Chris Argyris (1978) argues convincingly that managers have an enormous impact on their subordinates' growth and effectiveness or their lack thereof. However, he states that leaders often block employees' needs for self-direction and their sense of personal competence. He found that supportive and participative leadership creates the optimal work environment, and that authoritarianism causes employees to be "leader centered" at the expense of their own ideas, interests, and competence—they try to please the boss. Argyris stresses the importance of trust and people's ability to take risks in front of each other.

Schmuck et al. (1977) reported the success of projects that involved participative management as part of an organizational development effort. They found much support for participation in their review of the research related to applications of participative management in the schools. Sadler (1970) found that administrators who consult their subordinates during the planning process receive the highest ratings for being helpful, letting people know where they stand, assisting people to get ahead, inspiring subordinates with enthusiasm, building team spirit, being familiar with subordinates' work, and for forward planning, delegation, problem solving, and trust. They also achieved high scores on items reflecting efficiency.

PLANNING AND THE MANAGERIAL CONTINUUM

Although the research seems clearly to suggest that participation is important to the effectiveness of the planning and decision-making process, there is still much debate on exactly how much participation should occur.

McGregor (1960) established what he called a "range" of participation. At the one end, there is very little influence, with individuals being informed of decisions and the reasons behind them. Moving toward greater participation, the individual might be given some freedom in implementing objectives; the

FIGURE 7-2

Continuum of Manager and Nonmanager Leadership Behavior

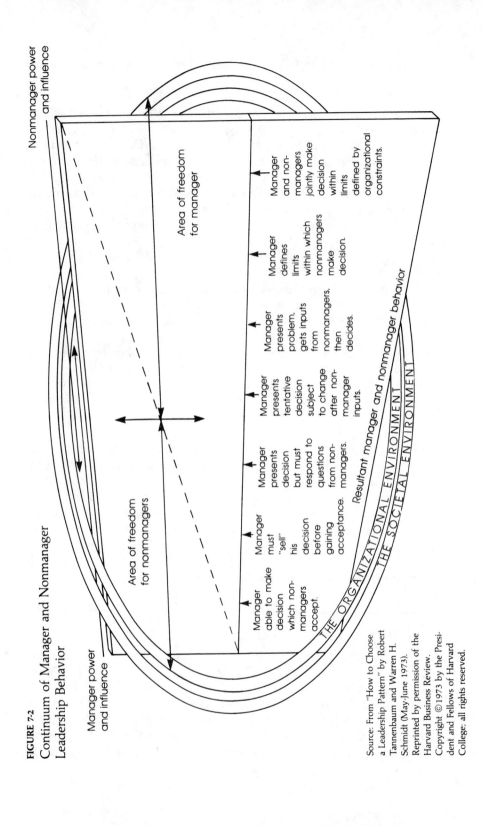

Manager power and influence

Nonmanager power and influence

Area of freedom for nonmanagers

Area of freedom for manager

Manager able to make decision which non-managers accept.

Manager must "sell" his decision before gaining acceptance.

Manager presents decision but must respond to questions from non-managers.

Manager presents tentative decision subject to change after non-manager inputs.

Manager presents problem, gets inputs from nonmanagers, then decides.

Manager defines limits within which nonmanagers make decision.

Manager and non-managers jointly make decision within limits defined by organizational constraints.

Resultant manager and nonmanager behavior

THE ORGANIZATIONAL ENVIRONMENT

THE SOCIETAL ENVIRONMENT

Source: From "How to Choose a Leadership Pattern" by Robert Tannenbaum and Warren H. Schmidt (May-June 1973). Reprinted by permission of the Harvard Business Review.

next step would include discussion with subordinates prior to making decisions final (after which managers might consider modification). Still greater participation would occur if the superior requested assistance in the form of input in developing solutions and setting objectives; next, the supervisor might request subordinates to help him or her find the best solution; and finally, the supervisor might accept the decision or objective upon which the subordinates were able to agree. Although McGregor argues effectively for the importance of participation, he does not define a point on his range where participation occurs or is satisfactory. Odiorne, in *Management by Objectives*, also seems to dodge this issue. The shortest chapter in Odiorne's book is on subordinate participation; it is very inconclusive.

At approximately the same time that McGregor published his work, Tannenbaum and Schmidt (1958) published the results of their examination of the same basic question that McGregor was concerned with; that is, what is the appropriate level of participation, given the possible range of behavior? They first published what they called their "continuum or range of possible leadership" in 1958 and then updated it again in 1973. Figure 7-2 presents the update of this continuum. It is very similar to the "ranges" described by McGregor. Each type of action is related to the authority used by the administrator and the amount of participation available to the subordinates in reaching decisions, making plans, and setting objectives. They suggest that participation is related to the administrator's power. Based on power, one's leadership style can vary from intimidation, through co-optation, to submission. The difference between the 1958 and 1973 articles is the change in control that managers were portrayed as having over where they operated along this continuum. In 1958, Tannenbaum and Schmidt viewed the manager as having almost unilateral control. In the 1973 article, they recognize the power available to all parties and the need to determine jointly the appropriate level of participation in order to achieve commitment and ultimate effectiveness in leadership efforts. In the 1973 article they view the total area of freedom shared by administrators and subordinates as being constantly redefined by interactions between interdependent organizational and human needs and influences. They concluded that "the new continuum is both more complex and more dynamic than the 1958 version, reflecting the organizational and societal realities of 1973" (1973, p. 164).

Fiedler (1967) believes that leadership depends on the situation, on what one is trying to accomplish, and on what one is up against. In Fiedler's conception of "situational" or "contingency" management, the administrator is counseled to accommodate and adapt, to move back and forth, to dominate and yield, to allow greater participation or none, depending on what he or she thinks best for the situation. Hersey and Blanchard (1977) support the contingency model and argue that the type of leadership style used should vary with the level of employee maturity existing in the situation being confronted. Contingency theorists repudiate the one-best-way idea (participation) for at least the following four reasons: (1) there are cases when there is no time to consult or to share problem solving in a participative way; (2) there are times when subordinates may not be competent to participate; (3) there are circumstances when the participation of subordinates would be wasteful because they have no stake in the situation and nothing to contribute; and (4) it is not wise to use a mechanical approach that is the same regardless of conditions.

Victor Vroom and Philip Yetton (1973) have developed a normative model of decision making based on five styles a manager can use, all based on the degree of subordinate participation necessary to choose an alternative. These styles are:

1. AI (Autocratic method #1): You solve the problem or make the decision yourself, using information available to you at the time.
2. AII (Autocratic method #2): You obtain the necessary information from your subordinates; you may or may not tell them what the problem is. The role your subordinates play in making the decision is clearly one of providing the necessary information to you rather than generating or evaluating solutions.
3. CI (Consultative method #1): You share the problem with relevant subordinates individually, getting their ideas and suggestions without bringing them together as a group. Then you make the decision, which may or may not reflect your subordinates' influence.
4. CII (Consultative method #2): You share the problem with your subordinates as a group, collectively obtaining their ideas and suggestions. Then you make the decision, which may or may not reflect your subordinates' influence.
5. GII (Group method #2): You share the problem with your subordinates as a group. Together you generate and evaluate alternatives and attempt to reach agreement (consensus) on a solution. Your role is essentially that of chairman—you do not try to influence the group to adopt your solution, and you are willing to accept and implement any solution that has the support of the entire group. (Vroom and Yetton, 1973, p. 69)

Given these five alternative decision-making styles, there has to be some method for choosing among them with respect to a specific decision-making situation such as the one that occurs in planning. Vroom and Yetton, after reviewing theory and research in the area, developed a set of situational characteristics, or what they call "problem attributes." In order to facilitate use of the rules and problem attributes in deciding the type of participative style, a decision tree was constructed (decision trees are discussed more fully in Chapter 10). In Figure 7-3, the problem attributes are arranged along the top. The rules are applied when one answers the diagnostic questions with respect to the particular situation. If you answered "no" to the first question (A), you would follow the line to the next node, answer question (D), and based on that answer, proceed until you reach an end point or terminal node. At the terminal node a decision style will be specified for that particular situation.

WHO SHOULD PARTICIPATE?

The question "Who should participate?" is one that has been debated by all planners and one that in the last analysis must be answered by each individual. The research tends to suggest that more participation in the planning process is best in the long run even though it is quite often much less efficient over the short haul. A higher level of commitment is achieved through participation, which results in more effective work performance even though there is considerably more time and effort involved in making the final plans.

The top-down approach to establishing objectives often creates confused perception regarding participation. Although the establishment of objectives flows from the top down, this does not mean that communication and participation regarding the establishment of objectives flows downward. The top-down approach to establishing objectives does not mean "communication down" with little or no participation in decision making. Authority and responsibility for setting objectives flows down but communication and participation in decision making must remain multi-directional. Each planner charged with establishing objectives at a given level must listen and give consideration to the thinking of those who have a legitimate interest in the decision. The debate regarding the degree of consideration and participation will probably continue into the next century; however, many would agree that the argument seems to favor a more active, broad level of participation.

Twenty years after the publication of *The Practice of Management*, Drucker (1976, pp. 12–19) has made a more precise statement about the point at which effective participation occurs. He believes that it is the manager's responsibility to set objectives and priorities after he or she understands the different and sometimes incompatible needs, objectives, goals, priorities, and strategies of the different people who are employed by and familiar with the organization. Only after such a mutual understanding has occurred will the administrator be prepared to make decisions regarding objectives.

Drucker analyzed the peak effectiveness of agencies that existed during the New Deal and that later occurred among certain Japanese organizations. He

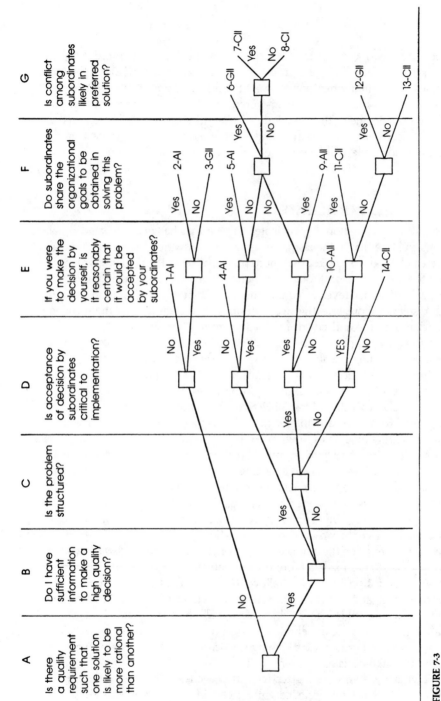

A	B	C	D	E	F	G
Is there a quality requirement such that one solution is likely to be more rational than another?	Do I have sufficient information to make a high quality decision?	Is the problem structured?	Is acceptance of decision by subordinates critical to implementation?	If you were to make the decision by yourself, is it reasonably certain that it would be accepted by your subordinates?	Do subordinates share the organizational goals to be obtained in solving this problem?	Is conflict among subordinates likely in preferred solution?

FIGURE 7-3
Decision Process Flowchart

Source: From V. Vroom and P. Yetton, "A New Look at Managerial Decision Making." Reprinted, by permission of the publisher, from *Organizational Dynamics*, Spring, 1973, ©1973 by AMACOM, a division of American Management Associations. p. 70.

found certain similarities regarding participation in both. He stated:

> Harold Ickes in Interior or Henry Wallace in Agriculture took infinite care to produce informed dissent within the organization and thus to obtain understanding for themselves and to create understanding for their associates. Thus, when decisions on goals and priorities were made unilaterally by the top man himself, and by no means democratically, they were understood throughout the organization; the top man himself understood what alternatives were available as well as the position of his people on them. (Drucker, 1976, p. 17)

Decisions were made so as to gain subordinate commitment and responsibility for performance and results and in the last analysis for the organization itself. In referring to the Japanese system of administration by objectives, Drucker states: "Consequently, they find out where their colleagues and associates stand, what they feel, and how they feel. Then a decision can be reached which the organization understands, even though large groups within it do not necessarily agree or would have preferred a different decision" (1976, p. 18).

J. B. Batten shared this view of how participation should occur in the development and establishment of objectives. He states:

> The work force—whether managerial, technical, or hourly paid—represents a vast amount of experience, ideas, and down-to-earth judgment. The top executive needs to use this, but with the understanding that he and he alone is accountable in the final tally for the results achieved. Thus, he listens, discusses, studies, and then approves objectives which embody the best thinking of his staff, but which he has paired, condensed, or expanded as may be advisable. These objectives of course stem directly from the corporate philosophy and are in full consonance with it; if this is not the case, something is clearly out of phase and needs attention. (Batten, 1966, p. 58)

The planner must obtain input and assistance through broad participation but can never lose sight of his or her own ultimate responsibility for making the final decisions. In the last analysis, it is the planner who has the lonely job of "biting the bullet," "taking the hard knocks," and making those final decisions. That is what the administrative decision-maker is paid to do, and that is what makes the job so fascinating and exciting.

GUIDELINES FOR PLANNING

1. The level of employee participation achieved during the planning process most often sets a precedence for the type of participation that occurs during all other phases of organizational activity.

2. Research tends to suggest that participative, collaborative, problem-solving, and team approaches to the planning and management process yield higher levels of achievement and satisfaction.

3. The hierarchical structure of organizations places authority and responsibility for final decision making regarding the development of plans with line managers. However, this should only occur after all interested participants have had a legitimate opportunity to have their views heard and considered, to find out the views and beliefs of others, and, most important, to determine if final decisions best meet the needs of the school system in general and the participants in particular. Only after such a mutual understanding has occurred will participants be willing to make commitments to the achievement of plans.

4. Although participative and collaborative approaches to planning are much more time-consuming and physically and emotionally draining than more autocratic approaches, they more than pay off, during the implementation of plans, as a result of increased commitment to one's work and to the school system in general.

8

Group Involvement and Communication

It takes two of us to create a truth, one to utter it and one to understand it.

—KAHLIL GIBRAN

Although much planning in school systems is accomplished through communication exchanges between two persons, the work of people in groups is very important as well. However, the more people who are involved in the group-planning process, the more complex are the group dynamics and the structures that must be used to gain the most from group participation. The planner needs to know alternative structures that can be used to facilitate the information flow so that groups of people can plan effectively.

Acting on a desire to expand participation in the planning process, organizations have attempted to amass the talents of groups of individuals in an effort to combine their individual skills to improve planning and decision making. Administrators have found that the adage "Two heads are better than one," or, more practically, "Several heads are better than one," is well founded. The group as a whole encompasses at least as much (and usually more) information than any single member. Educational planning, the kind involving future personnel and program development, requires accurate information, careful consideration, and involvement beyond a single decision-maker. Group decisions are necessary because the scope of planning problems is often such that no individual has sufficient expertise and knowledge to effect an appropriate solution. Through participation, group members can gain greater understanding of decisions and commit their support to plans.

THE COMMITTEE MEETING

One of the most common and widely used methods of obtaining group involvement is the committee meeting. The committee process is defined as a group meeting in which all communication acts take place directly between members with minimal controls or formal structuring (Delbecq, 1968). The typical process of decision making in the interacting group is (1) unstructured group discussion for obtaining and pooling ideas of participants; and/or (2) majority voting on priorities by hand count. The committee approach often brings people together across organizational lines in order that all views may be represented and a meaningful plan for action arrived at after the differing interests have been adequately expressed and advocated.

Committee meetings provide an opportunity for members interested in planning and decision making to come together and communicate, coordinate, and exchange relevant information related to contemplated plans. They also provide an opportunity to satisfy emotional needs for activity, participation, affiliation, and power. Those participating not only can have direct input into the planning process but also can gain greater understanding for the decisions that are finally reached. The experience, ideas, and values of a great number of individuals can be shaped into plans through committee efforts.

The success of the committee meeting is dependent on the competence of the committee chairperson to conduct an effective meeting or conference. The chairperson must be able to ensure that the group maintains direction, moves expediently toward the development and refinement of plans, and provides opportunities for all members to participate and contribute. To be successful in achieving these behaviors, the chairperson must be aware of the general needs of participating members and be adept at using appropriate procedural techniques to ensure that the committee completes the tasks at hand. This requires preparation to deal with both agenda and "hidden agenda" issues.

The preliminary consideration in preparing to conduct a planning meeting is determining the specific purpose of the meeting (problem solving, decision making, reporting, evaluation, or whatever). With this purpose in mind, the chairperson can make decisions about the composition and size of the committee, the frequency of meetings, and the process to be used. An agenda should always be set and distributed to members prior to the meeting so that they will be well prepared for the issues to be discussed. The leader should bear in mind the useful device of heading each agenda item "For information," "For discussion," or "For decision" so that those at the meeting know what they are expected to accomplish during the meeting.

In the meeting, the chairperson must fulfill task functions, which carry forward the meeting's purpose, and maintenance functions, which help group members develop satisfying interpersonal relationships. Task functions include initiating ideas on work procedures, giving/seeking information or opinion, elaborating, coordinating business, orienting participants, prodding the group, keeping records of what happened, and summarizing what has occurred in the meeting. Maintenance functions include ensuring that members have a chance to speak, ensuring that listeners have a chance to check on what they have heard, reconciling disagreements, sensing group mood, mediating differences, being responsive to others, clearing lines of communication, and helping attend to group and interpersonal processes.

It is the responsibility of the chairperson to stimulate discussion, maintain its focus, and redirect it if necessary. The leader must keep the discussion moving by interjecting comments when the group goes off on a tangent or when it gets hung up on an issue. The leader must ensure that arguments, which will naturally develop, help in terms of bringing out the points that have to be discussed. An argument should be legitimate, valuable, and nonpersonal. The leader must have a repertoire of responses in order to keep meetings on track and to eliminate unnecessary disruptions. Members must be given an opportunity for thinking, formulating ideas, analyzing prior comments, and tying facts together. Finally and perhaps of most importance, the chairperson must have the ability to manage feedback efficiently. Such feedback should be descriptive, specific, directed toward appropriate issues, well timed, and clear. Meetings should always try to close on a note of achievement.

Following the meeting, brief minutes should be distributed. They should tell the time and date of the meeting, where it was held, who chaired it, and who attended. All agenda items (and other items) discussed and all decisions reached or important information developed should be reported. The time when the meeting ended and the date, time, and place of any meetings planned for the future should also appear in the minutes of the meeting.

R. Alec MacKenzie (1975) has identified a number of ways to help ensure that meetings are productive and that minimal time is wasted. Before the meeting, establish purposes and the agenda in writing; see that the right people, time, and location are selected; provide adequate notice and requisite information; then, start on time; and finally, have no more or fewer meetings than necessary. During the meeting, reduce or eliminate socializing, wandering from the agenda, and "hidden agenda" ploys; limit the time for each item on the agenda; set and keep an ending time; and allow no interruptions except for clear-cut emergencies. Also, keep objectives in mind and move toward them; summarize conclusions drawn from the meeting and remind participants of any assignments. After the meeting, produce concise minutes recording decisions, assignments, and deadlines and distribute them within one day of the meeting. Ensure effective follow-up and list "unfinished business" at the beginning of the next agenda. Don't maintain the committee after a mission has been accomplished and it is no longer needed.

PROBLEMS IN GROUP DYNAMICS

There are certain inherent problems with committee meetings that are difficult even for the most skilled chairperson to counter. Meetings are considered, along with memos, to be an effective means of communicating, understanding, and digesting information. However, questions have been raised regarding the efficiency of meetings to support the creative and original thinking that is so important in effective planning (Delbeck, Van De Ven, and Gustafson, 1975).

Group theorists and practitioners are questioning the viability of committee meetings when used in planning, especially strategic planning (Van De Ven, 1974). With an increase in the size of organizations that perform a wider range of complex, uncertain, interacting functions, committees that truly represent all interests regarding the organization's future are often quite large and unwieldy. When committees grow to more than twelve people, a complete and free exchange of views within the allocated time and among all concerned is often too time-consuming and energy-absorbing (Jay, 1976). There is extensive lore about the ineffectiveness of such large committees; for example, "A large committee is one that, if you ask it to design a horse, will compromise on a camel."

Committee collaboration is often influenced by certain psychological factors that color the careful consideration of issues by the various committee members. Emerging leaders (high status, expressive, or strong individuals) tend to dominate activities because of either their knowledge or their informal influence. Personalities or organizational status may also interfere because ideas gain credibility through their association with the person advancing them and his or her position. Group processes often leave participants muddled, discouraged, and frustrated because of the endless meanderings and lack of resolution.

An area of group dynamics that has received considerable attention in recent years is the way in which committees reach decisions. Irving Janis (1975) has studied committee activity and identified negative characteristics of group dynamics that limit and interfere with effective critical thinking. He describes these negative characteristics as "groupthink."

Groupthink typically occurs in a very cohesive group whose members have strong positive feelings toward the group and are highly motivated to remain part of the group. There is a strong sense of solidarity, which makes the group strive for agreement and prevents it from seriously considering problems or possible consequences that might occur as a result of decisions being made. Janis points to Truman and his advisors' 1950 decision to cross the 38th parallel in North Korea and Kennedy and his advisors' 1962 Bay of Pigs invasion as examples of decisions that fell victim to groupthink.

Janis suggests nine major symptoms of groupthink. His first symptom is "mind-guarding"—the tendency of group members to protect the group from disturbing outside ideas or opinions. This problem can then be compounded by "rationalization," in which members defend and support one another by developing rationalizations that help the group maintain its self-respect. This often leads to the "illusion of morality," in which the group believes so strongly in its own morality that it disregards any ethical, value-laden, or moral objections that do not match the group's view. In an attempt to ensure agreement within the group, "direct pressure" is applied to any group member who provides a dissenting viewpoint. "Deviant members" soon learn not to speak out in the group, and rarely is there disagreement. This results in "self-censorship," as individual members restrict any doubts they might have.

There is an "illusion of unanimity," where members assume that everyone else's silence implies agreement; they are reluctant to disrupt the unity of the group and therefore appear to support positions about which they may have serious doubts. One does not become too concerned about whether the best decisions are being made because an illusion of "invulnerability" develops in which the group feels complacent and is secure in any decision it may make. The group becomes invulnerable because of its solidarity; it is felt that nothing it does could possibly harm the members of the group. This feeling is then expanded into the "we versus they" attitude, where any outside members are viewed as the enemy. The enemy must be manipulated, controlled, and cajoled to ensure that the group does not receive any disturbances from its adversaries. This leads us back to "mind-guarding"; the process will often continue to its own destruction.

The chairperson must make a conscious effort to reduce problems in group dynamics if quality planning decisions are to be made. In the committee process there are various methods or techniques that can be used to reduce these problems. Influential leaders might not be placed as the chairpersons of committees, and the membership periodically might be changed. The chairperson and others can invite in outside experts to give their opinions, can require every member of the group to be a critical evaluator, and can avoid exerting too much of their own influence, leaving members free to explore all alternatives and come to an informed decision. When important decisions are made, groups at all levels of the organization can be formed to discuss and move toward consensus of action. Also, a facilitator might be used in committees to take care of all procedural functions so as to free the committee members to maintain their involvement in the issues and decision making.

When an individual has time to work alone, his or her entire attention can be focused on the problem-solving tasks. When an individual works in the presence of continued committee discussion, he or she must also attend to the social interpersonal obstacles that are dictated by the needs of various personalities and that are present when committees meet face to face. One considerable obstacle is that of changing one's mind in front of the group. Some approaches make it much easier for participants to change their minds since they have less ego involvement in defending an original estimate. Participants are less subject to the "halo effect," where the opinions of one highly respected person influence the opinions of others. Also reduced is the "bandwagon effect" of joining in with the opinions of the majority. Consensus of opinion is facilitated by requiring justification for any significant deviation from the group average.

Murray Turoff (1970) and Norman Dalkey and Olaf Helmer (1963) argue in their respective studies that attempts to reduce the psychological effects of a group setting enhance creative decision making because respondents become more anonymous and fears of potential repercussions and embarrassment are removed. Campbell (1968) found that the greater the amount of effort a decision-making process demands of a group in maintaining social and emotional relationships, the less proportionate time and effort remain for task-instrumental problem-solving. In addition, written expression of ideas was found to induce a greater feeling of task commitment.

To reduce the influence of psychological factors associated with committee meetings—for example, the unwillingness to abandon publicly expressed opinion, the persuasive power of an articulate or loud advocate, and the bandwagon effect of majority opinion—other methods have been developed. The two most prominent are the Nominal group process and the Delphi technique. The Nominal group process is most similar to a committee meeting, requiring many of the same leadership skills. The Delphi technique is not similar to committee meetings at all and in fact does not require any form of face-to-face interaction.

THE NOMINAL GROUP PROCESS

The Nominal group process is an extension of the committee process. The Nominal group is a structured group meeting in which individuals work in the presence of others but do not verbally interact for periods of time. There are a number of variants of the Nominal group approach, but the Delbecq, Van De

Ven, and Gustafson (1975) model is most often used. First of all, this approach is typically used when the number of participants is less than fifteen, although there are some variations that allow for larger groups. The leader presents the question in writing and verbally reads the question—avoiding requests for clarification. The individuals sit in full view of each other; however, they do not speak to one another about the matter at hand. Instead, each individual writes ideas on a pad of paper in front of him. This is to map group thinking; the ideas should be stated in brief words or phrases. At the end of ten to twenty minutes, a very structured sharing of ideas takes place. Each individual in round-robin fashion provides one idea from his or her private list. This is important since it equalizes opportunities for all to present ideas. These are written by a recorder on a blackboard or flip-chart so that they are always visible to all group members. Ideas are provided verbally or by each participant passing his or her ideas to the moderator, who puts them on the blackboard or flip-chart as rapidly as possible. New ideas can be added even if they were not on the individual's worksheet. There is still no discussion, only the recording of privately generated ideas.

This round-robin listing is continued until each member indicates he or she has no further ideas to share. No one adds any ideas that have already been presented by others (group members may decide if a duplication has occurred). The output of this first step is the total set of ideas created during this structured process. Generally, spontaneous discussion then follows for a period (in the same fashion as an interacting committee meeting and with the chairperson serving the same functions) before Nominal voting. The leader must pace the group so all ideas receive sufficient time for clarification. "Nominal voting" simply means that the selection of priorities, rank-ordering, or rating (depending on the group's purpose) is done by each individual privately. Usually the participants are asked to select five to nine items for rank-ordering or rating and to record them on a three-by-five-inch card or rating form. The cards are collected and shuffled to retain anonymity. The votes are counted and the results are tallied in front of the group. The group decision is the pooled outcome of the individual votes. In some cases the first round of votes is discussed again for a specific period of time and then a second vote is taken, with the outcome of this vote being final. This allows for an accurate aggregation of group judgments and error reduction.

This Nominal group process has gained extensive use and recognition in health, social service, education, industry, and public administration (Van De Ven, 1974; Delbecq, Van De Ven, and Gustafson, 1975). The Nominal group process circumvents many of the inhibitory influences that plague nonstructured interacting groups involved in planning. The inhibitory influences that are reduced include individual domination, social pressure for conformity, status incongruities, self-opinion effects, and premature closure. Members have the time for uninterrupted thought as well as benefiting from the social facilitation of working in the presence of others. Minority opinions and ideas are represented and conflicting ideas are tolerated. This is important since everyone wants to have an opportunity for his or her ideas to be heard, recognized, and given consideration. Furthermore, the round-robin process facilitates disclosure of ideas even by reticent members. There is both visual and aural concentration on ideas. In general, the Nominal group process appears to mitigate many inhibitory factors in the committee setting and thus to enhance group functioning.

THE DELPHI TECHNIQUE

The Delphi technique "is a method to systematically solicit, collect, evaluate, and tabulate independent expert opinion without group discussion" (Tersine and Riggs, 1976, p. 51). The central purpose is to eliminate any direct confrontation of the experts and to allow them to reach a consensus based upon increasingly relevant information. The technique involves repeatedly consulting with numbers of informed persons as to their best judgment related to the planning problem at hand and providing them with systematic reports as to the judgment rendered by the group. The responses of all participants are assembled and returned to the participants, with invitations to reconsider and to offer any defense they may have for an estimate that seems out of line with others made by the group. This information and the revised estimates may then be circulated to the participants for further analysis. The process is continued through an iterative number of rounds until there seems to be sufficient convergence of opinion.

Delphi replaces direct debate with a carefully designed program of individual interrogations. Unlike the committee process, where close physical proximity of group members is required, participants in the Delphi process are physically dispersed and do not meet face to face. The control of the interaction among respondents represents a deliberate attempt to avoid the disadvantages of the more conventional approach—the committee process. Delphi is especially effective for decision making about highly charged issues such as program or staff cutbacks. It avoids the domino effect of emotional tension, which develops when groups are placed face to face in such situations. In the privacy of one's office or home, cool heads can prevail and the timing of decisions can be carefully controlled.

The Delphi concept is a spinoff of defense research. "Project Delphi" was the name given to an Air Force–sponsored Rand Corporation study started in the early 1950s. The study concerned the use of expert opinion. Norman Dalkey and Olaf Helmer of the Rand Corporation are given credit for developing Delphi for the purpose of estimating the probable effects of a massive atomic attack on the United States. Because of the topic of the first notable Delphi study, it took later effort to bring Delphi to the attention of individuals outside the defense community. A Rand paper developed by T. J. Gordon and Olaf Helmer (1964) provided the fundamentals, in the early and mid-1960s, for a number of individuals to begin experimentation with Delphi in nondefense areas.

One of the earliest applications of Delphi in education was in a study by Helmer (1966a). Helmer's work was part of the 1965 Kettering project to compile a list of preferred goals for future federal funding from a panel of education experts. Later, as part of a Virginia state educational needs assessment project, Gant (1969) used Delphi to determine educational standards for the elementary schools of Virginia. Donald Anderson (1970) used Delphi in a similar way in Ohio but limited the focus to a county school district. The technique has also been used to generate useful perspectives on changes in American education (Adelson, 1967).

Steps in the Delphi procedure

Delphi is essentially a series of questionnaires. The first asks each respondent to provide some initial input on the topic under investigation. The second consists of items developed from the first-round responses, and it requests individual judgment in the form of priority ratings on each item. The third provides the respondent with some average of the second-round responses for each item, usually in the form of an interquartile range, median, or mode. The participant is asked to reconsider his or her own second-round response in light of this information and either to move to the group judgment or to state a reason why he or she feels a minority position is in order. The fourth questionnaire provides each participant with new consensus data and a summary of minority opinions, and requests a final revision of responses. Figure 8-1 provides a basic flow diagram of the Delphi process.

The basic starting point is a clear definition of the problem to be solved, the expertise that is going to be required to solve the problem, and the use of the expert information in the planning process.

Since respondent selection is very important to the value of the process, care should be used in the selection of the group to be questioned.

It is unrealistic to expect effective participation unless respondents: (1) feel personally involved in the problem of concern to the decision makers; (2) have pertinent information to share; (3) are motivated to include the Delphi task in their schedule of compelling tasks; and (4) feel that the aggregation of judgments

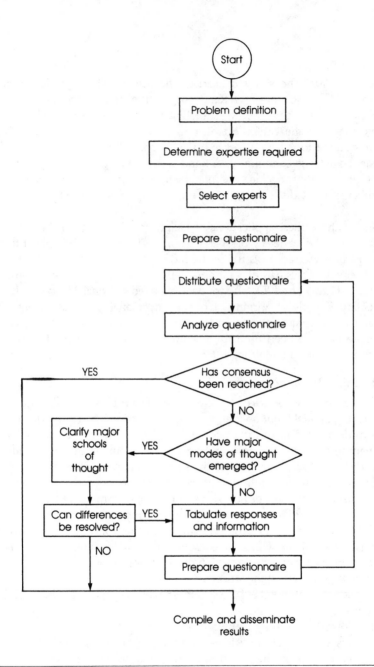

FIGURE 8-1

Steps in the Delphi Process

Source: Adapted from Tersine and Riggs, "The Delphi Techinque: A Long Range Planning Tool." *Business Horizons*, April 1976, p. 53. Reprinted by permission.

of a respondent panel will include information which they too value and to which they would not otherwise have access. (Delbecq, Van De Ven, and Gustafson, 1975, pp. 87-88)

One method for determining the composition of the respondents is to identify target groups likely to possess the needed expertise (for example, NEA, ASBA, PTA, city planners, or principals) and then select well-known and respected individuals from the target group. This, of course, is a good idea regardless of the group process used.

Stimulating responses of any kind from quality panelists is not easy. Few people like questionnaires, and from the participants' point of view, engaging in abstract speculation with people whom you do not meet and who do not know you is hardly compelling. Participants must be convinced of the importance of the objectives and the importance of their participation. The method of contact (telephone, face-to-face, or introductory letter with questionnaire) should clearly describe the purpose of the study, the nature of the respondent panel, the part they will play in reaching a solution, the information that will be shared among participants, the obligations of participants, the importance of a concerted effort to successful results, and the uniqueness of their abilities in the total effort. Soon after they agree to participate the first questionnaire should be mailed to them.

The first questionnaire asks participants to respond to a broad question. In cases in which the problem solution is already developed and concern is more with refinement and movement toward consensus, the questionnaire can be stated in a more detailed and specific form.

Some participants will not respond to the questionnaire the first time and will need further encouragement. Two forms of encouragement seem to be successful, and sometimes both may be needed. One is the "dunning letter," to be sent one day after the first questionnaire is due back. Along with reminding respondents of the deadline date, it should also offer to answer any questions by collect telephone. For those people who still do not respond, a further step may have to be taken. Respondents are telephoned to see if they are having any problem with the questionnaire and to remind them how important their input is.

Upon the receipt of the completed questionnaires, the tabulation process begins. This step requires attention to detail in the target group's responses and the feedback of this information along with overall movement, countervailing forces, or whatever unbiased macro-observations may be needed to describe what seems to be going on between and within individual responses. The analysis must capture and describe the reality that was negotiated by the respondents because this provides the perspective for remaining questionnaires. The exact form of the final analysis is left to the imagination of the moderator and depends both on the purpose to be achieved and the nature of the responses. There are a few major sources that suggest alternative approaches (Delbecq, Van De Ven, and Gustafson, 1975; Linstone and Turoff, 1975).

Many forms of voting scales can be used to rate the results from the first questionnaire—for example, desirable/undesirable, feasible/unfeasible, important/unimportant, certain/unreliable, as well as general votings such as high/low or rankings from first to last. The resolution of a Delphi sometimes requires that responses be rated by more than one voting scale. For instance, it might be important in planning to assess both the desirability and the feasibility of the responses. We often fail to distinguish what is desirable from what seems plausible. The voting scale is typically made up of four to five categories and seldom if ever more than twelve.

In the third follow-up questionnaire, a summary of the distribution of reponses is given to each respondent, usually as some measure of central tendency such as the mean, mode, or median and some measure of dispersion such as the interquartile range. Each respondent who, for instance, falls outside the interquartile range is asked to reconsider his or her own second-round response in light of this information and either to move to the group judgment or to state a reason why he or she feels a minority position is in order. It is customary to have respondents justify the reason for their "extreme" position. The responsibility for justifying extreme positions has the effect of causing a respondent without reason or strong convictions to move his or her estimates closer to the median. Those who feel they had a good argument for a "deviant" opinion tend to keep their original estimate and defend it.

The minority justifications are summarized, fed back, and counteragreements elicited on succeeding rounds. The purpose of information feedback is to produce more precise predictions and to encourage opinion convergence. The tabulation procedure is repeated in a similar manner for subsequent questionnaires until convergence of opinion is obtained. In the fourth questionnaire, participants are asked to reconsider their position in light of the minority justifications. Sometimes those who choose to remain with the old interquartile range may be requested to explain why they were unconvinced by the opposing minority arguments; however, this usually requires an extra questionnaire. The number of questionnaires varies, but generally an absolute minimum of three is necessary to achieve a reasonable consensus of opinion.

DEGREE OF CONSENSUS

"Degree of consensus" refers to the frequency of final agreement among respondents on the rating of each item. In most Delphis, consensus is assumed to be achieved when a certain percentage of votes, a consensus percent, occurs in the most frequent rating category. A cut-off percentage of from 70 to 90 percent is typically used in this case to determine if consensus has been achieved. If a larger rating scale is used, the consensus is reached when the interquartile range is no larger than two units. This rule is usually used on five to ten unit scales. Another simple measure for determining convergence is to determine when greater than 50 percent of the respondents agree on the most frequent rating and less than 25 percent of the respondents fall more than one category either direction from the most frequent response. When a majority category falls at an extreme, 75 percent of the responses must fall within two categories.

Measures of this sort do not allow for the possibility of a bimodal distribution. Bimodal distributions may occur that will not be registered as a consensus but rather indicate an important and apparently insoluble polarity of opinion. It is important that the administrator be aware of such differences when he or she sums up and presents the results. A measure that takes into account such variations from the norm is one that measures not consensus as such, but stability of the respondents' ratings over successive rounds of the Delphi. If the 15 percent change level is taken to represent a state of equilibrium, any two distributions that show marginal changes of less than 15 percent may be said to have reached stability. Use of this stability measure to develop a stopping criterion preserves any well-defined disagreement that may exist.

Experts (Gant, 1970) argue that there is often little change after the third questionnaire with most changes being a shift to the consensus; therefore, stability may be an excellent criteria for determining when the Delphi is ready for interpretation. When consensus has been reached, a report of the results is developed and provided to all participants. Armed with knowledge of the majority and minority views of all involved, administrators can then use the results of the Delphi to develop and make final strategic or operational plans.

EXAMPLE OF A DELPHI PROCEDURE

The superintendent of Akron City Schools decided she wanted to get broad-based input from the staff and community regarding strategic directions to be taken over the next five years. This seemed especially advantageous since a number of concerns had developed among parents, teachers, and members of the community at large. The first questionnaire was sent out to the select group of 339 — workers on the staff, citizens in the community, and state administrators (see Figure 8-2). This group agreed to participate in the Delphi in order to evaluate the relevance of school programs and to develop the most desirable purposes and goals for the schools. Respondents from the target group were asked to supply a minimum of two goal statements using one of the verbs in the questionnaire or their own verb. An introductory letter accompanied each of the questionnaires.

INSTRUCTIONS

1. Complete the sentence starting with the word supplied for each of the four items. You may supply the word for the last item if you so desire.
2. Complete the sentence in ten words or less with a goal that you consider of importance for a program for the schools in Akron.
3. Do not state more than five goals or less than two goals.
4. Each statement should be specific and not a generality.
5. The statements should deal with what should be accomplished and not why or how something should be accomplished.

- -

To provide quality education in the schools in the Akron City School System, effort and energy should be expended to:

1. Increase_____

_____

2. Decrease_____

_____

3. Promote_____

_____

4. Develop_____

_____

5. (   )_____

_____

FIGURE 8-2

Initial Questionnaire for the Development of a
Consensus on Goals in the Akron City School District

The synthesized goal statements developed from the individual goal statements submitted were used to form the second questionnaire. The respondents were asked to rate the goals according to their relative degree of importance for the school district. A semantic differential scale was used for rating the items as follows: (1) highest importance, (2) above-average importance, (3) average importance, (4) below-average importance, and (5) low or no importance. All 339 participants returned the second questionnaire. A one-page sample of the results of the analysis of this second questionnaire is presented in Table 8-1 in the form of a frequency distribution of the rating along with the consensus percentage.

It was necessary to determine if a consensus had been achieved on the second questionnaire. Consensus was defined as being achieved when greater than 80 percent of the votes of the consensus percentage occurred in the most frequent rating category. Only one of the forty-seven goals suggested by the participants had reached the consensus point on the second round on the basis of this criterion.

A third questionnaire was mailed, asking the participants to agree with the most frequent ratings of a goal or to give a reason for not accepting the consensus. In part the accompanying letter stated:

> The enclosed form is a duplicate of the second instrument with the most frequent rating for each goal and your previous response indicated. The *most frequent rating* of a goal by the more than three hundred persons who completed the previous instrument is marked with a *black square*. Your *previous response* is marked with a *red circle* unless your previous response was the same as the most frequent response. In that case, your previous response is not indicated. The purpose of this step is both to increase the consensus and to define more clearly minority opinion. Please mark the enclosed form according to the following instructions:
>
> 1. If a goal is marked with a black square only, do nothing.
> 2. If a goal is marked with a red circle and a black square *and* you *are willing to accept* the rating marked by the black square, do nothing.
> 3. If a goal is marked with a red circle and a black square *and you are not willing to accept* the rating marked with the black square, please state in one sentence your most important reason for not accepting the majority rating in the space provided below the goal.

The results of this third questionnaire revealed that the Delphi process had reached a consensus as defined by the test criteria. (If consensus had not been reached, a fourth questionnaire and the minority opinions would have been returned in order to find a consensus.) Eight of the goals had convergence on the low- to no-importance end of the scale, and twelve of the goals had convergence on the average importance category of the rating scale. This left

TABLE 8-1

Round 2 Goal Priorities as Determined by the Delphi Process (Sample Page)

GOAL NUMBER	GOAL STATEMENT	DISTRIBUTION OF RATINGS					NO RESPONSE	TOTAL	CONSENSUS PERCENTAGE
		1	2	3	4	5			
9.	Develop good citizens who possess qualities such as an appreciation and understanding of the United States government, pride in country, patriotism, respect for law and order, and understanding and appreciation of the American heritage.	218	70	34	10	3	4	339	64
10.	Develop better relationships including improved communication and understanding among faculty, administration, parents, students, community, government, and institutions of higher learning.	95	126	92	14	8	4	339	37
11.	Decrease the number of students assigned to each teacher.	106	99	97	24	11	2	339	31
12.	Increase the communication efficiency of students including the development of skills such as effective composition, legible writing, correct grammatical construction, correct speech, effective listening, comprehensive reading, and correct spelling.	167	105	52	11	0	4	339	49
13.	Develop curricula relevant to the contemporary world that will prepare students to function effectively in a modern technological society.	56	131	109	19	13	11	339	39

twenty-seven of the goals rated as being of above-average or highest importance.

Sample items from the final report appear in Table 8-2. Inclusions and priorities for the twenty-seven important goals were determined by considering both (1) highest importance rating and (2) above-average importance rating. Another approach to determining inclusions and priorities is to use the Delphi to identify the most important objectives and then to go back out again with a final questionnaire to have the objectives ranked. Some argue that the question of ranking objectives is quite different from defining and identifying the most important objectives and therefore must be dealt with in a separate step.

The data developed, including the minority opinions, was then used by Akron City Schools to develop a set of strategic objectives for the next five years. Many groups had felt a part in the process of developing the strategic plans and were interested in ensuring that they were a success. The disharmony and concerns in the districts were effectively diffused by giving an opportunity for all to be represented in the planning process.

Delphi Extensions

The possible extensions or modifications to the Delphi technique, as is true of the other techniques, are limited only by one's creativity. In fact, the greatest benefits often occur when the administrator modifies the technique to meet particular needs. For example, a local assistant superintendent may use a first and second Delphi questionnaire to get an initial ranking of critical issues and then place the lists on blackboards or flip-charts for open group discussion in a face-to-face format using the Nominal group process of discussion for clarification and voting on items of importance.

Another modification is known as System for Event Evaluation and Review (SEER). The SEER technique helps to make Delphi more efficient by developing initial lists of events through interviews prior to the beginning of the Delphi process. It can result in reducing the number of questionnaire rounds, thus saving time. Also, participants can be asked to answer questions only in their area of expertise. For instance, SEER can address the question of event "desirability" from the user's point of view and "event feasibility" from the organization's point of view.

Delphi conferencing via computer is possible but as yet is little publicized and not widely tested. It consists of linkage between individuals via a terminal (a keyboard with letters, numbers, and symbols linked to the control computer) plus a cathode ray tube (CRT) display device and/or printer. The central computer is programmed to sort, store, and transmit each conferree's messages. The individuals linked in this way may interact at the same time or, more typically, at their convenience with the computer holding all messages. This procedure could reduce the length of time of the Delphi process considerably (Rice, 1975).

Another rather complicated modification is called cross-impact analysis. This process takes into consideration the impact of the occurrence of one event on a subsequent event when several events are interrelated. Usually the analysis will develop a series of conditional probabilities for events. Through

TABLE 8-2

Final Goal Priorities as Determined by the
Delphi Process (Sample Page)

GOAL PRIORITY	(GOAL NUMBER)	GOAL STATEMENT	FINAL DISTRIBUTION OF RATINGS					TOTAL	CONSENSUS PERCENTAGE
			1	2	3	4	5		
A.	(5)	Promote the retention of qualified and experienced teachers.	298	19	18	3	1	339	88
C.	(9)	Develop good citizens who possess qualities such as an appreciation and understanding of the United States government, pride in country, patriotism, respect for law and order, and understanding and appreciation of the American heritage.	297	14	17	9	2	339	88
G.	(12)	Increase the communication efficiency of students including the development of skills such as effective composition, legible writing, correct grammatical construction, correct speech, effective listening, comprehensive reading, and correct spelling.	292	27	17	3	0	339	86
H.	(24)	Foster the attitude that parents must accept their responsibility for educating their children.	290	14	22	9	4	339	86
R.	(13)	Develop curricula relevant to the contemporary world that will prepare students to function effectively in a modern technological society.	12	295	22	3	7	339	87
S.	(28)	Develop and promote effective methods of diagnosing and working effectively with learning problems such as those associated with the handicapped, slow learners, underachievers, and others with learning disabilities.	24	290	18	5	2	339	86

an iterative process, the technique ensures that forecasts of interrelated events are consistent with individual probabilities of occurrence.

Participation in group process

Research suggests that the Delphi technique is effective. The absence of a group setting facilitates creativity because Delphi respondents are anonymous and experience less stress, domination, and fear of repercussions and embarrassment. Research indicates that interacting groups (face-to-face committees) produce a smaller number of problem dimensions, fewer high-quality suggestions, and a smaller number of different kinds of solutions than groups in which members are constrained from interaction during the generation of critical problem variables (Delbecq, Van De Ven, and Gustafson, 1975).

When an individual works alone, as in the Delphi process, he or she can focus his or her entire attention on the problem-solving task. When an individual works in the presence of others, as in committee meetings, he or she must also attend to the social interpersonal obstacles. Face-to-face discussion is usually centered around issues on which group members agree, often resulting in a lack of task accomplishment. This is caused by a predominant orientation toward stimulating and maintaining social and emotional cohesion among group members. In addition, members often fall into a rut and pursue a single train of thought for extended periods of discussion. Both Delphi and the Nominal group process tend to reduce the negative impact that occurs when group members play undesirable roles and deal with hidden agendas during the group process.

Delphi allows the inclusion of many more people in the planning process than can participate in committee meetings or in Nominal group processes. Typically, the larger the face-to-face group the less effectively it accomplishes tasks (Jay, 1976). This is not a problem in Delphi procedures, where as many as 400 respondents have been included in the problem-solving process. Although Delphi sometimes takes considerably longer in calendar time, it usually requires much less of the time of the individuals involved in the planning process. Delphi compares favorably to other group processes on such items as number of working hours required, cost of utilizing committees, and the proximity of group participants. It usually requires the least amount of time for participants. In addition, the Delphi process saves participants the additional time and cost of having to attend face-to-face meetings. However, the calendar time required to obtain judgments from respondents can be a disadvantage.

Committee meetings, the Nominal group process, and Delphi techniques are very useful tools in the planning process. Properly used, all three are powerful tools in the hands of an effective school administrator.

GUIDELINES FOR PLANNING

1. In order to obtain group participation and consensus, the planner may conduct meetings organized according to the traditional format or according to the Delphi and Nominal group process techniques.

2. Traditional committee meetings may fail to elicit fully a spectrum of opinion and ideas because of the dominance of prestigious persons, because of "hidden" agendas, or because of the inhibitory effect of the group process.

3. The Nominal group process is designed to overcome the common failings of traditional committee meetings by maintaining the individual's anonymity of opinion while permitting the stimulation of group interaction.

4. The Delphi technique allows for individuals to feed in information and opinions separately, anonymously, and on their own time; it preserves the consensus-reaching powers of a group meeting while avoiding the hazards of group dynamics. It lends itself well to communication by computer terminal as well as analysis of information by computer. Preparing and processing the minimum three rounds of Delphi questionnaires can, however, be much more time-consuming than one or two face-to-face meetings; on the other hand, it allows for the full participation of a far greater number of individuals.

9

Task Planning and Coordination

Plan Ahead

Operational objectives are the backbone of the school plan; everything from developing task plans to evaluating final performance should contribute to one or more of the school's operational objectives. The operational objectives, like the strategic objectives, are so fundamental that they do not communicate the specific task activities that are required for their achievement. Some school employees, with more experience and knowledge, may be able to convert the school objectives into specific task activities, but even they will have trouble managing the many and changing tasks in their head. For this reason, planning methodology is needed to develop individual programs, projects, and task activities that will make the whole planning process come to life through planned action. At this point, planning questions such as "How do we get there?" "When will it be done?" " and "Who will be responsible?" should be answered.

The need for more comprehensive task planning has increased with the complexity of the school. Not only is the margin for error between success and failure shrinking, but the activities to be coordinated often appear unmanageable, especially if all work activities are coordinated in the employee's head. Rapid technological change, increased expectations, decreased support, greater diversity, and a faster tempo combine to make task-planning efforts more difficult and demanding. To manage task plans, school employees must carefully organize the pertinent information. Failure to establish the interrelationship between tasks or to determine the status of a project activity can be costly and result in a failure to achieve objectives. Idle resources, time delays, and inefficient use of resources cannot be tolerated in a society that simultaneously faces increased educational challenge and dwindling resources. These changes have placed upon school employees a vastly increased responsibility for visualizing and documenting the various activities that will be expected of them in carrying out their tasks.

Wacaster (1979) found that school-system attempts to implement planned changes were sometimes unsuccessful because procedural details of the various programs were not spelled out. The absence of a task plan caused staff to implement, coordinate, and develop tasks as they went along. This lack of preparation created individual overload and confusion and often resulted in project failure. The lack of task plans was caused by administrators who did not believe that task plans would facilitate the implementation of operational plans. Failure in implementing projects was also caused by inadequate task plans. Task plans are inadequate if they are ambiguous at critical points or if they do not take into account the realities of the educational system in which they are to be implemented. Kent (1979) analyzed the change process in five school districts and found that failures of change efforts in these districts often occurred because the employees responsible for implementing the changes did not develop task plans that contained timetables, checkpoints, feedback loops, and clear specification of needed activities and expected (desired) results.

WHAT IS A TASK PLAN?

The task plan should include a time schedule and a procedure for monitoring progress against objectives.

> The person should be able to assure himself or herself that the individual projects are moving forward acceptably, but he or she does not have to have detailed knowledge of exactly what is going on at every point in time if he or she is not directly supervising the ultimate action steps. The person can develop program plans in whatever detail suits his or her style.
>
> Many people think of "project" plans in terms of discrete undertakings that have a beginning and an end—like building a plant or developing a new product. This does not have to be the case. You can "projectize" any task. All you have to do is put it in a time frame and put a finite objective at the end of it. (Kastens, 1976, p. 120)

In this way task planning establishes a unit of work accomplishment in contrast to a continuous operation. In any project there is a set of jobs that must be completed in order for the work to be completed and the objective to be achieved. Units of work are illustrated by such typical school activities as budget preparation, program implementation (such as in-school suspension programs), graduation exercises, opening school, closing school, converting from learning centers to mainstreamed programs, planning workshops, conferences, or assemblies, building a new school, closing a school no longer needed, eliminating a program, planning a basketball tournament, conversion of instructional programs, preparing lesson plans, and so on.

Essentially, task planning can be defined as the function of (1) selecting the work requirements to accomplish the objective, (2) developing a work plan or schedule of all work requirements, and (3) controlling to ensure that work activities are completed as scheduled and objectives are achieved. Task planning and coordination is an organized attack on an operational objective by breaking up and coordinating the work that must be completed in order for the objective to reach a successful milestone.

The trick in task planning is being able to visualize how a series of actions will progress before you ever start them. Perhaps the major advantage of this activity is that the kind of planning required to create a valid task plan represents a major contribution to the definition and ultimate successful control of the efforts required to achieve objectives. The creation of the task plan is a sure-fire indication of an organization's ability to visualize the number, kind, and sequence of activities needed to achieve an operational objective. This activity does, in fact, reveal interdependencies and problem areas that either were not obvious or not well defined during the objective-setting phase of planning. Such efforts should also provide for a large amount of data to be presented in a highly ordered and concise fashion.

A BRIEF HISTORY OF METHODOLOGICAL DEVELOPMENT

The need for coordinating techniques grew from the recognition that, in our modern complex society, administrators could no longer mentally coordinate the myriad activities that were required to accomplish objectives. As the complexity of the tasks being administered grew, so did the problems of planning, scheduling, coordinating, and controlling work strategy. It is out of this atmosphere of increased complexity, failure, and often frustration that the techniques of task planning, coordination, and review were born.

The original and most basic form of task planning is making activity lists, or action sequences as they are sometimes called. These are the lists of activities written down on sheets of paper or index-sized cards and carried around to remind us of the various tasks that still need to be performed. Usually there is some method of sequencing or assigning priorities to the tasks; as the tasks are completed they are crossed off. This method becomes slightly more sophisticated when activities are written on planning calendars that organize task sequences by days of the week. It is similar to the familiar lesson-plan book maintained by teachers and the executive calendar used by administrators.

The bar, or Gantt, chart was developed as an improvement on these basic forms of task planning. This technique was developed to aid administrators faced with tasks requiring many skilled persons and equipment all performing a number of activities that must be done in a prescribed sequence in order for predetermined objectives to be achieved. The bar chart was originally devised by H. L. Gantt and Frederick W. Taylor. The chart identifies resource capabilities, tasks to be performed by each resource, the period of time required to perform each task, and the sequence in which each task must be performed (a typical Gantt chart is shown in Figure 9-1, later in this chapter). The primary advantage of the Gantt chart is that it provides a graphic means of planning, coordinating, and portraying the plan, strategy, and progress of a project. As a graphic presentation device, the chart is particularly effective in showing the status of the various project elements. Its weaknesses are not taking into account the interdependencies of activities or coordinated functions and not providing any explicit means for adequately assessing the impact of a task on the entire project.

Program evaluation review techniques (PERT) were introduced collectively in 1958 by the Navy Special Projects Office; Booz, Allen, and Hamilton; and the Lockheed Aircraft Corporation as a method to eliminate many of the problems of Gantt charting. PERT management techniques were credited for helping cut several years from the Polaris Missile program. PERT was later used in the Saturn project and other space-related programs and was given partial credit for the U.S. success in the space program.

In 1957, paralleling the development of PERT, two engineers, Morgan Walker of DuPont and James Kelly, Jr., of Remington-Rand, developed the critical path method (CPM) as a direct result of work with the DuPont Corporation. This technique enabled the company to gain more than one million pounds of increased chemical production at no extra cost. The PERT and CPM methods were quickly incorporated by such large industries as Ford Motor Company, General Motors, Bell Telephone, Xerox, and many other businesses and educational institutions (see Schoderbek and Digman, 1967).

There is some benefit in the educational arena of combining the linear calendar format of the Gantt chart with the free-flow time format of the PERT/CPM technique. This modification is discussed in greater detail in a later section of this chapter. The need for such modifications is caused by differences between the industrial environment and the educational environment. For example, in industry a project can be planned using a PERT/CPM network by adjusting the length of time required to complete the project, always trying to reduce the required completion time, but with the general ability to set one's own project deadlines based on network feasibilities. Educators often do not have this luxury and must plan and sometimes reduce projects to fit within the time calendars available (often the academic year or funding cycle). For example, in an evaluation of an ESEA Title III project, one might wish to disregard time constraints in the evaluation work but, due to program duration and funding cycles, the time within which the evaluation is to be done becomes fixed. Therefore, in such cases, a linear calendar format proves to be a more realistic expression of the work plan.

THE TASK-PLANNING PROCESS

Activity list

The first step in any task-planning activity is merely to take a yellow pad and start listing all the things that are going to have to be done to complete the project and attain the established objective. List the activities in approximate chronological order. This is not like an appointment book that says what is going to happen every day or every hour, but rather is a listing by title of the various definable tasks that will have to be accomplished to complete a program or project. To a certain extent, the degree of detail will reflect the personality of the person(s) developing the list.

The activity list generally begins with a study of the operational objectives to determine the approach, methods, and work to be done, and a breakdown of the project into activities for scheduling purposes. The work breakdown consists of subdividing a total project into smaller and more easily managed elements. The process of subdivision and classification continues until the desired level of detail is reached.

The trick is to achieve a balance between detail and brevity so that the list is not so cumbersome or so vague that it becomes useless. If too many activities are spelled out in great detail the activity list becomes so cumbersome that it is much too difficult to work with. However, if too little detail is presented, the list becomes confused and difficult to interpret. The appropriate balance between detail and generality develops with practice.

Resource requirements

The next step is to determine what resources will be required to accomplish each of the activities. If only the administrator is involved, then this one resource will be listed. If other persons are involved, they should be included. The resources identified may be intellectual or skill resources, such as typists, statisticians, graphic arts people, computer programmers, teachers, curriculum consultants, supervisors, and assistant superintendents; or they may be equipment resources, such as stencil machines, video-tape equipment, computer availability, mag-card typewriters, or special classrooms; or, most likely the resources may be a combination: for instance, the physical education department, history department, music department, guidance counselors' office, printing and graphic arts department, or personnel department.

Time estimates

The next step is to estimate a reasonable amount of time for completing each task. These time estimates should be as accurate as possible and those who have to do the work should agree with them. It is important that time estimates be made by persons who: (1) are to perform the activities, (2) have performed and are experts, (3) are directly to supervise activity performance, or (4) are most familiar with and most qualified both to make the estimates and then to live by them. Time estimates imposed by uninformed management or higher authority might grossly exceed the personnel resources available. The accuracy of these time estimates adds to the usefulness of task planning. Other general considerations used in establishing time estimates are:

1. Time estimates assume that resources (including personnel) will be available on a normal basis or as requested in the project proposal.
2. Time estimates are based on a five-day work week and are established by weeks and tenths of weeks. A time estimate of 0.1 week would be equivalent to ½ of a day; an estimate of 0.2 would be equivalent to 1 day and so forth. Other time units may be used, but the weeks and tenths of a week are most common.
3. Schedule or calendar dates should have no effect on initial time estimates. By ignoring present calendar dates, the estimator avoids biasing his estimates in favor of these dates. (Cook, 1966, p. 21).

The most commonly used technique for determining time is simply to estimate the length of time it seems reasonable to expect the activity to take. For instance, if the administrator believes that it will take one day (0.2 weeks) to complete an audit of school books, then this becomes the activity's elapsed-time estimate, or "most likely time" estimate. A second commonly used method, especially when there is uncertainty regarding the scope of the work required, is the average or expected elapsed time. The expected elapsed time is based on a weighted average of the most likely time (M), optimistic time (a), and pessimistic time (b). The most likely time is the time that would normally be expected for completing the activity, the optimistic time is the least amount of time the activity could take assuming ideal conditions, and the pessimistic time is based on the assumption that anything that can possibly go wrong will go wrong. After the three time estimates have been made, average or expected elapsed time is calculated for each activity using the following equation:

$$t_e = \frac{a + 4M + b}{6}$$

where

t_e = expected elapsed time   M = most likely time

a = optimistic time

b = pessimistic time

If this method were used to estimate the time required to audit school books, one might estimate ½ day (0.1 week) as the most optimistic time, 1 day (0.2 weeks) as the most likely time, and 4½ days (0.9 week) as the most pessimistic time (subject to finding an error and checking all receipts and disbursements). With these three time estimates, we can use the above formula to give the following answer:

$$t_e = \frac{(0.1 + 4(0.2) + (0.9)}{6}$$

$$t_e = \frac{1.8}{6}$$

$$t_e = 0.3 \text{ weeks}$$

When we estimated the length of time required for this activity, simply using the most realistic time estimate, elapsed time was equal to one day (0.2 weeks). As can be seen, these two methods typically generate only small differences in elapsed time estimates. The first, and simpler method, using most realistic or most likely time, is recommended unless there is a good reason to believe that there is a great deal of uncertainty and variation regarding the time estimates.

Work plan

Now the administrator can begin to spread out the action steps along a time line. Start from today or the day of project initiation. Follow the initial conception of how the program or project should progress. Put down the activities that must be started first and then what can be started when the first activity is completed, then the next step and the next. Some activities may be nonsequential and can parallel the main sequence; their due dates can be entered at the point where the results will be required, and then by calculating back the latest possible starting date can be determined. The end result is a carefully laid-out plan for all work activities required to complete a program or project; all the pieces fit together in a dynamic flow, from work activities to task plan to operational objective to strategic objective.

Task planning may sound a little forbidding, rigid, or overorganized; a common complaint is "It takes too much time!" However, it really doesn't have to, and the odds are that it will save ten times as much time as it takes by eliminating lost motion. Actually, after a little practice, the "yellow sheet" task plan for most projects can be done in less than an hour.

What takes the most time is checking with the various people to see if they agree with the schedule and the time estimates. This would have to be done anyway, but without a task plan it might be done too late or so informally that there is no mutual appreciation of the commitment. That's how good ideas get fouled up, people get mad, and the alibis begin.

The entire work effort can be assessed by reviewing the task plan so that any unrecognized or hidden disagreements or misunderstandings will come to the forefront as participants question why certain activities are included when others are not and why activities have been sequenced one way rather than another. It is a tool that allows for greater participation because all individuals involved can see exactly what major tasks have been included and how they have been sequenced in order to achieve the objectives. Disagreements will be easily visualized when the action plans of participants are in conflict with the documented action plan for carrying out the project. These disagreements can be resolved before any action has been taken rather than after conflict, discrepancies, and inefficiencies have occurred during implementation. The benefits of developing a documented task plan—in reduced conflict and increase coordination and effectiveness—are well worth the time required to develop such a plan.

Sometimes during the review process, it is determined that the plan takes too long or is unsatisfactory for one reason or another. Such problems typically come to light during consultations with subordinates, staff departments, and other parallel organizations that must contribute to the successful completion of the project. If someone is unable to perform as scheduled, it is better for the administrator to find out about it before the work begins and try to provide for it rather than to get into a flap in the middle of the project when people both inside and outside the organization have emotional and conceivably political investments in the project.

Project replanning

The final step is replanning the project when problems develop. After having reviewed the plan, administrators may find project duration to be too long or the length of time to complete different tasks to be too unequal, or they may just not like the general sequence of activities required to complete the project. If such conditions exist, it often becomes necessary to replan the project. The task plan becomes an easy method to discuss project strengths and weaknesses when replanning with other administrators. It is one of the best methods to reduce misunderstanding and come to a common agreement on a project plan.

When the task plan is not feasible in terms of time, activities, and/or resources, certain established procedures can be applied for replanning the network. Some of these procedures are as follows:

1. *Removal of planned constraints.* Planned constraints are those work relationships which have been established as desirable but not absolutely necessary program relationships.

2. *Parallel activities.* Activities which are in sequential or linear order can, with the introduction of some management risk, be conducted in parallel. The decision to parallel activities will depend largely upon the availability of required resources as well as the degree of risk that the project administrator considers acceptable.

3. *Eliminate activities.* The project may contain activities whose accomplishments might be desirable but possibly more time consuming than is permissible. If not essential, they can be eliminated.

4. *Reallocate resources.* The addition of resources (personnel, equipment, or material) to critical activities usually will result in a reduction of activity times. In using this technique, a determination must be made that the time savings will justify the increased cost.

5. *Revision of time estimates.* Careful examination of activities often may reveal specific activities which can be assigned a shorter cumulative time estimate. It is important to stress that activity time estimates must not be shortened or "crashed" arbitrarily to meet a schedule or directed date. (Cook, 1966, p. 31)

THE FORMAT FOR GANTT CHARTS

Although simpler methods can be used effectively in task planning, a Gantt chart is often very helpful. The Gantt chart simply provides a systematic method for graphically representing the results of the task-planning effort. In the Gantt chart, the tasks to be performed by each resource are identified horizontally on the time axis (called a schedule bar), which shows the periods of time required to perform each task; the actual work to be accomplished is written on the schedule bar. All resource requirements are listed down the left side of the chart, and the time, usually expressed in either days, weeks, or months, is written along the top of the chart. Each activity is placed next to the required resource and on its schedule bar according to its duration and sequence.

The last step in the construction of a Gantt chart is progress posting. Progress is normally posted at regular intervals so that those activities that are behind schedule can be identified and corrective action taken. The nature of such corrective action is usually to add more personnel, use overtime, or make alternative plans. Work on project activities that are ahead of schedule can often be slowed or temporarily suspended by transferring personnel to those elements that are behind schedule.

Progress is posted to the Gantt chart by showing the estimated amount of time required to complete each of the various project activities. Work that has been accomplished is indicated by a heavy line below the schedule line. Large V's, or upside-down carets, are posted on the top horizontal time scale to indicate the last date on which progress has been posted. The estimated time required to complete a task is represented by the span of time between the righthand end of the work-accomplished heavy (or dark) line and the planned completion date designated by the closing angle of the task or schedule light line. Then this data can be used to compare actual completion to planned completion.

EXAMPLE: PRESENTING A "FAMILY-LIFE" PROGRAM

The development of task plans can be best understood by considering a very simple example that is common for most administrators—presenting an idea and getting reactions from a broad audience. A principal is to present a new curricular program entitled "Family-Life Education" to a select group of principals, supervisors, teachers, and parents for their reactions. Some may consider such an application of Gantt charting to be overkill, but the example is chosen for its simplicity and common understanding, not because it necessarily is needed in this case. This same example will also be used to demonstrate PERT/CPM analysis so that the similarities and differences between it and Gantt charting can be most readily observed.

Figure 9-1 is an example of the project planning or Gantt chart for the principal's "Family-Life Presentation." The resource requirements for the project are listed on the lefthand side of the chart. The workday, based on a five-day work week, is used as the unit of time and is placed as the horizontal axis at the top of the chart. The light horizontal schedule lines indicate when work is scheduled for the project tasks. The specific activities to be performed are written above the schedule line, and the start and completion times are indicated by the use of opening (and closing) angles respectively. The tasks are sequenced in time, with the planner taking into consideration those tasks that must be performed sequentially as well as those tasks that can be performed simultaneously.

In this example, the report to the board would not be available until the end of the last week in April—probably the morning of April 29. In a few very

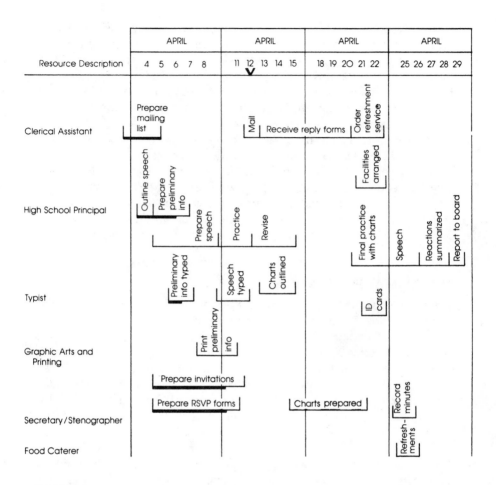

FIGURE 9-1

Gantt Chart for the Family-Life Presentation

special cases when a project completion date has been specified in advance, the tasks can be planned and sequenced on the chart by working backward from that completion date. This often requires some adjustments in the time required to perform certain tasks.

Figure 9-1 also shows the results of posting after seven days from the start of the project. The project is already behind schedule since the invitations have not been mailed. However, we can see that this is caused by the fact that the high school principal has not prepared the preliminary information that is to be enclosed with the invitations and the graphic arts person has not completed the invitations or the RSVP forms. The principal is already one day behind schedule on the preliminary information and has not begun to prepare or practice the speech, the graphic arts person is one day behind schedule on the invitations and RSVP forms and hasn't started the preliminary information, and the typist is one and a half days behind on the preliminary information and has not begun to type the speech. The impact of these delays on the entire project cannot be determined by Gantt charting.

In Gantt charting, jobs using each resource are placed horizontally without regard to all the interrelationships and interdependencies between each task using each resource. Therefore, the Gantt chart cannot answer questions regarding the sequence and relationship between each job (Handy and Hussain, 1969). For example, the question is unanswered as to whether one job can or cannot be started before the end of another job or whether the utilization of one resource is in any way related to the utilization of another resource.

THE FORMAT FOR PERT/CPM

The PERT network describes the task plan in terms of a graphic model that shows the work activity that must be performed. It illustrates, by diagram, the sequential relationships among the activities that must be completed in order to achieve an objective. The CPM calculations determine the time necessary to complete the project. They control the project's duration. One path of the sequential work flow (out of many possible paths) requires the most time and is, therefore, critical to the completion of the project. This path is called the "critical path" and represents the minimum time required to complete the action plan.

The PERT/CPM network is composed of events and activities. An event, which is graphically represented by a circle, denotes the start or completion of an activity; an event does not normally consume a resource such as time, material, or personnel. Events are instantaneous points in time where an action has been started or completed. An activity, represented by a straight line with an arrow on one end, is a task or job in the project requiring utilization of personnel and resources over a period of time. An activity consists of a single task in the work process, leading from one event to another. Activities coincide with the tasks identified in the activity list and are written on the arrow in the PERT/CPM network.

The length of the arrow underlying an activity has no significance. This is an important difference between a Gantt chart and a network plan. In Gantt charts, the time required to perform an activity is read from the horizontal time line on the basis of the length of the schedule bar for the task. In a network plan, the time required to perform a task will be represented by a time estimate

FIGURE 9-2
Series Construction in PERT/CPM

placed on the directed activity arrow for the task rather than by the length of the arrow itself.

Dummy activities are used for the convenience of the administrator in developing relationships between activities. They are often used in cases in which one activity must precede the start of two or more other activities, which can occur simultaneously. A dummy activity, which is represented by a dotted line with an arrow head on one end, does not consume time or resources. Dummy activities are used for convenience in chart construction to show that one activity must follow a preceding activity.

The network plan is constructed by drawing circles and arrows in the sequence in which the events and activities are to be accomplished. The network always begins with one event, called the origin, and must always end with another event, called the terminal event. Each activity in the network must begin with an event and end with an event. In adding an activity to the network, it is necessary to answer three questions:

1. Which activities must be completed before this activity can start?
2. Which activities must start after this activity is completed?
3. What other activities can be performed at the same time as this activity?

One activity must follow another activity on the network if that activity cannot take place until the preceding activity has been accomplished or if the administrator decides that it would be desirable, even if not absolutely necessary, for the one activity to follow the other. When activities are dependent on one another, they form a progressive or additive chain called a series construction (see Figure 9-2).

Two or more activities can go on at the same time if those activities are not dependent on one another and the completion of one activity has no effect on the completion of another. Thus, activities that are performed concurrently must be independent of one another. In making these decisions one should not consider the human resources required for the work but simply whether the activities could be performed at the same time. The sharing of common human resources can be considered after the entire PERT/CPM network has been constructed; this is usually a major part of computer-developed PERT/CPM networks. When activities are not dependent on one another, they form a parallel construction (see Figure 9-3). The activity following event 5 cannot begin until all activities that terminate at event 5 are completed. Notice that a dummy activity (shown by the dotted arrow) was used for convenience to properly sequence the activities; however, no time is consumed by this dummy activity.

For the PERT/CPM network to be useful in project scheduling and evaluation, time estimates must be assigned to the network activities and a time analysis of the network performed. The activities in a network plan represent the time-consuming elements of the project. By assigning time estimates to each activity, the network can be analyzed to determine time-dependent characteristics. These times are placed right on the PERT/CPM network next to the activity. Each of the time estimates is enclosed in parentheses.

After all the time estimates have been placed on the network, it is necessary to calculate a network time and to find the critical path. There is usually more than one path from the origin event to the terminal event. The sum total of all the elapsed times for each activity along a series construction is called a time path. The lengths of time required to complete each of the network time paths may be equal or unequal. If they are unequal, the longest path through the network, which is thus the duration of the entire project, becomes the critical path. In other words, the critical path is defined as the longest or most time-consuming path through the network. If there are two paths through the network that are both equal in length, then the network is said to have a dual critical path. The critical path is graphically displayed on the network with a double-line arrow.

The determination of the critical path and the length of time through each of the paths of the network is an important part of the PERT/CPM analysis. Administrators can often spend money and effort trying to reduce the duration of a total project by decreasing the length of time required to complete a noncritical activity. But the reduction of noncritical activities will in no way decrease the length of the project duration, since noncritical activities do not lie on the longest path through the network. But without a PERT/CPM analysis and the computation of the critical path, it is often impossible to determine which activities are critical to the duration of the entire project.

To schedule the project and determine completion dates, a planner must depend on the network time calculation for the critical path. As the project progresses and the network is updated to reflect progress and changes in the plan, the activities and events through which the critical path passes may change. Periodic updating of the network ensures that the time significance of project changes will not go unnoticed.

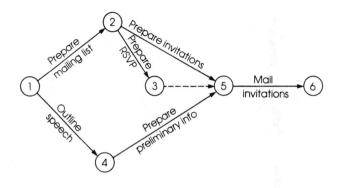

FIGURE 9-3
Parallel Construction in PERT/CPM

In more complex analyses, it may be necessary to calculate both slack and float. This is especially useful when the administrator wishes to know how much excess time is available to complete an activity that is not on the critical path. Slack and float are usually calculated on earliest expected (start) time and latest allowable (start) time. Since these concepts are often not necessary to the application of PERT/CPM in educational administration and since much of the information provided by these additional calculations can be understood and determined from the network itself, these concepts will not be discussed here. This is not to minimize their importance, since they are needed to provide information regarding and earliest and latest times when an activity may start.

EXAMPLE: THE "FAMILY-LIFE" PROGRAM USING PERT/CPM

To illustrate the construction of an entire PERT network, we will use the "Family-Life" example previously developed. Figure 9-4 shows the network plan. Events 1 and 19 are the origin and terminal events, respectively. The logical relationship of all activities between these two events is shown. It should be noted that descriptive labels and time estimates (in the parentheses) for each activity are located on the arrows. Using the information provided in Figure 9-4, we can calculate the critical path, which is graphically displayed on the network by the double line. The various times for each of the serial time paths through the network are shown at the bottom of the figure (the critical path is marked with an asterisk).

The total duration of the project—the sum of all elapsed times along the critical path—is found to be 3.6, or three weeks and three days. If the ad-

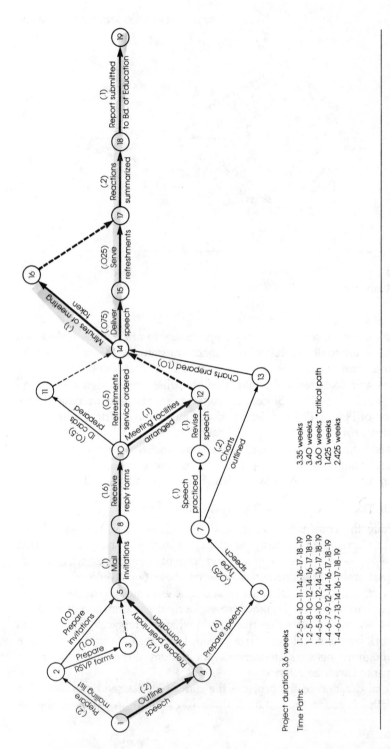

Project duration 3.6 weeks

Time Paths:

1-2-5-8-10-11-14-16-17-18-19	3.35 weeks
1-2-5-8-10-12-14-16-17-18-19	3.40 weeks
1-4-5-8-10-12-14-16-17-18-19	3.60 weeks *critical path
1-4-6-7-9-12-14-16-17-18-19	1.425 weeks
1-4-6-7-13-14-16-17-18-19	2.425 weeks

FIGURE 9-4

PERT/CPM Network with Critical Path
Calculations for the Family-Life Presentation

ministrator wishes to reduce the total duration of the project, it would be necessary to replan one of the activities along the critical path since activities on the critical path in the network provide the most rigid time constraint on completion of the project. This network provides a simply organized, graphic display of all project activities from preparing the mailing list and outlining the speech, to summarizing reactions and reporting them to the board. It can be used to further discuss or replan the project or to monitor the completion of each of the activities. It also provides excellent documentation of the project.

EXAMPLE: HIGH SCHOOL GRADUATION

The planning and carrying out of commencement exercises is a common example of a recurring activity that requires considerable planning and coordination. The high school graduation problem provides an example of how PERT/CPM can be used to document projects, allowing the administrator to use the same network for planning and managing projects year after year.

Let us assume that you are the principal of a high school and have the responsibility of overseeing the planning and carrying out of your high school's graduation. You can assign the various tasks to different people, but you must coordinate all the activities to ensure that they result in a successful commencement exercise. The planning and carrying out of a graduation begins with such activities as compiling a graduation list, determining time and date, developing and ordering various components from student announcements to graduation programs, and arranging speakers; it finally ends with such activities as cleaning up after graduation, collecting caps and gowns, and mailing out unclaimed diplomas. The activities are diverse, interrelated, and must be completed at the appropriate time if the commencement exercise is to occur as scheduled. It is often difficult for those involved in planning and carrying out the graduation project to see how their tasks are related to others and to the project in general. It is your responsibility to coordinate all these activities and to make sure they are completed on time.

The network in Figure 9-5 contains the forty-nine activities required to carry out a graduation ceremony. The absolute minimum amount of time needed to plan, prepare for, and hold a graduation ceremony is approximately 14 weeks (13.625 weeks). If the graduation ceremonies are to be held on June 7, the very latest that the graduation plans could be started is by the end of the third week in February. Of course, this would allow no extra time for any unforeseen delays in any critical tasks.

There are three critical paths that would need to be carefully monitored. They are (1) measuring, ordering, awaiting arrival of, and fitting caps and gowns; (2) planning graduation, ordering, awaiting arrival of, and disbursing student admission tickets; and (3) setting graduation time, ordering, awaiting arrival of, and disbursing student invitations and announcements. Activities

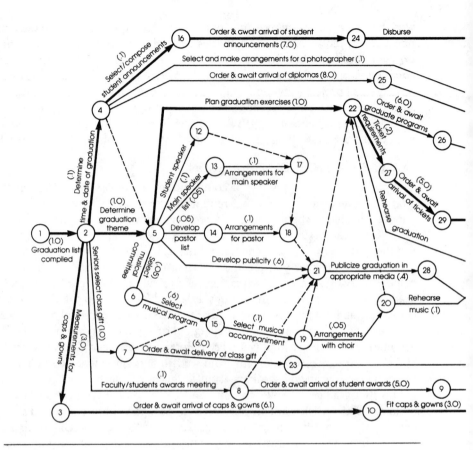

FIGURE 9-5
PERT/CPM Network with Three Critical Paths for
High School Graduation

such as selecting the student speaker, arranging for the main speaker and a
member of the clergy, selecting and arranging music, determining and ordering
student awards, rehearsing, preparing the high school stadium or auditorium
and so on, although very important, are not critical to completing all tasks on
time. However, these noncritical tasks could become critical if they are allowed
to slide for too long. Again, the PERT network can be used to determine the
latest time a noncritical activity can start. Latest starting times are computed by
beginning at the end (or right side of the network) and working backward

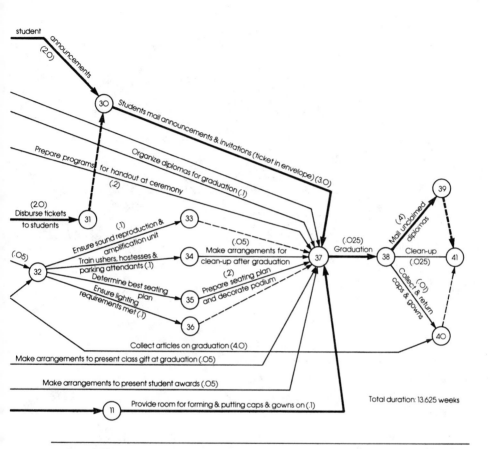

toward the beginning (or left side of the network). For instance, graduate programs must be ordered at least six and a half weeks prior to the graduation ceremony (time path 37-26-22).

PERT/CPM MODIFICATIONS

The preceding two examples demonstrate all the steps in the development of a PERT/CPM analysis. There are some minor modifications that can be added to solve more sophisticated problems, but these steps will be all that are necessary for most of the typical applications of PERT/CPM analysis in educational administration.

Much of the PERT/CPM network analysis can be done on the computer. In computer solutions, typically a network is developed and elapsed times are

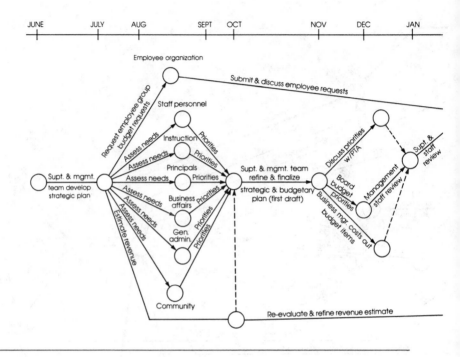

FIGURE 9-6
Budget Preparation, Using a Combination of Gantt
Charting with PERT Analysis

assigned to the activities. These data are put into the computer, which will then construct all additional networks and calculate the critical path, slack, and float. In one variety of PERT analysis, the administrator provides the computer with information about resource availability and about the resources that will be used in each activity, and the computer will figure the critical path based on elapsed-time estimates and resource availability.

Another modification that proves useful to educators, because they are often on a fairly fixed time schedule, is the combination of PERT analysis with Gantt charting. In this type of analysis a horizontal time axis, called a time line, is placed along the top of the PERT network and activities are placed in the network so as to fall along the horizontal time axis at the point when they must be scheduled to occur. This analysis does not allow for the calculations of a critical path but shows the interrelationships of activities and the time periods within which each activity must be completed. This is an especially handy method when the project must be scheduled within fixed time limitations. An example of such an application is budget preparation.

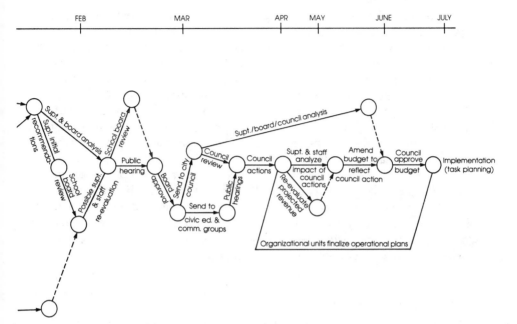

EXAMPLE: BUDGET PREPARATION

Let us consider the preparation of the operating budget for a school system as an example of a modified PERT time schedule. Figure 9-6 is an example of a PERT time schedule for budget preparation. There is a time line along the top of the PERT time schedule; this is used exactly as discussed in relation to the preparation of Gantt charts. The PERT network is drawn below the time line, with each activity appearing directly below the time interval in which it must occur. There are no time estimates shown on the network; they are read directly from the time line above. There is no critical path; however, the superintendent's initial budget recommendations must be made to the school board by January 20 or there is a good chance that the budget will not be able to be approved by June 1 or that other activities will have to be rushed, possibly resulting in poorer relations among the various interested parties. The PERT time schedule keeps everyone appraised of all activities required in budget preparation as well as the time when each of the activities must occur.

The various divisions, schools, and interest groups assess their strategic needs from April through July (of the school year preceding budget adoption), providing input into the development of the strategic educational plan, which is completed in July. Once the strategic plan has been completed, the budget groups go back and begin to refine and develop their specific operational plans and priorities to fit in with the strategic plans. The budget groups make their operating budgets final by the first week in October and employee organizations do so sometime in January. The superintendent and management team then refine the budget and draw up a rough draft. From November through May the budget is reviewed and modified by the public, school board, and city council and is finally approved in mid-June for implementation the following school year. But the administrator can never finish planning; in May the management team begins the process all over again.

The PERT task plan documents and coordinates the activities of all those involved in the budgetary process. The plan provides information on the timing of activities and notification of when activities must begin, displays responsibilities for particular activities, shows the importance of their completion, and compares actual completion with expected completion dates, showing how delays will affect the completion of the budgetary cycle.

APPLICATIONS OF TASK PLANNING

Task planning can be applied to almost any program/project where logical planning and coordination are required. Applications can be made to a single-person project or to one involving many persons, institutions, or agencies. Task planning works as effectively in planning for expansion as it does in planning for cutbacks. It is limited only by the creativity of the administrator who is applying it.

Task plans help the administrator effectively to manage more projects simultaneously than can be administered by other methods. The implementation of planning technology to multi-project management has converted some administrative positions from loci of unmanageable frustrations and failures to manageable, challenging, and rewarding positions. The methods of task planning provide permanent documentation for recurring projects. Possibly one of the least mentioned but most powerful benefits is its characteristic of documenting projects and allowing the administrator to use the same plan for discussing, replanning, and managing projects year after year. It is a very effective vehicle for communication. Using its techniques, participants can visualize the entire project with greater ease and clarity. In this way, task planning provides the entire organization with a stylized "road map."

The final task-planning session is apt to be as much a stock-taking session as anything else. If the strategic and operational commitments have held up through the completion of the task plan, there is much happiness and time for mutual congratulations. If they have not, it is a time to resolve to do better during next year's planning cycle.

GUIDELINES FOR PLANNING

1. Without a task plan, planners are forced to implement, coordinate, and develop required task activity as they go along, often creating organizational overload, confusion, and failure.

2. A task plan is a simplified visualization of the number, kind, and sequences of activities required to achieve a specific operational objective.

3. The task plan is developed by: (1) creating a list of activities needed to achieve a specified objective; (2) determining what resources will be required to accomplish each of the activities; (3) estimating a reasonable amount of time that must be allowed to complete each activity; (4) developing a work plan that shows the interdependency, sequence, and dynamic flow of the activities required to achieve operational objectives; and (5) replanning the task when problems develop.

4. A Gantt or bar chart is a form of task plan that provides a graphic means of planning, coordinating, and portraying the plan, strategy, and progress of a project. The activities to be performed by each resource are identified horizontally on a time axis called a schedule bar. Progress for each activity is posted at regular time intervals so that those activities which are behind schedule can be identified and corrective action taken.

5. A program evaluation review technique/critical path network provides all the information that appears on the Gantt or bar chart as well as the sequential interrelationships among the activities, the duration of the project, and the activities that are most critical to completing the task plan on time. The network is constructed by drawing circles and directed activity arrows in the sequence in which events and activities are to be accomplished, attaching time estimates to the network activities, and calculating time estimates for each path in the network in order to find the critical path. Scheduling of the project and promised completion dates are based on the network time calculation for the critical path. The network is used to discuss and monitor the task activities.

6. The final task plan provides a surefire means of determining if operational personnel have the ability to convert school objectives into operational work plans. It provides a stylized guide for all discussion regarding a project and serves as an excellent documentation to be used over and over again in carrying out reoccurring types of tasks. Final task plans are especially handy for administrators who must manage a diversity of different tasks because they provide a quick and easy reference to various different work plans and their status.

10

Decision Making

"The cause of lightning," Alice said very decidedly, for she felt quite certain about this, "is the thunder—no, no!" she hastily corrected herself. "I meant the other way."

"It's too late to correct it," said the Red Queen: "when you've once said a thing, that fixes it, and you must take the consequences."

—LEWIS CARROLL, Through the Looking Glass

In this book, we have drawn a distinction between strategic and operational planning; this same distinction can be made for decision making. At the strategic level, decisions are made to determine the major directions the organization should take—for example, "What should our school system be doing?" At the operational level, decisions are being made concerning the most efficient and effective means of achieving the strategic plan—for example, "What is the best course of action to achieve a desired (planned) result?"

The strategic decisions provide direction to and limits on the answers that will be arrived at during operational decision making. Thus, decision making is viewed as a flow, from more general long-range decisions to specific short-range ones. Each decision further specifies the direction, scale, character, and sequence of efforts that will follow. In this way, decision making begins with core questions of purpose and flows into technical considerations about operational activity. Each decision serves as a guide indicating how the next decision in the sequence will be made. The final test of this process is how well the decisions can be implemented and how well they achieve the desired results.

THE ESSENCE OF DECISIONS

Decision making can be defined simply as the selection of a course of action from among many possible competing alternatives. It is rarely a choice between right and wrong. It is at best a choice between "almost right" and "probably wrong," but more likely it is a choice of action that appears simply to be more nearly right than the others. Thus, decision making is the identification of one alternative that seems to be most appropriate from among all possible recognizable alternatives.

The essence of a decision is that it is an event of choice. Dale Mann states:

> If, for example, one alternative within a set has such compelling and attractive features that there is no point in comparing it with other alternatives, then there is really no "choice." In that case, the perceived excellence of one course of action forecloses any necessity to make a decision. There are many examples in which excellence or inevitability or compulsion vitiates the need for decision. It does not require a decision to take an absolutely outstanding option, to accept an irrevocable or unavoidable event, or to "choose" to do what is forced upon us. Decisions are a response to situations of choice in which the choice is guided by standards extrinsic to the alternatives. (Mann, 1975a, p. 20)

Decision making does not, as so many studies of decision making proclaim, flow from a "consensus on the facts." Decision making requires a judgment related to alternative strategies. Decisions are based on various conditions that the decision-maker is not always sure about and on the different realities and values of people viewing the decision. The final decision grows out of the clash and conflict of divergent opinions and out of the serious consideration of competing alternatives. It is not through consensus but through the appropriate managing of conflict that creative alternatives and appropriate choices are made.

This is why ready-made decisions that are handed down by authorities often become very narrow decisions. They are narrow in that they may only reflect the values and interests of a select few. If the only justifications for a decision are nice, glowing, but meaningless words such as management expertise or expedience, then decisions become commands, efforts become obstructions, and long-run organizational efficiency is reduced. "Decision making is something that is just done. A choice is made—so what?" It is a dangerous practice for value-laden and judgmental planning decisions to be made by a single or small group of decision-makers (task forces) with little conscious effort to determine how the decisions were made. Such expertise takes the form of narrow-minded technocracy rather than enlightened leadership; thus, it inspires substantial distrust.

Values play a crucial role in the decision-making process. The appropriateness of a decision is based on the capacity to assess preferences, to trade off advantages and disadvantages, and to examine the future consequence of present decisions. Such assessments and choices are based on multiple and conflicting value systems, without which planning would be impossible or unnecessary. It is tension, created by the pressure to select from among multiple and conflicting values, that can force administrators to make innovative decisions.

Since value systems are so important, decisions are improved by broadening the base of people who are aware of the variables that the planning decisions must address. The aim is to enlarge the range of options to be considered within sufficient time for sound decision making. This can only occur if the administrator sees to it that the broadest possible population has gained understanding of the questions being addressed and has had a chance to clarify and express its value systems before problem simplification and decision making begin.

> Effective participation, however, relies much more on developing a common understanding to a problem. Solutions then become almost self-evident, are better supported, can be more readily implemented, and are less likely to generate unwanted repercussions. The common search to understand a problem also generates less conflict, allowing more meaningful participation than jumping to proposed solutions whose originators are then put into conflictual positions, thereby impeding the subsequent implementation of any solutions adopted. Creative participation thus emphasizes problem detecting, problem perceiving, problem formulating and common understanding, and is not restricted merely to problem solving. (Botkin, Elmandjra, Malitya, 1979, p. 30)

The effective decision-maker encourages deliberation, differing opinions, and disagreement. However, the effective decision-maker insists that people who voice an opinion also take responsibility for defining the facts that are needed to support it. Disagreement, especially if it is thoroughly discussed, analyzed, and documented, is the most effective stimulus for effective decision making. It ensures that the decision-maker is not lost in the fog if decisions prove deficient or wrong in execution.

These concepts are described by Peter F. Drucker in his book on management tasks:

> The effective decision-maker does not start out with the assumption that one proposed course of action is right and that all others must be wrong. Nor does he start out with the assumption "I am right and he is wrong." He starts out with the commitment to find out why people disagree.
>
> Effective executives know, of course, that there are fools around and that there are mischief-makers. But they do not assume that the man who disagrees

with what they themselves see as clear and obvious is, therefore, either a fool or a knave. They know that unless proven otherwise, the dissenter has to be assumed to be reasonably intelligent and reasonably fair-minded. Therefore, it has to be assumed that he has reached his so obviously wrong conclusion because he sees a different reality and is concerned with a different problem. The effective executive, therefore, always asks "What does this fellow have to see if his position were, after all, tenable, rational, intelligent?" The effective executive is concerned first with *understanding*. Only then does he even think about who is right and who is wrong.

Needless to say, this is not done by a great many people, whether executives or not. Most people start out with the certainty that how they see is the only way to see at all. As a result, they never understand what the decision—and indeed the whole argument—is really all about. . . . No matter how high his emotions run, no matter how certain he is that the other side is completely wrong and has no case at all, the executive who wants to make the right decision forces himself to see opposition and *his* means to think through the alternatives. He uses conflict of opinion as his tool to make sure all major aspects of an important matter are looked at carefully. (Drucker, 1974, pp. 474-475)

It is the conflict of opinion or opposing points of view that makes the decision-making process so difficult. While it is not usually possible to combine the content knowledge of one teacher with the human understanding of another to secure greater precision in the teaching–learning process, it is often possible to add the knowledge of a curriculum specialist to that of a business specialist in order to improve the quality of a particular decision. But the cost of such combinations is the increased difficulty they present in structure and integration. Therefore, the issue becomes clear and well-reasoned communication with one another; that is, how to complement and support creative thinking without losing track of the final purpose—the decision.

THINKING AND EFFECTIVE DECISION MAKING

The way in which individual participants in the decision-making process view decisions has a major influence on the quality of the decisions finally made. It is obvious that one's values influence the decision but so also do one's thinking and reasoning. Our thinking, though more difficult to observe than our values, has a profound influence on the quality of our final choices. For this reason, authors like James L. Adams (1979) have stressed the importance of and attempted to cultivate the thinking and problem-solving abilities of decision-makers.

Psychologists believe that the way decision-makers conceptually structure decisions has a significant influence on their effectiveness during the decision-making process. For example, "abstract" thinkers are better prepared to cope with the uncertainty and disjointedness in the decision environment as well as conditions of inadequate information than are concrete thinkers.

Those who are better at mental conceptualization and recognizing conflicting information are better equipped for the decision process. Adams identified four basic conceptual blockages to effective decision making: (1) perceptual, (2) emotional, (3) cultural and environmental, and (4) intellectual and expressive. Perceptual blocks "are obstacles that prevent the problem-solver from clearly perceiving either the problem itself or the information needed to solve the problem" (Adams, 1979, p. 13). Some examples of perceptual blocks are seeing what you expect to see—stereotyping; inflexibility or dogmatism; creating what we see; perceptually selecting what fits our mind set; narrow thinking; delimiting the problem area too closely; inability to see the problem from various viewpoints; closed-mindedness; saturation; and failure to utilize all sensory inputs.

Emotional blocks may "interfere with the freedom with which we explore and manipulate ideas, with our ability to conceptualize fluently and flexibly—and prevent us from communicating ideas to others in a manner which will gain their acceptance" (Adams, 1979, p. 42). Examples of emotional blocks are fear to make a mistake or to fail; inability to tolerate ambiguity; overreliance on feelings; preference for judging rather than generating ideas; inability to relax and incubate thought; rationalizing or withdrawing; inability to deal with pressure; worrying; excessive zeal; and inability to distinguish between reality and fantasy.

Cultural and environmental blocks are similar to each other in that one's thought becomes bound by cultural patterns or by the immediate physical and social environment. Cultural blocks come from learned beliefs—for example, believing that fantasy and reflection are a waste of time or a sign of laziness; that playfulness is for children; that problem solving is serious and humor has no place; that rationality is good and feelings and emotions are bad; or that tradition is preferable to change. Prejudice is also a cultural block. Some environmental blocks are lack of cooperation and trust; distractions; and lack of support.

Finally, intellectual and expressive blocks are caused by a lack of intellectual or verbal ability. Some examples are inability to generate solutions; lack of ability to follow alternative logic; inability to interpret information; inadequate language skills; inability to convert imaginary thought to verbal expression; and lack of logic and rational ability.

These four kinds of conceptual blocks have a very negative impact on the decision-making process. The worst impact is that they create "mental walls that block the problem-solver from correctly perceiving a problem or conceiving its solutions" (Adams, 1979, p. 11). The emotional blocks can be used to show how the decision-maker's doubt about a decision can create anxiety and ultimately reduce one's ability to deal effectively with decision making.

Decision-makers often do not make good decisions as a result of adverse emotional reactions to the decision-making process itself. Those who are afraid of making mistakes will tend to procrastinate, putting decisions off to collect more and more information. However, people who are unable to tolerate ambiguity may very quickly come to a solution just to put the decision behind them. Such people cannot stand not having the answer right now, and so they jump to a solution to eliminate discomfort at not obtaining the best solution. Both these kinds of decision-makers are overly controlled by their emotions, which influence their objectivity and judgment.

Another form of emotional blockage occurs when a decision-maker feels uncomfortable and shaky unless on very familiar ground. Uncertainty causes such people to play it safe and be biased toward ideas and solutions that they have already experienced, know, and like. In decision making, one needs to be aware of such blockages and know how they influence the decision-making process. Perhaps even more important, decision-makers must feel healthy and secure with themselves. Self-respect, respect for others, optimism, trust, and willingness to invest energy and take risks go a long way in reducing barriers to effective decision making.

TRADITIONAL APPROACHES

Administrators have traditionally drawn upon authority, personal experience, and logical reasoning to aid them in making decisions. To refer to authority is to seek advice from an expert or powerful source. Such authority comes from tradition, position, or status within an organization, or from expert opinion. The statement that "everybody has always done it that way" is a form of appeal to tradition that decision-makers have long relied on.

Personal experience is used when one is confronted with a new problem. Administrators often try to recall or to seek a personal experience that will help them reach a solution. Reasoning is making choices or drawing conclusions on the basis of known or assumed facts. It usually takes the form of either deductive or inductive reasoning.

Modern methods of decision making developed from the criticism that decisions reached on the basis of authoritative premises, experience, and rationality did not always match observed facts. The future has not followed the ordered perception of the past. The amount of uncertainty with which administrators must deal, the dynamics and interdependence of organizations, and the complexity of decisions have all increased rapidly, while at the same time the possible consequences of errors have also multiplied. Decisions have become much more difficult as the number of students dealt with has increased, then leveled off and declined; as the state and federal role in education has changed and as public funds have become scarce; as the expectations for schools have increased; as the numbers and kinds of professionals having legitimate roles in education have expanded; as teacher dissatisfaction has grown; as the needs of a technological society have been clarified; as global awareness has developed; and as the roles of church, family, and neighborhood have decreased. No one could argue that today's educational decisions are less complex than those that have ever been faced by educators.

PROBLEM-SOLVING APPROACHES

The classical administrative theorists did not generally view decision making in a central role. Henry Fayol (1949) and Lyndall Urwich (1952) considered decision making in relation to its impact on delegation and authority. Frederick W. Taylor only alluded to scientific methods as an approach to decision making. However, Herbert A. Simon, probably the best known and most widely quoted decision theorist, gave considerable attention to decision making. He described three major phases in the decision-making process. These are:

1. Intelligence activity. Borrowing from the military meaning of intelligence—this initial phase consists of searching the environment for conditions calling for decisions.
2. Design activity. In this second phase, inventing, developing, and analyzing possible courses of action take place.
3. Choice activity. The third and final phase is the actual choice, selecting a particular course of action from those available. (Simon, 1960, p. 2)

From these modest beginnings have developed a flood of literature on decision making. Much of this literature focuses on the decision process itself and a technique that is described as the "problem-solving process" (Ackoff, 1978). Problem solving is much broader than either planning or decision making. Problem solving is a tool that is used any time you want to change something. Problem solving becomes planning when it is future oriented and it becomes planning and decision making when there is a pressure to make a future-oriented decision. Decision making actually is a step in the problem-solving process, but it is an important step that requires all the other steps in order to be effective. In this way, decision making is considered a subset of problem solving, with decision making dealing primarily with evaluation and choice from a set of alternatives, and problem solving dealing with the whole process of problem formulation, alternative generation, and information processing, and culminating in implementing and evaluating final choices.

Difficulties may develop in problem solving if a structural approach is not followed. For example, the desire to make a decision, to resolve the problem, to move on quickly, all may lead to making decisions by "shooting from the hip." Often in such a situation an essential stage of problem-solving activity may be omitted. For example, if one does not generate quality alternatives, then choosing the best of several mediocre alternatives still leaves one with a mediocre solution. Mediocre decisions increase tension or stress concerning future decisions and cause the problem-solving capacity to diminish.

The impact of hastily selecting one alternative without carefully weighing its possible outcomes can be devastating. When a solution is formulated hastily and is a consequence of inadequate search and limited participation, those asked to implement it will feel that they do not want to bear the responsibility for that decision and will psychologically withdraw from the situation and the solution.

Problem-solving stages

In broad terms, there are five stages in the problem-solving process. The basic stages are problem definition, search for alternatives, exploring the consequences of alternatives, choosing among alternatives, and implementing and evaluating the decision.

The problem-solving approach begins with defining a problem situation—with generating information and clarifying the problem about which a decision is to be made. This is not as simple as it seems on the surface, since decision-makers begin by having only a symptom or, at best, only part of the problem. From this small part, they must work to generate a clear presentation of the entire problem. The next stage involves a search for alternative solutions by brainstorming, reviewing, revising, elaborating, and recombining solution ideas. Research has shown that solutions can be greatly improved by looking at as many alternatives as possible. In the third stage of problem solving, all of the consequences of the alternatives, given the organizational context, are explored and evaluated. The benefits and detriments of each alternative are constructed and weighed.

The next stage is the one most often thought about when we reflect upon decision making. This step requires the selection of a preferred course of action and a firm commitment to carry out the decision. This final step is the implementation and evaluation of the chosen course of action. This includes

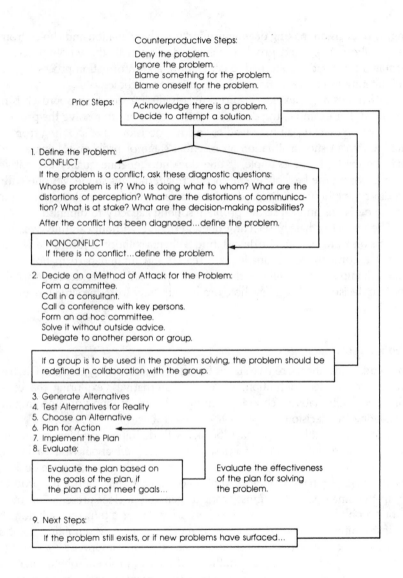

FIGURE 10-1

The Nine-Step Problem-Solving Model

Source: Reprinted from John E. Jones and J. William Pfeiffer (Eds.), *The 1973 Annual Handbook for Group Facilitators.* San Diego, CA: University Associates, 1980. Used with permission.

preparing a task plan, with names of persons responsible for each task, developing a coordinating plan, reviewing desired outcomes, developing measures of effectiveness, and creating a monitoring plan for gathering evaluation data as the solution is put into action. The decision will work more smoothly if the actions needed to put it into operation are carefully planned and evaluated through a task plan.

Earley and Rutledge (1980) provide a specific nine-step problem-solving model based on the generalized problem-solving structure. Their model is presented in Figure 10-1. They suggest that the nine-step model is not dependent on a group to be effective and can be used by individuals, consultants, or with key leaders to work through a problem. The key to using the problem-solving procedure, however, is to follow each step in each stage to the point at which all involved parties can agree that the step and stage are fully accomplished. The final solution should be the most effective decision the group can generate and one that is well understood and supported by the entire organization.

THE DECISION-MAKING PROCESS

Although decision making is only one stage of the problem-solving process, it is a most important one. Since many of the other steps in the problem-solving process are developed in other chapters, decision making will receive central attention in the remainder of this one.

Decision making is the most dramatic stage of problem solving, the stage where we commit ourselves to a specific course of action. For this reason, decision making is the essence of all problem-solving efforts.

The creation and development of courses of action should have been completed in previous stages, so in methodological decision making we are no longer concerned about whether the courses of action are as good as can be. We are only interested in evaluating the utility of choice and event outcomes and picking out the best of the available choices. Probably the most common method of doing this is by just thinking and talking about the solution alternatives until we feel that we have made up our minds. However, it is wise to understand the elements and the ramifications of the decision-making process itself in order to fully understand why we actually choose alternatives. Also, when the problem is important and there is time to exercise greater care, we can be more deliberate in our considerations.

Decisions in their basic form require some system in which a decision-maker can weigh alternatives and choose the one that seems most desirable. The development of a system through which the weighted value of alternatives can be evaluated, has been the subject of a massive body of literature that generally is classified as Bayesian statistics. In its simplest form, a system of points is set up by constructing a list of advantages and disadvantages, relating them to each alternative, and awarding points to each course of action. The alternative with the highest number of points is selected. A more complex, formal device not only takes into account points for advantages and disadvantages, it captures the structure of decisions and the impact of chance events on the advantages and disadvantages of outcomes. This method is described as decision-tree analysis. Perhaps its strength lies as much in helping one conceptualize and share the decision as it does in helping one make it.

DECISION-TREE ANALYSIS

Von Neumann and Morgenstern (1947), in their work on game theory, suggested the idea of representing possible future behavior as a "tree" with branches radiating from each choice point so that individuals might select at each such point the appropriate branch to follow.

Most of the literature that has followed this "tree" concept can be traced to the work of two of the most respected decision theorists, Howard Raiffa (1970) and Robert Schlaifer (1969), both from Harvard University. These two men have made substantive contributions regarding the application of Bayesian statistics and decision-tree analysis to the administrative decision-making process. Much of their contribution has become the basis of Bayesian statistics courses and management science programs that have become popular over the past twenty years. Most students of business and an ever increasing number of educational administrators are being exposed to decision theory as a means to better understand the analytical technique and the basic process of decisions. In one of his latest books, Simon states: "One cannot help being impressed by the virtuosity that has been exhibited in formal decision theory during the past generation, the beauty of some of the results, and the applicability of these results as normative rules for decision making under certain rather restricted circumstances" (1976, p. 32).

Only a few U.S. companies appear to have used decision-tree analysis in their operations for any length of time. Two of these companies are DuPont and Pillsbury. At DuPont, middle and even senior management increasingly will take action or submit recommendations that include DTA along with more conventional analyses. At Pillsbury, many divisions use DTA in decision-making situations. When recommendations come to be considered, DTA analysis is the vehicle for discussion. At Ford Motor Company, some 200 senior executives have passed through a brief DTA-oriented program during the past ten years. The program has been followed up in some divisions by intensive workshops for junior executives.

Howard Raiffa's work related to this topic was first published in a book entitled *Games and Decisions* that he co-authored in 1957 with R. D. Luce. His 1970 *Decision-Tree Analysis* is his most thorough treatment of decision making. Robert Schlaifer's first work related to Bayesian statistics and decision making appeared in 1959; a 1969 book, *Analysis of Decisions Under Uncertainty*, is his most comprehensive treatment of decision-tree analysis.

Decision-tree analysis may be defined as a method to compare alternative strategies in simple but quantitative terms, using a logical sequence of steps that can be easily retraced and verified by others. It provides a systematic way to assist administrators in identifying and ordering the differentiated strategies, relationships, possible outcomes, and probabilities related to outcomes that may be conceived as part of a decision. It facilitates the structuring, discussing, and evaluating of strategies and the making of final decisions.

Decision analysis accommodates the same types of considerations as informal decision making; however, it imposes logical structure and discipline on the reasoning process. Decision-tree analysis helps individual decision-makers to structure their thinking, to recognize needed information, and ultimately to provide a vehicle for communicating thoughts related to the decision. It provides a method to communicate the grounds for a decision and to identify the areas of potential disagreement. It helps to focus different types of expertise on different parts of the problem and to isolate areas of disagreement.

Major steps in DTA

Decision-tree analysis is made up of four stages or steps, which should be followed in logical order. These four steps are:

Step 1: Organize and exhibit the anatomy of the problem in terms of a decision-tree diagram.

Step 2: Evaluate the consequences at the terminal forks.

Step 3: Assign probabilities to the branches of the tree.

Step 4: Determine the optimal strategy by averaging out and folding back.

In general, a decision-tree is rather like a road map. It is a map of a decision problem that includes actions and events considered relevant to the problem. In developing a decision tree, the combinations of alternative events can be examined at several levels of detail. The problem in laying out the decision tree is to strike the right level, the one that permits administrators to consider major alternatives without becoming so concerned with detail and refinement that the crucial issues are clouded.

The development of a decision tree can be best understood by considering a series of examples of its application. We will start with a very simple example and go on to a more difficult application. The application of DTA to such a simple problem might seem to be so much overkill; however, the simple example will clearly illustrate the characteristics of the decision-tree approach.

EXAMPLE: LOCATION OF HIGH SCHOOL GRADUATION

The first example is inspired by an illustration that was used by John F. Magee (1964) in his discussion of decision trees. Let us suppose that you are involved in planning the graduation for one of the senior high schools in your school district. This high school has recently built a new football stadium and the school personnel, parents, and students are very proud of it. The senior class, in fact, was particularly responsible for the stadium because they had very good football teams that created a great deal of community spirit. The high school also has a basketball fieldhouse, which is much smaller and has less seating capacity.

The football stadium is new and pleasant while the basketball fieldhouse is old and very cramped for space. If weather permits, you and most others would prefer to hold the graduation exercises and serve refreshments in the new football stadium. It would be most pleasant, more people could attend, and they would be more comfortable. On the other hand, if you set the graduation for the football stadium and all students and guests are assembled and it begins to rain, the refreshments will be ruined, your students and guests will get damp, and you and everyone else will heartily wish you had decided to have the graduation in the fieldhouse.

Step 1: Organize and exhibit the anatomy of the problem

This is possibly the most complex and yet the most important step in decision-tree analysis because it requires the description of the entire problem, including all perceived relevant alternatives, all possible events, and all likely outcomes.

This step requires one to organize all information and to appropriately bring that information together as it will bear on the decision. In this step, the decision-makers consider the state of affairs and the alternative courses of action and graphically display their relationships. This step requires some compromise since only the most "plausible" alternatives and events become a part of the analysis and are worked out in detail. In the present example, there are but two alternatives and two possible events. Figure 10-2 illustrates a decision tree for the graduation problem.

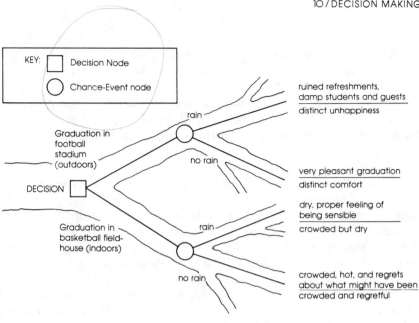

FIGURE 10-2

Decision Tree for Location of Graduation
Ceremony

Source: From "Decision Trees for Decision Making" by John F. Magee (July-August 1964). Reprinted by permission of the Harvard Business Review. Copyright © 1964 by the President and Fellows of Harvard College; all rights reserved.

In this first step, it is necessary to present the anatomy or the qualitative structure of our simple example as a chronological arrangement of those choices that are controlled by the decision-maker (decision nodes are represented by a box or square) and those choices that are determined by chance (chance-event nodes are represented by a circle). In the graduation problem, the decision-maker has a choice at the very start. At the first node on the left, the school administrator has the choice of holding the graduation ceremony in the football stadium or the basketball fieldhouse. Each branch represents an alternative course of action or decision. At the end of each branch or action course is another node representing a chance event—whether or not it will rain. At this point on the decision tree, the decision-maker must relinquish control to chance. Each subsequent alternative course to the right represents an alternative outcome of the combination of a decision and chance event.

Associated with each alternative-event sequence through the tree is a pay-off, shown at the end of the rightmost or terminal fork. For instance, holding graduation in the football stadium when it does not rain results in a pleasant graduation environment and distinct comfort for those involved. A decision tree of any size will always combine alternatives with different possible events to determine the final outcomes—outcomes at the end of the terminal forks.

Step 2: Assign utility values

To evaluate the consequences at the terminal forks requires coming up with a quantitative measure for each of the outcomes. In our example, the terminal fork outcomes are distinct unhappiness, distinct comfort, crowded but dry, and crowded and regretful. Since some outcomes are clearly preferable to others, we need a quantitative measure that reflects how much we value the outcome of each alternative event sequence. This can most easily be done in cases such as this one by using a unit of measure called "utility value."

The desirability, to the decision-makers, of any end position (terminal fork) of their decision-tree diagram can be completely described by a single number, which is called the utility of the outcome. All that is really required is to find some way of replacing detailed descriptions of consequences by meaningful numerical values; in some problems the most suitable values may well be monetary (see Kaiffa, 1970; Schlaifer, 1959). However, in our example, and in most cases in education and in this chapter, we will consider utility as a numerical description of consequences and not monetary values.

Utility can be defined as the values that outcomes, from alternative-event sequences, have to the decision-maker. The utility that an outcome has for a decision-maker is its desirability or usefulness to the decision-maker and is measured in terms of "utils." In assigning utility to outcomes, it is first necessary to determine what are considered to be the most preferable and the least preferable outcomes. Then a value of 1 is assigned to the most preferable outcome and a value of 0 to the least preferable outcome. Outcomes of intermediate desirability are given values between 0 and 1. One might assign a desirable intermediate consequence a value of 0.7 and a less desirable intermediate consequence a value of 0.2.

It is difficult to briefly explain how such "utils" should be interpreted, but basically the value of 0.7 means that one considers the desirable intermediate consequence as being worth exactly the same as a hypothetical lottery that would give a 70 percent chance at the most preferable outcome and a 30 percent chance at the least preferable outcome. Similarly, the value 0.2 for the less desirable intermediate consequence implies that one considers this outcome to be equal in desirability to a hypothetical lottery that yields a 20 percent chance at the most preferable outcome and an 80 percent chance at the least desirable

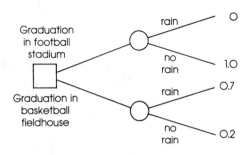

FIGURE 10-3
Utils Assigned to Decision Tree for Location of
Graduation—Step 2

outcome. However, for all practical purposes, the decision-maker can consider
them as relative weights for the desirability of outcomes.

The decision-maker must assign "utils" to all outcomes of alternative-event
sequences. Figure 10-3 presents the graduation problem with utility values
noted at the terminal forks. A utility appraisal of 0.7, even if it is just a guess, is
a more informative mode of expression than a phrase like "crowded but dry."

It is important to note that different individuals may have different utilities
for the same outcome of an alternative-event sequence. Decision-tree analysis
becomes an excellent mechanism to bring such differences to the forefront to
be discussed before they become confused and create indecision or greater
disagreement at a later point.

Step 3: Assign probabilities to the branches

At each fork where chance is in control, it is crucial to know what the probability is that chance will choose any particular one of the alternative branches
available. Since each chance event has some probability of occurring, it is
necessary to assess that probability. The probability estimates are assigned to
each of the events.

If an individual knew the exact state of affairs or events, the choice of an
alternative would be easy. In our present decision problem there are two possible actions: hold graduation in the stadium or hold graduation in the basketball fieldhouse. If the decision-maker knew for certain that it would rain, then
he or she would decide to hold graduation in the fieldhouse. If the decision-
maker knew for certain that it would not rain, then graduation would be held
in the stadium. Under these circumstances, the principal is making a decision

under the condition of certainty. However, most decisions are made under conditions of uncertainty—the decision-maker does not know the state of affairs with certainty.

Most often, however, decision-makers do have some information regarding conditions influencing the decision. The decision-maker introduces intuitive judgments and feelings directly into the formal analysis of the decision problem. (For an extended discussion of this concept, see any good book on Bayesian statistics: McGeer, 1971; Newman, 1971; Schlaifer, 1969; and Winkler, 1972.)

Basing judgment on a combination of facts and belief—history, predictions, experience, intuition, wisdom, and sometimes scientific inquiry—the decision-maker must formally or informally predict the probability of events. In the example, the decision on where graduation will be held must be made by Wednesday in order to allow enough time for all the necessary arrangements. On Wednesday morning you may not be at all certain whether or not it will rain the following Saturday; indeed, technically, you can never be absolutely certain about the weather, although you may often feel certain for all practical purposes. You might get the best possible weather report from the weather bureau. You may collect information on weather conditions at that same time of year over the past three to five years. You may look at the sky and reflect on your own experience about weather at graduation time. Using any number or combination of procedures, you can determine your degree-of-belief related to the two events, "rain" and "no rain."

Figure 10-4 represents our decision problem with the probabilities added. We estimate the probability of rain not by using terms such as "a good chance" or "less than likely" but by using numbers such as "80 percent chance" or "20 percent chance." This gives us the probability that chance will choose one particular chance-event branch over another, in our case, rain over no rain. These probabilities are written in parentheses right on the chance-event branches.

Step 4: Determine the optimal strategy

This last step is used to make the final decision. The final choice is the best decision that can be made based on the information provided. If the information provided is close to being correct, decision-tree analysis, on the average, will result in the best possible decision—over time no other approach could come up with more correct decisions based on the same set of information.

Some might argue that it is easy to make decisions once the information is available, but this has not always proven to be true. Information and facts are not adequate tools for solving problems or making decisions because facts do not speak by themselves unless relationships between them have been established. The way one structures the information—that is, supplies the missing link—is the process of effective decision making. Decision-tree analysis not

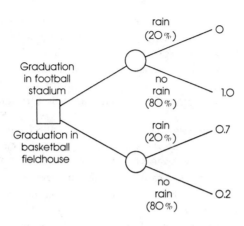

FIGURE 10-4
Probabilities Assigned to Location of Graduation
Ceremony—Step 3

only points out the information needed in a decision problem but provides the mechanism to structure that information so as to make the best possible decision given the information available.

Step 4 is basically a technical procedure in which the expected values of each decision strategy are compared to determine which is the most favorable strategy. "Expected value" is the average value, in our case utility, that would be obtained from a set of decisions given the utility and the probability of all possible outcome-chance combinations.

Before we continue with Step 4, let us take stock as to where we are. The basic problem has been organized in terms of a decision-tree diagram, or stylized road map, that depicts in chronological order the alternatives that the decision-maker may choose and the outcomes that are governed by chance. This road map exhibits the utility for following any road to its end. It indicates the probability assessments of the various possible branches at each chance fork.

The problem can now be stated: Given the road map, the utilities, and the probabilities at each chance fork, which is the best strategy? In our particular example, you now must choose whether you should begin final preparation for graduation in the football stadium or in the basketball fieldhouse.

The final decision is made by "averaging out and folding back." The purpose of averaging out and folding back is to determine which decision or set of decisions will result in the highest expected value to the decision-makers. To determine this, one must average out the expected value at each chance-event node starting at the terminal fork or the extreme right side of the tree and fold this information back to each decision node. All alternatives that are not considered to have as high a utility are pruned from the tree until the best set of decisions (the optimal strategy) is selected. According to Raiffa:

> We first transport ourselves in conceptual time out to the very tips of the tree where the evaluations are given directly in terms of the data of the problem. We then work our way backwards by successive use of two devices:
> 1. an averaging-out process at each chance juncture, and
> 2. a choice process that selects the path yielding the maximum future evaluation at each decision juncture.
>
> We call this the "averaging out and folding back" procedure. (Raiffa, 1970, p. 231)

The decision-maker always averages out at a chance-outcome fork and folds back at a decision fork.

Averaging out

Figure 10-5 shows the decision tree after the completion of the averaging-out and folding-back procedures. We begin by going to the tips of the tree (or terminal forks) and determining the expected value of the various chance outcomes. If you follow the graduation-in-football-stadium branch you end at the chance-event node for the terminal branch rain/no rain. If you place yourself conceptually in time at that point and sight down the chance outcomes, you know that 20 percent of the time it will rain in this situation, giving you no utility, and 80 percent of the time it will not rain, giving you the maximum utility of 1.0. Averaging out is based on the average utility at that point in time; this is called the expected value (EV) of the decision. To a decision-maker perched at this chance-event node, the future looks as though it is worth:

$$.20 \, (0) + .80 \, (1.0) = 0.8$$

This is the expected or average utility we get from the chance events.

If we now do the same thing for the other decision strategy, graduation in the basketball fieldhouse, we will have averaged out all the terminal forks. To a decision-maker perched at this chance-event node, the future looks as though it is worth:

$$.20 \, (0.7) + .80 \, (0.2) = 0.3$$

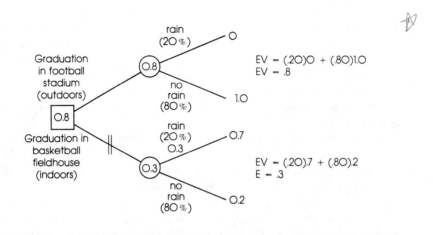

FIGURE 10-5
Decision Tree for Location of Graduation
Ceremony—Step 4

This is the expected or average utility we will get from these chance events. The expected-value figures are written within the circles that graphically represent the chance-event nodes for each terminal fork.

Folding back

We are now ready to begin the folding-back process. Let us now back up and place ourselves at the decision node where we sight down the branch graduation-in-football-stadium or the branch graduation-in-basketball-fieldhouse. We must look to see what is down the road. We see two risky events for each decision but we also see the average utility that these decisions have for the decision-maker. One risky option has an evaluation sign of 0.8 and the other risky option has an evaluation sign of 0.3. The decision to hold graduation in the football stadium has greater utility than the decision to hold graduation in the gym and therefore is the optimum strategy. The utility of 0.8 is folded back and placed within the box that graphically represents the decision node. The decision to hold graduation in the stadium eliminates the decision to hold graduation in the fieldhouse; therefore, this decision is pruned. This is indicated on the diagram by the double vertical slashes.

Sensivity analysis

Such an analysis usually begins with the remark, "I don't believe the conclusions." When such a problem arises, the decision-maker must decide where he or she went wrong in the DTA analysis. If the decision-maker believes the estimates of the probabilities or utilities are in error, then he or she must try to improve them. However, if no realistic adjustments to the analysis change the decision, then the decision-maker should very carefully examine the basis for his or her disbelief in the solution because, in all probability, it is wrong.

If the chance of rain shifted to anywhere close to 54 percent, then sensitivity analysis would suggest that the decision should be reanalyzed and possibly shifted. Such data might be revealed prior to making the decision or at a point when it would not be too late to change the decision. Again, if the utility for holding graduation in the stadium without rain was changed to less than .37 or if the utility of holding graduation in the fieldhouse with no rain was raised to .85 or above, the decision would shift.

Knowledge of the sensitivity of a decision to changes in probability and/or utility values may be helpful in deciding whether to engage in further analysis. If small changes in estimates of utility or probability could change a decision, then the expected benefits of further analysis would more than likely be worth the additional time and cost. In our example, the shifts in the estimates are large and would not justify reanalysis. Of course, all of this is finally determined by the importance of the decision.

EXAMPLE: EXCEPTIONAL EDUCATION

The graduation problem, though involving only a single stage of decision, illustrates all the major principles on which larger, more complex decision trees are built. The real payoff of such analysis is likely to occur when the problems become more complex. Let us take a slightly more complicated situation.

You are trying to determine whether you should screen all children entering the kindergarten program for various forms of exceptionality. Your school system has been aware for a long time of students with "exceptions" that influence their learning; you want to be able to identify the exceptional student early in his or her school career. However, due to limited funds you must critically determine if screening children for exceptionality is really necessary. The total cost for screening each first-grade child is approximately 45 cents plus ten minutes of the teacher's time. The alternative is to allow the classroom teacher, counselor, or principal to refer the child for testing when they suspect that the child has an exceptionality. This requires only about 32 percent of the money and time required to screen all kindergarten children.

At the same time, you are also considering three possible programs for dealing with exceptional children. One approach consists of a team for diagnosis, prescription, and monitoring plus exceptional-education teachers for implementation. Each team will service a geographical area that will include twelve schools; each of these schools will have an exceptional-education teacher who implements aspects of the team's prescription in a learning lab and works with the classroom teacher to strengthen or reinforce the prescription. The second approach includes an exceptional-education teacher for every three schools in addition to a supervisor who covers twelve different schools (the diagnostic team is eliminated). The exceptional-education teacher is used in much the same manner as in the team approach and existing central office staff are called in as necessary. This plan costs only about 28 percent as much as the team approach. The last approach is to provide in-service training to existing classroom teachers as well as a special-education supervisor who covers twelve schools and works with the classroom teacher to set up classroom approaches for dealing with the children's exceptionality. This procedure would add very little cost to the existing operation and would be about 12 percent as expensive as the first approach.

To assist you in making these decisions, you complete a decision-tree analysis that looks something like the one in Figure 10-6. In this example, cost-effectiveness relations may have been the best method of measuring consequences at the terminal forks; however, since the purpose of the example is to demonstrate methodology, the details of the problem are minimized.

A child's success in his or her school work as a result of a small expenditure of money is identified as the most favorable outcome and a child's failure with the expenditure of a large sum of money is identified as the worst outcome. The tree shows that the screening instrument is only 94 percent accurate in identifying the 30 percent of the students who are actually exceptional learners. On the other hand, teachers not using the screening device can only identify about 40 percent of the exceptional students. In addition, the most expensive method results in a 98 percent success factor in working with exceptional children. Examination of the decision tree shows that the best decision is to screen kindergarten children and to provide in-service training and a special-education supervisor to assist the regular classroom teacher (option 3). However, small changes in the probability and/or utilities could easily shift either of these decisions. Therefore, it would be advisable to double-check all data and possibly to do a sensitivity analysis on this decision-tree.

WHY DTA?

In the final analysis, judgment is the most important determiner of effective educational decision making. Yet, responsible judgment cannot be exercised unless the basis for judgment rests upon a sound examination of the facts pertaining to the decision. Decision-tree analysis allows the administrator to struc-

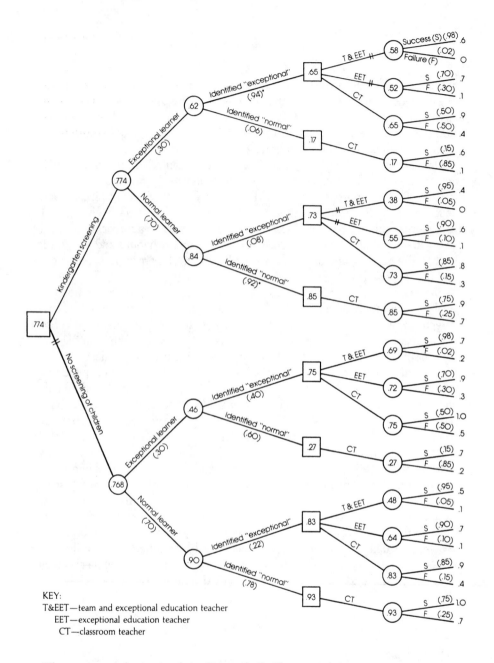

KEY:
T&EET—team and exceptional education teacher
EET—exceptional education teacher
CT—classroom teacher

*The screening procedure is not perfect and incorrectly identifies some students.

FIGURE 10-6
Decision Tree for the Exceptional
Education Program

ture information related to a decision so as to facilitate the application of sound judgment. Dale Mann makes this point very well:

> The attempted use of any formal model of rationality requires that we make explicit what we usually leave implicit with uneven and haphazard results. In addition, because the forms of rationality are familiar to many people, they can facilitate communication. Because of the explicitness and commonality with which the problem is stated, additional people may be able to participate in its solution. For example, if the analyst asks only "which program is best," she will get only relatively unenlightening recommendations—"A is best," "B is best," and so on. But if the problem is stated in any more explicit and expanded form, it becomes possible to make more precise comparisons and, hopefully, also more precisely useful recommendations. (Mann, 1975a, pp. 43-44)

Using decision-tree analysis, administrators can consider various courses of action with greater ease and clarity. The interactions between present decision alternatives, uncertain events, future choices, and final outcomes become more visible. Differences in assumptions or standards of value that underlie differences in judgment or choice are forced into the open. Such differences are usually recognized as those involved in decisions realize that they have different utilities for outcomes or different probability assessments for events or even possibly a slightly different way in which they structure the decision. However, the explicit recognition of such differences is usually the beginning of greater understanding and agreement. When the causes of such differences are only vaguely recognized, they tend to drain off much of the energy and spirit in maintaining sociopsychological homeostasis.

Decision-tree analysis can be used to communicate the rationale for a decision and to rally support for it. Howard Raffia states:

> Analysis helps put the arguments of an opposing point of view in perspective. "Yes, these factors are cogent but we incorporated them into our analysis and found that they were outweighed by consideration of this, this, and this." By the same token, if the factors have not been included this is immediately laid bare. (Raiffa, 1970, p. 269)

Decision-tree analysis focuses thinking on the critical elements of a decision. It forces into the open hidden assumptions behind a decision and makes clear their logical implications. The decision-maker does not need to keep in his or her head all the considerations that are taken into account, and, indeed, all the considerations do not need to be evaluated by the same person. It provides an effective vehicle for communicating the reasoning that underlies a recommendation. This is the benefit that best summarizes all others. By forcing meaningful structure on the information and reasoning related to a decision, others can better understand that reasoning and see how their reasoning and judgments relate to the decision.

Decision-tree analysis encourages the decision-maker to scrutinize his or her problem as an organic whole and to come to quantitative grips with the interactions that influence the decision. Decision-tree analysis helps to suggest what data need to be gathered and how they should be compiled and organized so as best to facilitate the decision-making process. Decision-tree analysis, when the problem requires, suggests what could happen in the future and prepares a rationale for ensuing action. The documentation can help the decision-maker keep the problem and decision in mind, providing a framework for continuous reevaluation. The completed analysis provides documentation of the decision for a new administrator who might be assigned after the decisions are put into action.

Obviously, the administrator faces too many different decisions to apply in all cases such a formalized time-consuming method as DTA. In addition, many of these decisions are simple or recur often enough so that they really do not require such a formalized system. However, when administrators face difficult choices among alternatives, complex structure, and/or vagueness related to possible future events and resulting outcomes, the conditions are ideal for the application of decision-tree analysis. Such conditions often exist in the planning environment, where administrators must make difficult choices regarding goals, objectives, resource allocations, action plans, and many other factors that have a significant impact on future organizational success. Decision-tree analysis provides a commonly understood mechanism upon which to open up administrative rationale to greater scrutiny and ultimately communicate the basis upon which decisions related to educational plans are founded.

GUIDELINES FOR PLANNING

1. Creative decision-makers emphasize problem detecting, problem perceiving, problem formulating, and common understanding as well as decision making. It has been frequently suggested that decisions must not be made by examining "green apples" if the organization is to avoid future stomach aches. Decision-makers must allow the "apples to fully ripen" before final decisions are made. This occurs as conflicts of opinion and opposing points of view are given sufficient time to develop.

2. Decision making has evolved into the most important subset of considerations involved in the broader problem-solving process. Decision making deals primarily with evaluation and choice from a set of alternatives; problem solving deals with the whole process of problem formulation, alternatives generation, and information and decision processing, which culminates in implementing and evaluating final choices.

3. Decision making is the selection of one course of action from among many possible competing alternatives and is based on the capacity to assess preferences, to trade off advantages and disadvantages, and to examine the future consequences of present decisions.

4. The way that people conceptually structure decisions has a significant influence on their effectiveness during the decision-making process. One must guard against the perceptual, emotional, cultural, environmental, intellectual, and expressive blockages to effective decision making.

5. Administrators have traditionally drawn upon authority, personal experience, and logical reasoning to aid them in making decisions.

6. Decision-tree analysis is a method of making decisions by comparing alternative strategies, in simple but quantitative terms, using a logical sequence of steps—organizing and exhibiting the anatomy of the problem, evaluating the consequences, assigning probabilities to the branches, and determining optimal strategy by averaging out and folding back—that can be easily retraced and verified by others. This process accommodates the same types of consideration as traditional approaches; however, it imposes logical structure and discipline on the reasoning process.

7. Decision-tree analysis helps individuals to structure their thinking, to recognize needed information, and ultimately to provide a vehicle for communicating thoughts related to the decision. It provides an effective means for communicating the reasoning underlying an organizational decision. Others can better understand that reasoning and see how their reasoning and judgments relate to the decision.

11

Reducing Resistance Through Organizational Development

The very difficulties which it [change] presents derive from growth in understanding, in skill, in power. To assail the changes that have unmoored us from the past is futile, and in a deep sense, I think, it is wicked. We need to recognize the change and learn what resources we have.

–ROBERT OPPENHEIMER

This book stresses the importance of environmental context, goals, objectives, policies, budgets, task coordination, communication, and decision making in effective planning. However, effective planning must go beyond operational issues and structure if the carefully laid plans for the organization are ever to become a reality. Problems are not always caused by a lack of strategic and operational planning or even by lack of an appropriate structure by which participation in planning is possible.

Plans must be implemented if they are to be deemed successful, and their implementation is dependent upon the attitudes and behavior of the individuals within the organization. If those within the organization support each other and the plans, that support goes a long way toward ensuring successful implementation. Conversely, if those working within the organization do not support one another or the plans, there is an increased likelihood that all planning efforts will ultimately fail. For this reason, it is very important that the behavioral norms of the organizational culture support the successful implementation of plans. Sometimes, this may require a change in employees; in other cases, the attitudes of employees already working in the organization must be changed.

For example, if the board of a private school decides to implement a school desegregation plan, it will need the support of the headmaster in order for the plan to be successful. If the headmaster does not support the plan and resists implementation, the board has two possible alternatives available in order to get the plan implemented. The first is to fire the individual and hire a new headmaster who will implement the plan. However, if the existing headmaster is a very good one that the organization does not want to lose, this may not be the most ideal solution. In fact, the new headmaster may have similar attitudes as the one the board fired, be much less efficient as an administrator, and simply word his intentions to meet what he believes the board most desires. For this reason, there is considerable merit in working with the existing individual in order to try to change or modify his or her behavior to better fit the needs of the organization. Instead of firing the headmaster, an effort might be made to change his values and attitudes so he becomes more supportive of the planned change.

Administrators must be consciously aware that there will come a time when existing organizational structure, interpersonal relations, and group norms will no longer suit the goals, objectives, and financial resources of the organization. When this occurs, resistance is often expressed in destructive ways: administrators no longer seem to support the plans; points of reference become outdated; authorities and responsibilities no longer seem to be clearly defined; relationships within units and between units become distorted and strained; and irrelevant activities and information seem to increase. These difficulties manifest themselves through frictions between individuals within a department and between departments; neglect and duplication of tasks required to achieve objectives; confused lines of communication; and a general lack of coordination. Even if planned structures have been satisfactory in the past, such conditions usually indicate the impending need for adjustments within the work groups and/or the individual. Efficiency is usually doomed if the individual and his or her work group remain static during the implementation of plans.

In order to plan for organizational and human resource requirements, it is necessary to understand the culture of organizational life. This is not an easy task because much of that culture is suppressed and not easily visible to the untrained eye. French and Bell (1973, p. 18) portrayed the organization as an iceberg with formal (visible) and informal (nonvisible or covered) systems. Figure 11-1 shows this organizational iceberg. Much of the planning structure discussed in this book is about the formal aspects of the planning process—or the tip of the iceberg. However, when discussing the organizational and human

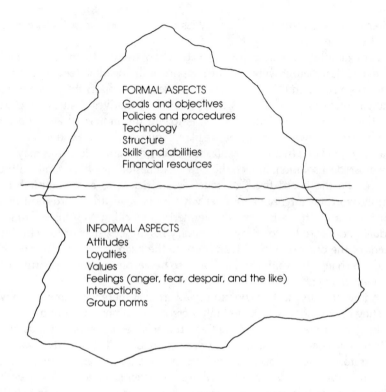

FORMAL ASPECTS
Goals and objectives
Policies and procedures
Technology
Structure
Skills and abilities
Financial resources

INFORMAL ASPECTS
Attitudes
Loyalties
Values
Feelings (anger, fear, despair, and the like)
Interactions
Group norms

FIGURE 11-1
Organizational Iceberg

Source: Wendell L. French/Cecil H. Bell, *Organization Development: Behavioral Science Interventions for Organization Improvement*, Second Edition, © 1978, p. 16. Reprinted by permission of Prentice-Hall, Inc., Englewood Cliffs, N.J.

resources required for implementing plans, the informal aspects become increasingly important.

Kurt Lewin's (1948) model is most often used to describe the types of changes that must occur in order to influence the informal aspects of an organization. According to Levin, in order to effect changes in the informal aspects, it is necessary to first break the equilibrium in the individual's "force field." The force field is a somewhat firmly set belief regarding behavioral norms. He describes this first step as "unfreezing." Unfreezing results in a decrease in the strength of old attitudes, values, or behaviors resulting from information or experiences that disconfirm one's perception of self, others, or events. Once this has been done, it becomes possible to introduce change. This second step—of introducing change—results in the development of new attitudes, values, or behaviors through identification and/or internalization. However, change can be very fragile (one quickly slips back into old ways), and therefore it is necessary to "refreeze" the changes within the individual and the organization. This helps to protect and ensure the long-range retention of the changes. Refreezing is the stabilization of change at a new equilibrium state by supporting new behaviors in reference-group norms, cultures, processes, and structures. The concept of organizational development (OD) is based on this three-stage change process. Organizational development (OD) focuses on what French and Bell call the informal aspects of organizations. There are other umbrella terms for the techniques classified here as OD: human resource development (HRD) is one, and "quality of work life" is another; the latter has gained favor in federal circles. However, the most common name under which to find much of the literature is organizational development.

HISTORICAL PERSPECTIVE

Organizational development was created as a tool to help human beings to better understand and deal with complex human relationships and the resulting problems that often develop in organizations. It encompasses a wide range of approaches that social and behavioral scientists have developed to achieve desired organizational changes. OD begins with the assumption that the organization already exists but may need some modification to become more effective or to successfully implement suggested plans. In fact, organizations are always developing or at least going through planned or unplanned evolution. OD developed out of the belief that improved performance is possible "through the planning and controlling of organizational evolution."

The body of OD literature has grown so fast and there have been so many significant contributions that it is impossible to give much more than a cursory survey of its development. Those who wish to better understand the development of OD will want to refer to the several recent attempts to synthesize the available knowledge (Alderfer, 1974; Beer, 1976; Buchanan, 1969; Friedlander, 1976; Friedlander and Brown, 1974; Fullan, Miles, and Taylor, 1980; Patten and Vail, 1975; and Strauss, 1973).

The field of organizational development deals with organizations as functional, ongoing, total systems. What today is called OD can be traced back to what is most often called the human relations view, which was first presented in 1933 by Elton Mayo and his colleagues in order to bridge the gap between individual needs and organizational reality. Those involved in the human relations movement suggested that the organization is a social and psychological institution made up of people and groups glued together by interpersonal relations. It is from this beginning that the two major components of OD's heritage initially began: the development of T-groups or laboratory learning, and the establishment of action–research–feedback methodologies. Both began in the late 1940s and early 1950s.

Laboratory learning is essentially an unstructured small-group situation in which participants learn from their own interactions and the evolving dynamics of the group. In the summer of 1947 a group of individuals met in Bethel, Maine, under the sponsorship of the National Education Association and the Office of Naval Research and developed an idea that evolved into the National Training Laboratories for group development and contemporary T-group training. The leadership team in this effort consisted of Kurt Lewin, Kenneth Benne, Leland Bradford, and Ronald Lippitt.

T-group training quickly came under fire and was criticized as only dealing with a small part of the problem—interpersonal relations. Individuals who participated might feel very good about the experience but when they returned to their organization, their behavior would revert back to the normal, problem-provoking type because the T-group had failed (most often) to deal with the fundamental problems (organizational culture and group norms). It was in this climate that the broader, more functional concept of action–research–feedback techniques gained greater popularity. Perhaps the late 1950s or early 1960s mark the first use of the term; George Strauss explains the differences:

> As mentioned earlier, OD is derived largely from the T-group movement. T-groups are still utilized as part of an OD effort, though perhaps less frequently than in the past. Yet by my definition, T-groups alone do not constitute OD, since T-groups are concerned with individual and group development, not organizational development.
>
> T-groups seek to increase their participants' ability to be good group members in any situation; OD seeks actual improvement in interpersonal relations in a specific organization. T-groups are essentially artificial groups, and they deal with tensions that arise in their own little world—tensions that in a sense are artificially created. OD, by contrast, is concerned with the real world, and it deals with tensions that arise on real jobs. It takes as its bailiwick not just relations within groups, but also relations among groups and even among organizations. (Strauss, 1973, p. 3)

OD efforts resulted in the development of many action–research–feedback methodologies.

The *Journal of Applied Behavioral Sciences* seems to have been the main house organ of the OD movements during the 1960s and 1970s; the journal's "Landmarks" issue of April 1967 contains articles by such luminaries in the field as

Chris Argyris, Warren G. Bennis, Bernard Bass, and H. Shepard. Perhaps the best single introduction to OD is the *Series on Organization Development* (published by Addison-Wesley).

Many studies of OD suggest that very positive results can be obtained—productivity can be improved from 20 to 43 percent; turnover can decline from 10 to 90 percent; defects can be reduced from 20 to 39 percent; and returns on investments can be increased (Bowers, 1977). In addition, there are reports of increased trust, greater job satisfaction, improved relations between supervisors and subordinates, and better inter- and intra-group relations, to name a few. Success stories have occurred at AT&T, Procter and Gamble, Volvo, IBM, Corning, GM, and many other corporations. Although many of the research efforts to date have been very promising, much more carefully controlled studies of organizational development are needed (Porras and Olafberg, 1978).

Fullan, Miles, and Taylor (1980) reviewed the research on the use of organizational development in schools and concluded that OD held considerable promise for school improvement:

> Given our existing state of knowledge, we conclude that OD is a useful strategy for school improvement. The best general guidelines for use seem to be threefold: (1) use OD in school districts that meet (or can come to meet) certain readiness criteria and introduce OD in these settings following guidelines suggested in this review; (2) develop and adopt new models of OD, which are more appropriate to changing conditions and to divergent settings, and (3) use other strategies (planned curriculum change, new hiring, new policies and legislation, political lobbying) for organizational change where (1) or (2) cannot be achieved (although components of OD, especially its underlying principles, such as reflexivity, valid data, and participatory problem-solving process, can be incorporated into any change strategy).
>
> Whether the future of OD in education will result in its demise, absorption or renewal, there is little doubt in our minds about its significance as a change strategy—a strategy which will, if its own reflexive, self-evaluative character is maintained, become increasingly well-adapted to the task of improving schools. (Fullan, Miles, and Taylor, 1980, p. 178)

ORGANIZATIONAL DEVELOPMENT: SOME DEFINITIONS

Organizational development refers to a rather loose collection of training and therapeutic techniques whose purpose is to improve the operational functioning of the organization and the interactions of members within it. Organizational development is planned change through a coordinated attack on the interpersonal problems of the organization. Its purpose is not just to develop individuals within the organization but the organization as a whole. OD is designed to effect change through altering attitudes and values and improving interactions. By contrast with many of the other techniques discussed in this book, organizational development techniques are unlikely to have a direct influence on financial or compensation systems, planning and management technologies, or the formal aspects of organization, even though the organization may eventually make such changes as a result of the attitudinal changes that result from the OD effort. Its primary emphasis is on helping individuals and groups within the organization learn how to face interpersonal problems directly so that they can be solved, rather than trying to avoid, smooth over, or compromise them in a way that may not result in the best solution.

Although specific definitions vary greatly, there is a common thread of agreement that seems to weave through most. Harvey and Brown reviewed a number of definitions of OD and devised their own: OD is an "effort to introduce planned change throughout an organization based on a diagnosis shared by its members for the purpose of improving organizational effectiveness through the application of behavioral science techniques" (Harvey and Brown, 1976, p. 55). Harvey and Brown stress that OD is a consciously planned process.

Warren Bennis (1969, p. 2) defines organizational development as "a response to change, a complex educational strategy intended to change the beliefs, attitudes, values, and structure of organizations so that they can better adapt to new technologies, markets, and challenges, and the dizzying rate of change itself." Bennis focuses primarily on the submerged portion of the organizational iceberg and its relation to any planned changes. He stresses the concept of an educational strategy to bring about planned organizational change—strategy that emphasizes experiential behavior such as data feedback, sensitivity training, confrontation meetings, and team-building activities.

Perhaps the most widely used concept of organizational development is that of Blake and Mouton. Their definition is actually more a statement of purposes—in fact, of what should be eliminated:

1. Common sense–based management assumptions . . . replace them with systematic management concepts that increase individual involvement, commitment, and creativity towards sound problem-solving and production.

2. Unproductive thought patterns within each individual . . . replace them with mental attitudes that result in a better identification of problems and novel solutions.

3. Interpersonal and intergroup blockages which prevent effective discussions . . . replace them with interpersonal openness and candid communication that can sustain sound deliberation and insure effective problem-solving between individuals and groups.

4. Organizational traditions, precedents, and past practices which stifle productivity, effort and creative thinking . . . replace them with standards and values which promote efforts of excellence and innovation.
5. Unresolved problems preventing attainment of organization competence . . . [eliminate them by] (a) defining what they are, (b) designing solutions to them, and (c) insuring their elimination by executing the plans. (Blake and Mouton, 1968, pp. 255-256)

Blake and Mouton see organizational development as an approach by which the entire organization studies itself and the workings of its various parts. As a result of this study, concrete arrangements for executing agreed-upon changes are implemented under a carefully designed program. Organizational development is self-administered by the organization membership, except for broad consultation regarding major issues of strategy and tactics. Blake and Mouton stress the concept of developing an open and honest environment whereby individual and/or group problems and conflicts can be examined, reconciled, and resolved.

THE NEED FOR ORGANIZATIONAL DEVELOPMENT

Appropriate OD interventions most often require a number of different approaches depending on the process and task needs of the organization. OD is primarily a set of mechanisms—social interventions—for identifying and solving problems in intact, complex organizations such as school systems:

OD strategy rests on several assumptions, of which perhaps the most basic is that many of the problems confronting changing schools arise from the nature of the groups or organization in which change is occurring. It is the dynamics of the group, not the skills of its individual members, that is both the major source of problems and the primary determiner of the quality of solutions. Although group process and procedures often obstruct the full use of human potential, they can, if coordinated smoothly, allow the release of latent energy needed for responsiveness and creativity. (Schmuck et al., 1977, p. 3)

Negative group dynamics can drain the energy of employees, leaving little or no time left for the accomplishment of organizational objectives.

There are a number of different organizational conditions or symptoms that call for OD intervention. Following are examples of some of the types that have triggered organizational developmental efforts:

1. *A belief that people within the organization are playing dangerous games.* For instance, teachers or principals may have strong opinions or thoughts regarding a program or objectives but refuse to reveal those thoughts.

An unwritten but generally accepted policy is that you seldom or never disagree with a superior, or you only tell the boss good things or what you and others believe that he or she wants to hear. The results of these games are the same as if administrators had never opened up the channels of communication to participation in the first place. Effective planning requires three-way communication—up, down, and across organizational lines. Organizational games can destroy the integrity of three-way communication.

2. *A general belief that the organization has become too mechanistic, leaving little room for initiative, self-discipline, and creativity.* For example, teachers or other staff members may express a sincere concern for the level of paper work and/or restrictions on professional behavior. There may be complaints about a lack of flexibility compounded by too many built-in controls and predetermined methods. No one may be willing to make relatively simple decisions unless "the boss approves it." There may be a lack of ability to be creative and modify the system to meet unique school or departmental needs. There may be oversupervision of professional employees. Such an environment creates pessimistic attitudes regarding the accomplishment of new objectives, and often the result is a total lack of motivation even to try.

3. *Dissatisfaction with the suitability of the workplace, work arrangements, or design of the job for meeting the needs of employees or individuals being serviced.* For instance, there may be complaints that teachers have no chance to get to know and understand children, especially children with behavioral problems; or the complaints may be about the diversity of responsibilities (testing, grading standard tests, recording desired information, report production, counseling, discipline, committee work, and so on), all of which are having a detrimental effect on the teachers' role and should be reduced or modified to leave more time for higher-level responsibilities.

4. *Changes in both the content and context of employees' roles such that there is a high level of ambiguity and resulting insecurity and rivalry.* Such conditions create a highly uncertain environment that often decreases productivity. Some adjust to the changes relatively quickly; others, particularly those with a low tolerance for ambiguity, tend to have difficulty with them. The changing attitudes of society toward education and teachers in general may lower teachers' self-esteem unless they understand these changes.

5. *An increasing number of complaints concerning communication problems.* There may be a lack of communication between individuals or about specific issues or problems, or between departments or divisions. Duplication of work effort and jurisdictional disputes between individuals and departments is

a normal but distressing organizational error. Employees may complain that reports never seem to include the right information or to be sent to the right individuals.

6. *An inability or unwillingness of managers to move away from authoritarian, hierarchical models of leadership.* This is a style of leadership that often closes off subordinates' feelings about their work and provides little or no opportunity to participate in the planning process. The end result is often fear, insecurity, counterorganization, and a general lack of trust between superior and subordinates. This typically occurs when objectives and decisions are developed exclusively "up the ladder" and are not clearly communicated or understood by subordinates.

7. *Decision making that is painstakingly slow.*

8. *Values, ground rules, norms, and power structures that no longer serve the organization.*

9. *A high level of inter- and intra-group conflict.* There may be very little friendliness and a seemingly high level of animosity between members and groups within the organization; there may also be a lack of vitality, dedication, and loyalty among the employees of an organization.

The end result of all these symptoms is poor morale and a general lack of motivation and commitment.

OD METHODS

In applying OD methodology, it would be a mistake to think of it in terms of techniques; rather, the administrator should concentrate on meeting the needs and objectives of the organization. However, by discussing OD techniques separately here, we can better understand their purpose and when and in what cases to use them.

Organizational development comes in a wide variety of forms. Some approaches continue to use nothing other than T-groups. Others range from the flexible ad hoc approach of Schein (1969) to the coordinated six-phase approach of Blake and Mouton (1978a) or the integrated plan of Likert (1967). Figure 11-2 presents a typology of some of the major categories of intervention in organizational development.

Since 1973, when French and Bell published their chart of intervention strategies, there have been a number of new developments; the following list catalogs many OD strategies. The intervention approach ultimately selected is determined by the aspect of the organization being changed and the problem condition being addressed.

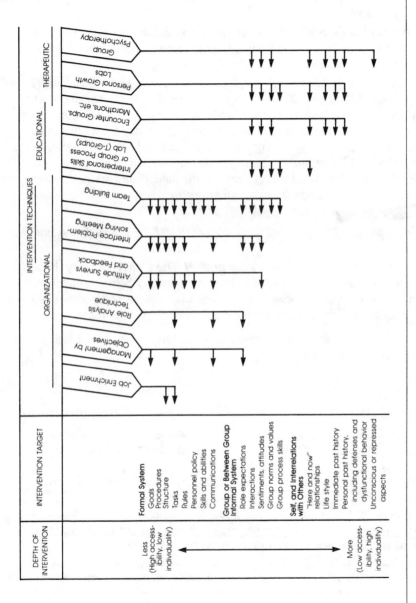

FIGURE 11-2

Categories of OD Intervention

Source: Wendell L. French/Cecil H. Bell, *Organization Development: Behavioral Science Interventions for Organization Improvement*, Second Edition. ©1978, p. 208. Reprinted by permission of Prentice-Hall, Inc., Englewood Cliffs, N.J.

Laboratory Training (individual development):
Unstructured
T-groups
Encounter groups
Instrumented Groups

Diagnostic Intervention (general):
Data gathering and data sharing
Survey feedback
Interview feedback
Confrontation meeting
Diagnostic meeting

Process Intervention (specific):
Diagnostic meetings
Team development
Process consultation
Intergroup intervention
   Leadership
   Problem solving and decision making
   Assertiveness
   Transactional analysis
   Group-think
   Peacemaking
   Communication

Environmental Intervention (organization):
Organizational design and roles analysis
Structural consultation
Job design and enrichment
Personnel systems

Employee Conditioning (problem orientation):
Employee assistance programs
Conflict and stress management
Gestalt therapy
Hooks and irrational thoughts
Conflict management
Abrasiveness
Meditation and muscle relaxation
Behavior modification

Positive reframing
Career planning
Time management
Influencing skills
Centering

Change
Quality circles
Management by objectives
Breakthrough analysis
Futuring and planning

Integrated Technologies
Grid organizational development
Quality-of-work-life programs

In selecting a specific OD technique, the change agent and client consider a number of factors, including the nature of the problem, the objectives of the change effort, the cultural norms of the client system, and the expected degree of resistance. Selecting a technique involves comparing and testing possible intervention techniques against some criteria. The selection of any given technique is the result of a systematic process of deliberation.

THE FRAMEWORK FOR APPLYING AN OD METHOD

Organizational development is usually seen as a system made up of a number of steps or stages that are needed for successful implementation. These steps provide the framework through which most OD efforts are tailored specifically to the particular circumstances and needs of the organization. The haphazard introduction of bits and pieces of OD technology without a clear framework for its implementation usually results in unbalanced results at best. The framework includes a number of specific and clearly identifiable stages that flow into one another. The typical steps are:

Pre-entry: who, theories, expectations

Initial contact: objective of intervention, cost, relation with client, forces, contracting

Entry and data collection: questions to be explored, organizational units to be included, preparation, method, data collection

Diagnosis: evaluate data, interpret, problem recognition, feedback, and recommendation

TABLE 11-1
Risks in Choosing OD Strategies

	PROBLEM	MODE OF RESOLUTION
Risk in diagnosis	Identify factors responsible for symptoms or observed variation and/or likely to lead to organizational improvement.	Assessment mode: Explore alternative causes of symptoms and/or areas of possible improvement. Gather opinions of others. Seek consensus through discussion. Identify possible approaches.
Risk in analysis	Choose approach or philosophy most appropriate for the elimination of casual factors and/or improving the organization.	Decision mode: Isolate target area or areas. Identify important organizational and individual parameters. Examine the impact of selected approaches on these parameters. Make group decisions.
Risk in implementation	Ensure that technique or program is correctly implemented. Generate feedback on results. Consider rediagnosis or analysis.	Implementation mode: Concentrate on target area or areas. Build commitment. Use management techniques.

Reprinted, by permission of the publisher, from *Personnel*, Nov.-Dec. 1977, ©1977 by AMACOM, a Division of American Management Associations, pp. 26-27. All rights reserved.

Intervention design: key variables are success or failure; change and values; change strategy; behavioral theory, technology, and methods; elements and techniques

Intervention: acceptance, timing, logistics, implementation, evaluation, feedback

Follow-up: need for future-action planning, recycle and design

Separation: future commitments, follow-up, client satisfaction

For each step there are questions that must be answered in order to design substrategies for that stage. The answers to the questions at one stage typically become the input to the next stage. These steps are necessary to ensure that the intervention technique selected best meets the needs of the organization.

There are three broad factors, or what Meglina and Mobley (1977, pp. 26-27) call risks, in determining what specific technique should be selected. These are outlined in Table 11.1. Each of these risk factors should be considered carefully prior to making a final decision on the selection and implementation of an intervention strategy. The specific technique or techniques selected become the action plan for the OD program. Chapter 12 discusses this in greater detail.

Often factors inside organizations weaken the effectiveness of very capable individuals and complicate or even sabotage an excellent plan. Unrealized expectations; lack of involvement; dissatisfaction with job, colleagues, or superiors; disappointment of one sort or another—all can reduce individual and, ultimately, organizational effectiveness. Yet, such problems are easy to overlook because they are expressed in indirect ways such as morale, loyalty, satisfaction, climate, disenchantment, lack of commitment, and so on. However, such informal conditions serve as indicators of the success an organization will have in accomplishing its organizational goals and objectives. The importance of individual commitment becomes clearest when considered in relation to its positive contributions toward the achievement of plans—what is often referred to as bottom-line considerations.

Organizational development provides a methodology to help both individuals and organizations to confront, understand, and eliminate the socioemotional barriers that often beset people as they function in groups. The techniques of organizational development can help individuals to remove ineffective norms for behavior within the organization's culture and within their own interpersonal style of dealing with peers, superiors, and subordinates. This is not an easy task, but at the heart of the matter is a realization that such efforts are inextricably linked with individual growth and development and with organizational success in achieving goals. The technology of OD facilitates intervention and change. Ultimately, it creates the needed organizational culture in which planning and management structures can be most effective.

GUIDELINES FOR PLANNING

1. The successful implementation of educational plans often depends upon the commitment of school employees and the behavioral norms under which they operate. The explicit planned policy of the school system and the implicit organizational and professional norms of behavior define the range of permissible behavior within which school employees can operate. If the behavior required to achieve a plan deviates from the range of permissible behaviors, the normative pressure to conform increases. School board policy can be altered as part of the planning process; however, behavioral norms are much more difficult to change since they depend upon the attitudes and behaviors of individuals within the organization.

2. Organizational development (OD) is needed when existing organizational structures, interpersonal relations, and group norms no longer suit the goals, objectives, and resources of the organization. Organizational development focuses attention on the attitudes, loyalties, values, and feelings of individuals within the organization and their communication patterns, interactions, and group norms.

3. The OD process is based upon a three-step change model—unfreezing, identification and/or internalization, and refreezing. Unfreezing results in a decrease in the strength of old attitudes, values, or behaviors; internalization results in the development of new, more supportive attitudes, values, or behaviors; and refreezing is the stabilization of this change at a new equilibrium state.

4. OD is primarily a set of mechanisms, social interventions, and behavioral science techniques for identifying and solving behavioral problems in intact complex organizations such as school systems. Organizational development is made up of a wide variety of techniques including such diverse technologies as laboratory training, diagnostic intervention, process intervention, environment intervention, employee conditioning, change strategy, and integrated technologies.

12

OD Diagnosis and Intervention

You cannot teach a man anything. You can only help
him discover it within himself.

—GALILEO

The first step of any OD intervention is generating valid and useful information. One rule for the organizational development consultant is to question the client's diagnosis of the organizational problem or needs. The client may have some preconceived ideas as to what the problem is, but these ideas should be accepted only after a careful analysis (Argyris and Schon, 1978). The purpose of the diagnosis is to specify the nature of the exact problem requiring solution, to identify the underlying causal forces, and to provide a basis for selecting effective change strategies and techniques. The consultant must be able to sort out opinions, inferences, hypotheses, and assumptions from factual evidence. In the process, the consultant must identify the underlying causal forces—forces that lie at the heart of organizational problems (Harvey and Brown, 1976, pp. 135–159).

To facilitate the diagnostic effort, an elaborate technology has been developed to measure the sociopsychological state existing within organizations. However, Schmuck states: "The underlying strategy is reasonably simple, and the methods employed—interviewing, questionnaires, direct observation, poring over documents, and others—need not be sophisticated if consultants persistently obtain enough of the right information to meet their purposes" (Schmuck et al., 1977, p. 41).

A typical diagnostic sequence might start with semistructured observation, followed by semistructured interviews, and completed with a structured questionnaire intended to measure precisely the problems identified by the earlier diagnostic steps. A sampling of some OD questionnaires appears in Appendix B. For a more complete discussion and guide to collecting organizational and behavioral information of many kinds, see Levinson (1972).

After the organizational diagnosis has been completed, it is necessary to begin evaluating the data. This data will be organized during the analysis and implementation stages of OD so that the three-stage change process discussed by Lewin—unfreezing, change, and refreezing—will actually occur. Many of the OD techniques are briefly listed in Chapter 11. The remainder of this chapter is devoted to a discussion in detail of seven of the analyses and implementation techniques. Nine of the questionnaires and survey instruments used in various OD procedures are extracted in Appendix B.

SURVEY FEEDBACK

The survey feedback technique is one of the oldest and most popular approaches to OD (it is listed in Chapter 11 under the heading "Diagnostic intervention"). It was originally developed by Floyd Mann and Rensis Likert (1952) at the University of Michigan's Survey Research Center. It is still today one of the most important intervention methods. The major purpose of survey feedback is to make sure that organizational members understand the data collected and have an awareness of causal relationships and organizational behavior. Typically survey feedback presents information in a clear and understandable form for interpretation but does little to assist an organization in determining what action or strategy should be taken as a result of the findings. It is more of a reporting function. In most cases it is the first step in a more comprehensive OD effort. It is used to unfreeze existing behavior.

In survey feedback, most of the data are objective and are related to things that have happened on the job prior to the beginning of the diagnostic effort. The role of survey data is to corroborate the client's beliefs about the state of the organization or to "disconfirm" beliefs, thereby unfreezing the client and encouraging inquiry concerning the reasons for the data. The greater the relevancy of the survey data, the greater the likelihood that organizational members will be involved with the data and committed to subsequent change.

Survey feedback usually works best when data are turned over to work teams in what Mann calls family or group meetings with member diagnosis and action planning. Michael Beer states:

> Meetings are effective because they probably have an unfreezing effect by creating pressure on individuals to own up and clarify their views for the group. The group meeting also creates pressure on individuals to evaluate their views about problems in light of the prevailing viewpoint in the group. Thus, if effective problem solving is done by the group, members are likely to arrive at greater agreement about the real problem and develop more change momentum. The group meeting can unfreeze existing beliefs about problems, change individual and group perceptions of these problems, and refreeze a new group awareness and belief through group pressure. (Beer, 1976, p. 948)

A spin-off benefit of survey feedback is that once problems have been openly discussed in front of and with authority figures, it is easier to do it again in the future.

Survey feedback may increase communication, openness, information flow, confrontation of problems—all important dimensions of the planning process. In many organizations there is an accumulation of pent-up and hidden frustration, irritations, and resentments that participants are afraid to expose. Sometimes these build up to such interfering levels that members within the organization cannot confront each other with anything other than the simplest small talk without fear of being overwhelmed emotionally. Such a build-up of interpersonal tensions leads to totally ineffective collaboration and the draining of a great deal of emotional energy in nonproductive and sometimes actually destructive deceptions (games). Many of these frustrations—"gunny sacks" of pent-up emotions—can be reduced when a consultant is involved in survey feedback techniques (Schmuck et al., 1977, pp. 428-432; Chase, 1968).

Interpersonal tensions can be reduced by talking openly and directly about them, especially if a consultant is present. Open discussion may be difficult to achieve immediately and may only develop with the help of the consultant. However, the end result will be a significantly different, more open, and ultimately more effective planning process than the organization has ever achieved as well as a release of a significant amount of energy, cooperation, and commitment to the achievement of objectives.

CONFRONTATION MEETING

The confrontation meeting, an intervention technique developed by Richard Beckhard (1967), is designed to bring together a large segment of an organization so that members are directly involved in problem identification and action planning for organizational improvement. A major benefit of the confrontation meeting is that it can mobilize an organization much more quickly than other OD designs, such as survey feedback. Therefore, it is probably best used when an organization faces some sort of crisis or stress requiring immediate action. In these situations there is often a wide gap between the perceptions of the various individuals and groups; an example is a total breakdown of communication and trust between central management and school building personnel (Beer, 1976, pp. 950-951).

For confrontation meetings, the organization is usually broken into smaller groups consisting of different organizational units and levels. A diagonal slice is taken from the organization so that bosses and subordinates are not placed in the same group. The meeting begins with a message such as "Think of yourself as a person with needs and goals in this organization and think of the total organization. What are the behaviors, procedures, ways of work, attitudes, etc., that should be different so that life would be better around here?" (Beckhard, 1967).

Harvey and Brown describe six steps that serve as a guide for conducting confrontation meetings. However, they are quick to point out that the steps must be modified to fit particular client situations.

1. *Climate setting.* The first step involves setting the ground rules that will be used in the confrontation meeting. The facilitator shares with the participants the need for open discussion of issues and problems and outlines the broad goals he or she has for the meeting.

2. *Information collecting.* Small groups are formed of people from different functional areas and managerial levels. It is stipulated that bosses and subordinates not be on the same work group. Top management generally meets as a separate group. Usually it is preferable to use a diagonal slice from the organization, that is, individuals representing different functional areas and different levels of the organization. The groups work on the task of identifying problems for about an hour, and a recorder lists the results of the discussion.

3. *Information sharing.* Reporters from each small group place that group's findings on pieces of newsprint which are taped to the wall. The total list of items is categorized and reported to the entire group. At this point the numerous problems that have been identified are categorized into basic problem areas so that they can be worked upon and problem solutions developed.

4. *Priority setting and action planning.* In a brief general session the meeting leader goes through the list of items, and the participants then form into functional work teams reflecting the way they are organized in the organization. Each group is headed by the top manager in the group, and they are charged with these tasks: (1) to identify the problems related to their area and develop a list of priorities for these problems, (2) to identify problems and priority issues

for top management, and (3) to determine action plans for solving these problems, giving first consideration to highest-priority items.

5. *Follow-up by top team.* The top management team meets after the groups have completed Step 4 to review the first action steps and evolve a set of follow-up action plans, which are then communicated to the rest of the group within the next few days.

6. *Progress review.* A follow-up meeting with the total management group is held periodically, generally beginning four to six weeks after the initial meeting to review the outcome of action plans resulting from the confrontation meeting. Top management plays an important part here by showing that it is committed to following up on problems that emerge from the confrontation meeting. (Harvey and Brown, (1976, p. 307)

Crisis situations, which seem to generate willingness to take personal risks and to tackle problems, are regarded as the best environment for a confrontation meeting. A climate of openness is crucial for a successful confrontation meeting. In short, the meeting is an attempt to stimulate the type of communicating that should have been occurring in the organization all along by creating a special situation where openness can occur. In fact, some observers say that the major purpose of OD is to make confrontation an organizational way of life.

TEAM BUILDING

All work teams (departments, schools, division, project teams, committees, or whatever) without exception have their own culture. The clarity of their goals and objectives, the commitment of individuals to achieve them, the norms and standards of conduct that each expects of all the others, are some of the properties of the cultural patterns. Other cultural aspects include the ways by which joint efforts are coordinated, the manner in which disagreements and conflict are resolved, the way decisions are made, and the degree of candor with which people express their convictions. Dysfunctional behavior within this culture alters these properties and creates dysfunctional symptoms.

In team building all members of the team are given an opportunity, indeed are expected, to become involved in the process of examining how they function together, the way they communicate with each other, how various decisions are arrived at, the arppropriateness of the reward system, and especially the group norms, which more than anything else determine their behavior. Team building might be viewed as a social contract in which each member of the group, including the boss, renegotiates the norms that influence the group's behavior. The power of the contract is that it is openly agreed upon and witnessed by all members of the team.

The contract is developed by bringing to the surface the attitudes and feelings of the members of the team and identifying obstacles to group action and performance. The obstacles include the effectiveness of communication, the adequacy of planning and decision making, usefulness of controls, the appropriateness of the systems of rewards, and ownership of goals and objectives. The kind of team desired is openly and thoroughly discussed. Such discussion results in answers to questions such as the following: How is the team coping with problems or tasks at hand? How can it become more effective? Who needs to do what? What is getting in the way of our functioning effectively? How can we learn from this process of how we work together to function even more effectively in the future?

The problems are discussed in relation to the desired team, usually beginning by focusing on problems caused by the boss. In this way the boss serves as an example of the open kind of discussion that is needed in order to first clarify and then improve group norms. One should be aware that the process of team building is as difficult to get started as it is to stop once under way, and therefore the members of the team must be adequately prepared for what is to come and willing to follow it to a successful conclusion. The use of a consultant can be very helpful in this process.

Team building should ensure that the members have a clear understanding of what is expected of them in the accomplishment of objectives. Members should not be expected to perform activities out of sequence, such as having team members coordinate the details of a plan before seeking final approval. Authority and responsibility should be clear to all members of the team and should facilitate the accomplishment of plans and not present obstacles. Isolation, parochial thinking, self-interest, abrasiveness, and the like should be minimized within the groups and between groups. Conflict should be accepted when it is related to real differences associated to important issues.

New people must be brought into the team as needed to meet planned objectives; jobs should not be created around existing subordinates. Relevant expertise and information should facilitate the team-building process by enlarging the base of information. Rewards should encourage collaboration and mutual support. Group members should listen to and own up to honest feelings and beliefs and not just say and hear what is politically expedient. All members of the team should be involved in decisions that affect the team. The team must always take time to focus on the process by which the team functions. Such practices lie at the heart of team-building efforts.

The team-building approach usually uses the action–research–feedback model of intervention. The process typically includes analysis, feedback, and action planning. The purpose of the analysis is to conduct an open discussion and critique of the performance of the group. These discussions are used to uncover problems that may be hindering group performance. The discussions can be coupled with self-report questionnaires. The work team is asked to identify problems that require correction. If the group, administrator, and consultant believe that working through the problems by group discussion would be worthwhile, a formal diagnostic meeting is scheduled.

The purpose of the diagnostic meeting is to conduct a general critique of the performance of the group, that is, to determine how well the objectives have been established, to determine how the team works together to support one another in task accomplishment, to determine generally how well the work group is doing, and to bring to the surface problems that may be interfering with work accomplishment. The group, supervisor, and consultant meet for approximately one to three days to discuss the findings and to try to develop an action plan to eliminate any problems identified. Data discussed in the meeting may include, but not be inclusive to, leadership behavior, interpersonal problems and process, roles, trust, communication, planning and decision making, goals, delegation, technical and task problems, and barriers to effective group and organizational functioning. It is typically difficult to break the ice on—to "unfreeze"—these issues, so the "open data sharing approach" selected is very important.

OPEN DATA SHARING

There are several ways to get the diagnostic data out, that is, to make the information known to the work group. One approach to sharing the diagnostic data is for the consultant to present all the information collected anonymously; then each person will have a chance to comment or to talk about the data and join in the discussion. Since the data are presented anonymously, there will be less guilt in regard to comments about the different team members. The consultant might put the names of each member of the team on a large board and then place around each name the problems others had said they had with that particular team member. For example, some of the types of problems that might appear around the administrator might include such items as "doesn't delegate properly," "gives contradictory instructions," "makes unilateral decisions affecting us all without getting our opinions or telling us," "keeps group members ignorant of one another's activities," "doesn't like confrontations and conflict," "is manipulative," and "has too many irons in the fire at one time."

As one would imagine, this might be a very difficult list to face. But each member of the team must be prepared to face these lists by being very clear on the purpose of the meeting. It is best to make sure that the list includes some positive points about each member so that he or she is able to see that there is a little of both in all of us—a point most of us hate to admit but know is true. The climate of the meeting should be one of trust, warmth, caring for each other, and an honest interest in helping one another and the group to learn to appreciate one another and to function as a team.

EXAMPLE OF OPEN DATA SHARING

The best way to get a real feel for open data sharing is through the eyes of a participant. William J. Crockett, who was involved in a team-building experience when he was an assistant secretary of state during the Kennedy administration, shares his views of open data sharing:

> And then the anonymity would disappear because the person who had put this item on the list would come in hard to justify his stand. And so with illustration of time and place and circumstance he would prove when I had not delegated properly or how I would fall back after I had given them authority, or how I had made a decision unknown to them or how, before evidence had come in, I had changed their decision, and so on. This kind of confrontation only started the conversation. Chuck would not let any of us off so easily. He probed deeply. How did my action make them feel? How did they see me? What were my motives? How did this affect the group's work together? This and many more questions that he asked would give me the opportunity to reply, "Yes, but you don't realize the pressure I am under from the White House . . . or from the Congress . . . or from the Secretary. . . ." And the whole complexity of relationships, the pressures upon me, and explanations for my seemingly erratic behavior would come out. From such explanations and probings came understanding and a sense of sharing that had never before existed in the group. . . .
>
> I also realized that I had not fooled them about the real me. The group had had the data all along. But due to the climate of the group—its norms—we had not been able to be open with one another; we had not been able to face confrontation, and so the group could not share the data with me earlier. It would have hurt me too much at the time. It would have asked them to risk too much at the time. As "tough minded" as we thought our own management to have been, we soon learned that it had not been tough enough to deal with real conflict, deep personal feelings, or confrontation. Instead of this kind of confrontation's causing my leadership to dissipate, I saw a new excitement born of involvement emerging within the group. There could be no question of their total commitment to me as their leader and to the concept of the "Executive Group" which we had been discussing. Out of this meeting we all saw the phenomenon of a new group come into being before our very eyes! We were a united group— trusting and caring and sharing as never before. (Crockett, 1970, pp. 300–303)

An action plan for the future will usually be necessary to sustain the benefits derived during open data sharing. The group must learn to maintain the united group climate without the consultant or with only a minor consulting intervention. Periodic meetings to discuss crucial issues in the same open and trusting way of the open data sharing meeting should be part of the action plan.

Team development makes sense intuitively. There is a recognizable need for a process such as team development that attempts, through open communication and confrontation of conflict, to develop a better fit between people, tasks, and group process. William Crockett concludes his discussion of his experience with team building by stating:

> The lesson that was most impressive to us all was that the so-called Theory Y style of management—management by participation—is neither soft-headed nor "easy." It is much easier to sit in the big office and issue directives. It is much easier to avoid confrontation by issuing orders. It is easier to avoid personal involvement and conflict by smoothing over the surface. Theory Y management is not for the executive who likes surface serenity and obsequiousness. Theory Y management is for those managers who are willing to take the gut punishment of a truly tough-minded approach to management. It is for those who believe that conflict can be handled best by confronting it openly and for those who understand that real commitment of their people can be secured only by their continuing participation in making plans and setting objectives. (Crockett, 1970, p. 306)

PROCESS CONSULTATION

Process consultation is another approach for helping work groups to improve their functioning. Edgar Schein (1969) pulled together much of the practices and procedures of process consultation in a comprehensive and coherent book; he defines process consultation as "a set of activities on the part of the consultant which help the client to perceive, understand, and act upon process events which occur in the client's environment" (Schein, 1969, p. 9). The consultant identifies the events within an episode and traces the impact of each event upon succeeding events. Knowing the likely effects of behavior upon outcomes helps individuals to better manage their behavior so as to ensure that it is directed toward the achievement of a desirable outcome.

Process consultation can be applied to a number of different environments where a group of two or more members are working and interacting together. Primary emphasis is on processes such as communication, leader and member roles in groups, problem solving and decision making, group norms and group growth, leadership and authority, and intergroup cooperation and competition.

This method often is used to analyze the effectiveness of committee meetings. This usually is done by having the consultant either attend a group meeting and/or tape record the meeting in order to observe and analyze the interactions that take place between people. The purpose is more to make people who attended the meeting aware of the influence that interactions are having on the process. It is usually left up to the individual to evaluate this impact and decide if he or she wishes to alter this behavior.

Meetings are a very important aspect of the planning and management process in education. But unless they are effective and efficient, they have little usefulness. Meetings provide a means of communicating, problem solving, sharing information, decision making and coordinating—all of which are essential elements of planning. In trying to improve the effectiveness of meetings, the consultant gathers impressions about the process he or she is observing while the meeting is in progress or at its conclusion. Not only does the consultant observe the process but he or she also listens for assumptions about human behavior, whether they relate to an individual, a particular group, or people in general.

Feedback by the consultant can cover the content of the meeting, quality of communication, interaction patterns, nature of conflict resolution, relationships between the chairperson and members of the committee, intergroup relations, and/or assumptions about human behavior. The consultant may also provide feedback to specific individuals concerning their unique behavior during the meeting (Beer, 1976, pp. 954–955).

EXAMPLE OF PROCESS CONSULTATION

Chris Argyris and Donald Schon (1978) provide an example of a corporate executive who tended to cut short the discussion of members who attended meetings he chaired. The result was that few ideas were contributed and the meetings tended to be ritualistic; information was shared in short bursts, and decisions were primarily controlled by the chief executive. Argyris stresses the value of making individuals aware of their behavior but of only assisting in changing their behavior if they see that their actual behavior differs from their ideal. This concept of actual versus ideal managing style—what Argyris calls "theory-in-use" versus "espoused theory"—is often used as a basis for process consultation.

Process consultation is based on the belief that (1) behavior has a cognitive basis, that it reflects norms, strategies, assumptions, theories, and models that influence our human action and learning; and (2) that this cognitive basis for action may be different from the conceptual basis of what we define as an ideal pattern. What we have learned from childhood on as our natural behavior patterns may not match with what we see as the ideal behavior required as an administrator. Argyris and Schon stated:

When someone is asked how he would behave under certain circumstances, the answer he usually gives is his espoused theory of action for that situation. This is the theory of action to which he gives allegiance and which, upon request, he communicates to others. However, the theory that actually governs his actions is his theory-in-use, which may or may not be compatible with his espoused theory; furthermore, the individual may or may not be aware of the incompatibility of the two theories. (Argyris and Schon, 1978, p. 11)

Argyris suggests that the best way to change behavior is not to focus on the behavior; what you need to do is help people discover and make explicit their theory-in-use. If you help people discover what their theory-in-use is, then they can decide whether to alter it. If a person learns to alter the theory-in-use to the more ideal theory in an actual, on-going situation, then that person has been helped more than if you say, "You ought to be less autocratic." The foundation upon which actual behavior rests will have been altered.

In the example of the domineering executive, the administrator might wish to reduce the control he is exerting. His action plan might be that he will not say anything and will allow his subordinates to develop plans. This is the opposite of control—it is withdrawal. But it certainly is not an effective approach to administration. It is not a very helpful action plan, and it is unlikely that it can be sustained. Part of the consultation process requires that the consultant point out fatal flaws in one's action plan.

A better solution would be for the administrator to learn problem-solving skills. Argyris suggests that the domineering administrator might begin by involving his peer group in his problem by saying, "Look, I'm beginning to see some of my behavior; here's the theory I've been operating under among you people, and it doesn't make any sense to me now. However, I'm not going to change these values overnight, and therefore I don't expect real changes overnight in the way I work with you. I need your understanding and your help." In this way members of the organization can work together to plan and better prepare for behavioral and, often as a result, structural changes.

STRUCTURAL MODEL

Organizational development does not limit its focus to individual, interpersonal, group, and organizational process but includes the examination of the existing organizational structure in its broadest sense. It has thus been the object of some debate since traditionally structural changes have been the role of management consulting. However, structure is one area where both approaches to organizational improvement tend to overlap. Considerable attention has been paid to structural change as part of the technology of OD

(Friedlander and Brown, 1974). The major emphasis of OD technology is on altering the environment of the individual as a means of changing his or her behavior. The key elements of the structural model are the identification and improvement of interdependencies among the strategic parts of the organizational structure.

Organizational behavior is improved by studying how underlying structural conditions shape events. The objective is to identify parameters that influence or shape behavior and to specify the form of that influence. The structural model is especially concerned with pressures and constraints as they influence the behavior of the individual within the organization. Behavior is viewed as the result of pressures and constraints, and behavioral change is seen as the consequence of changes in the configuration of these variables. If structural influences are believed to be undesirable, changes will be recommended and tested.

The structural model examines many of the parameters that are identified in Chapters 2, 3, and 4 of this book. Kenneth Thomas (1976) suggests a set of diagnostic questions for practitioners interested in taking a structural approach to understanding and managing organizational conflict. These questions examine behavioral predispositions, social pressures, incentives, and rules and procedures. Some of the key questions from this structural model include:

1. Are the individuals' predispositions regarding conflict-handling compatible with the requirements of their positions?
2. Are any parties acting as representatives for a larger set of individuals with specific expectations?
3. How much is at stake for the various parties involved and what are the areas of competitive and common interests?
4. Are there any rules, formats, or procedures that dictate or constrain settlements of specific issues?

In this way the structural model focuses upon the conditions that shape undesirable behavior in a relationship. It is useful in restructuring a situation to facilitate improved behavior. Structural changes also deal with roles, workflow procedures, and the design and enrichment of the job.

Role analysis technique (RAT)

One form of structural intervention is called the role analysis technique (RAT) and is designed to clarify role expectations and obligations of team members to improve team effectiveness. It is used when individuals within the organization lack a clear understanding of what behaviors are expected of them. This lack of role clarity can hinder involvement and performance and result in dysfunctional levels of anxiety and stress. This is often caused by role ambiguity and role conflict.

This problem is confronted by asking the people in a work team, each in turn, to define their focal role, its place in the group, why it is needed, and how it adds to group performance. These specifications are listed in front of the group members and openly discussed. Agreement is sought on the makeup of the role. When the group tentatively agrees, the individual lists his or her expectations of each role occupant in the group who, he or she believes, affects the individual's own role performance. Behaviors are added and deleted from all lists until the role incumbents are satisfied with the defined roles. The written role profile is briefly reviewed at the following meeting before another focal role is analyzed. This intervention can be a nonthreatening activity with major benefits since this approach can resolve major conflicts and group problems without having to get into feelings and emotions.

Job enrichment

Job enrichment is a structural method by which the individual structures the job so that it maximizes both satisfaction and production. Job enrichment is based on the simple assumption that people who like their work are likely to be more productive and put more effort into it. Job enrichment focuses on innovations in the work place. It is based on the question, "Can we improve the work environments of our teachers, counselors, librarians, special-education teachers, supervisors, administrators, and everyone else?"

Job enrichment began in the United States with the pioneering research of Frederich Herzberg (1966). Early tests of the techniques, such as the studies at AT&T spearheaded by Robert Ford (1973), were highly successful. Lawler (1969), in reviewing ten studies where jobs had been enriched, concluded that job enrichment did have positive effects on behavior and quality of performance.

The basic premise of job enrichment is that more interesting and challenging work provides primary incentives for employees to improve performance. The explanation for such improvements is that when jobs have been properly enriched, job satisfaction increases and employees work more earnestly and show more commitment and loyalty in response to the new challenge and interest provided by the job. It is based on the belief that many employees suffer from severe "job-impoverishment."

Job enrichment requires the deliberate upgrading of responsibility, scope, and challenge in work. It is sometimes confused with job enlargement, or horizontal job loading, which means that the job is redesigned to include additional tasks or operations of about the same difficulty as the core job. This typically has little or no positive effect on motivation and more often means more work, few benefits, and decreased motivation. For example, one might add knives, forks, and spoons to the task of someone who is washing the plates. By contrast, job enrichment, or vertical job loading, involves building into the job greater motivation by delegating some of the planning and controlling aspects as well as the "doing" of the job.

Job enrichment is usually defined as follows:

> Job enrichment is concerned with designing jobs that include a greater variety *def*·
> of work content; require a higher level of knowledge and skill; give the worker
> more autonomy and responsibility for planning, directing, and controlling his own
> performance; and provide the opportunity for personal growth and meaningful
> work experience. (Luthans and Reif, 1978, p. 31)

The objective of job enrichment is to provide for the employees' psychological growth and development rather than just for their economic growth and development.

Argyris (1964) suggests that, in many cases, when people join the work force, they are kept from maturing by the organizational culture and administrative practices utilized in the organization. They are given minimal control over their environment and are encouraged to be passive, dependent, and subordinate; therefore, they behave immaturely. Job expectations in many organizations have resulted in the oversimplification of the job so that it becomes repetitive, routine, unchallenging, and strictly controlled by superiors and/or organizational policy. In education, the jobs of teachers must be modified to provide opportunity for influence, challenge, chances for growth (competence and skills), and a sense of contribution to goals. Teachers must be provided optimal class sizes and workloads, capacity to mobilize and utilize resources, opportunity for planning time and work breaks, availability of supplies and equipment to accomplish tasks efficiently, elimination of nonteaching duties, noise reduction, duty-free lunches, outlets for aspirations, recognition, clerical support, and improved professional work environments. Such changes will require structural modifications in school systems—to provide improved work designs—and in teaching roles—to provide for higher-level motivators.

Teachers might be given the freedom to choose subject topics within broad guidelines, to purchase materials directly, to determine with the class specifics to be covered in greater detail, to establish classroom climate and instructional strategy, to work with parents, to organize opportunities for students with special needs, and so on. At the same time, routine matters, such as administering and scoring standardized tests, hall duty, producing instructional materials, maintaining funds, and the like, would be removed from the teacher. On the principal and central-office side, instructional and curriculum responsibilities would be given away, piece by piece, to teachers ready to take on the responsibility.

Teachers could be provided an opportunity for increased interaction, support, and promotion through a hierarchy of positions that make it possible for them to assume authority and responsibility, take initiative, and receive salary commensurate with their interests, talents, and abilities. Promotion would be based on ambition, commitment, motivation, and performance. Teachers would begin their careers by implementing educational plans under close supervision. They would move not only to positions where they would serve as resource persons, diagnose learning disabilities, and develop instructional activities, but ultimately to higher-level positions where they would have major planning and supervisory responsibility over other teachers in their grade or subject area. Thus, teachers would have an opportunity to move into more complex, demanding, and better-paying teaching roles as assessment determined their readiness for responsibility and increased status.

Through differentiation, teachers would have daily contacts with and receive assistance from teaching professionals, who would enhance their growth, simplify their work, provide instructional ideas and support, and recommend ways to save time, cover course essentials, and improve teaching effectiveness. Classroom teachers would have a mentor who provides support, perspective, and understanding, and shares responsibility. Functioning as a mentor, master teachers supervise from seven to twelve teachers in their own school, focusing on curricular and instructional strategy as well as on unique student needs. In addition, teachers who enter teaching because they enjoy working with students and developing curricular and instructional strategy are provided channels for promotion within teaching, while at the same time they are experiencing greater assistance and less isolation in the classroom (Cunningham, 1981).

Finally, "feedback" should go directly to the employee responsible for the work so that he or she can have immediate knowledge of how well he or she is doing the job. People have a great capacity for midflight correction when they know where they stand.

Job satisfaction occurs when a worker experiences a sense of meaningfulness and responsibility and gets information about results. Table 12-1 presents a list of the core dimensions that typically produce job satisfaction as well as some of the implementation concepts that might be used for increasing the core dimensions. Hackman and Aldham (1975) have developed an overall "motivating potential score" (MPS) that can be computed from scores of a given job on the five dimensions. The scores are obtained from a "job diagnostic survey" they developed. It is computed as follows:

$$MPS = \left[\frac{\text{skill variety} + \text{task identity} + \text{task significance}}{3} \right] \times \text{autonomy} \times \text{feedback}$$

The MPS is a summary indicator of the overall "richness" of the job.

TABLE 12-1

Core Dimensions and Implementing Concepts for Job Enrichment

CORE DIMENSIONS	IMPLEMENTING CONCEPTS
1. *Skill Variety.* The job requires the worker to perform different activities calling for different skills.	1. *Task Combination.* Where possible, put together separate tasks and assign them to one worker.
2. *Task Identity.* The job requires completion of a "whole" identifiable outcome.	2. *Natural Units of Work.* The tasks combined should have a relationship that is logical and inherent in terms of some identifiable outcome.
3. *Task Significance.* The job has substantial impact on other people or their jobs.	3. *Client Relationships.* Users of the product or service should be identified and continuing working relationships should be set up between them and the worker.
4. *Autonomy.* The worker has freedom and independence in planning, performing, and checking his work.	4. *Vertical Loading.* To increase autonomy the job design should expand the worker's responsibility to include elements of control and decision making which were formerly reserved to higher levels.
5. *Feedback.* The worker receives regular and timely information about the results of his efforts. The feedback may come from aspects of the task itself, from supervisors, from users of his product, or from higher management.	5. *Feedback Channels.* Information on results should be provided regularly— created, if it is not inherent in the tasks themselves.

Source: Robert, Janson "Job Design for Quality," *The Personnel Administrator,* October 1974, p. 15. Copyright © 1974 by American Society for Personnel Administration.

T-GROUPS

When we begin to talk about T-groups we are at the extreme right of the French and Bell continuum of OD intervention strategies (see Figure 11-2, in the preceding chapter)—what they describe as the educational/therapeutic area of organizational interventions. It is the area, often also described as laboratory techniques, that includes such interventions as T-groups, encounter groups, personal-growth labs, and group and individual psychotherapy. Such approaches are usually needed when there is significant conflict within the organization regarding appropriate individual behavior.

The previous six methods discussed in this chapter are directed at helping the organization to recognize existing conditions, to describe ideal conditions, and to move in the direction toward the ideal. The purpose of the laboratory method is to help an individual to change what he or she sees as already ideal behavior. The method is for cases in which individuals see their behavior as ideal even though it may be having a negative effect on the group process and the organization as a whole. T-groups and the like go much deeper than previously discussed methods because these types of interventions deal with value collisions. The values of a group within the organization, or of a particular individual, are in conflict with the mission and strategic objectives of the organization; this is creating disharmony, a breakdown in the team, and lack of effective participation in and implementation of plans.

This might be the type of problem exhibited by the headmaster described in the beginning of Chapter 11, who had certain prejudices and would not implement an integration plan. Individuals whose value systems are in conflict with organizational directions must re-examine those values and resulting behaviors to determine if they are comfortable with the behaviors and with their effects on others and on the organization. The laboratory method is thus a way of avoiding sabotage of planning efforts without firing otherwise capable employees.

But, it is very difficult to change behavior and usually requires a much more intense approach such as that used in Gestalt therapy. This typically is a difficult process requiring extended efforts and social and psychological expertise well beyond the ability of the average or even very skillful administrator. Because of the intense effort and the unique expertise required, this kind of therapy does not fall under the normal range of organizational activities. However, some organizations, such as IBM, have hired full-time psychologists to help work out such problems. The need for such activities seems to be very pressing among educators—much has been written on teacher stress and burnout.

Because physical and psychological energy and enthusiasm are such important parts of teaching, it is necessary that teachers be physically and emotionally well and health- and happiness-oriented. Teachers should be provided confidential diagnoses; counseling, training, and conditioning; referral services; and laboratory types of techniques to help them deal with physical, emotional, and attitudinal exhaustion. Schools must expand their traditional employee benefits to include systemwide physical and social activities, expanded professional services, programs to improve teacher conditioning, and free confidential professional counseling and hot-lines for troubled teachers. Programs should be encouraged to increase contact among teachers while stimulating positive health behaviors. In-service activities are needed to promote good nutrition, health, exercise, stress control, and effective social interaction, all of which result in improved patterns of moving, speaking, and dealing with people, and in increased vitality. Good experimental programs presently exist in the La Canada-Flintridge school district in California and the Butler City school district in Pennsylvania.

T-group models

A T-group may be defined as an unstructured group meeting of no more than twelve members and a professional facilitator, in which members experiment with behavior. The concept of the laboratory approach is that the individual experiments with behavior and, based on responses received, can continue to modify that behavior to a more effective mode. The main mechanism of learning is nonevaluative feedback received by each individual from other group members. This feedback creates a certain amount of anxiety and tension, which causes the individual to unfreeze and begin to consider alternative values, attitudes, and behavior. An atmosphere of "psychological safety" is necessary for this unfreezing to occur. The individual must be willing to do a self-examination and to experiment with new attitudes, values, assumptions, and actual behavior, thus allowing the development of new internal states and external behaviors, provided they are reinforced by the group.

There are three types of groups: stranger groups, which include members who do not know each other; cousin groups, made up of members in the same organization who do not work together; and family groups, whose members belong to the same work unit. These groups meet with a trainer who may or may not choose to structure the content of the discussion. Regardless of the type of group, it is essential that the individual feel safe enough within the group to experiment with behavior and to provide honest feedback in regard to others' behavior. In relation to this psychological safety, Argyris states:

> How does one create the conditions to encourage valid information and accurate consensual validation? The answer is by creating conditions where he and the others are minimally defensive. The less the defensiveness, the higher the probability that the information generated within and among the human beings will be valid. Defensiveness "in" people, and among them, tends to be minimal when the self-acceptance of the individuals involved is high. The higher the self-acceptance, the less the probability that the individuals will generate defensive conditions or be seduced by them. (Argyris, 1967, p. 155)

Argyris further states that no matter what the preference of the consultant, the learning experiences created should tend to maximize psychological success, confirmation, and essentiality. The group usually comes to see the difference between providing help and attempting to control or punish a member; between analyzing and interpreting a member's adjustment (which is not helpful) and informing him or her of the impact it has on others. Typically, certain features of everyday group activity are blurred or removed. The consultant, for example, does not provide the leadership a group would normally expect. This produces a kind of "power vacuum" and a great deal of behavior that, in time, becomes the basis of learning. All learning dilemmas (for example, the power vacuum), if created properly, should leave the primary responsibility to the participants of what will be learned and how.

Argyris sees "group interactions in an unstructured setting" as the first characteristic of laboratory designs. Other characteristics are emphasis on the here-and-now, the giving and receiving of "minimally evaluative feedback," and the creating of learning conditions that can be transferred beyond the laboratory.

A modification of the T-group approach incorporates some of the lessons of OD data analysis and substitutes exercises that generate organizational phenomena and discussions about these phenomena. The exercises are an effort to provide realistic organizational experiences that participants can profitably critique. The exercises may involve organizational issues such as the multiplicity of management, budgeting goals, expectations and satisfactions, compensation, leadership style, information flow, or planning versus operating. Or the structured approach may deal with individual concerns such as abrasiveness, stress, assertiveness, hurry sickness, prejudice, personnel responsibility, and so on.

Researchers have generally agreed upon the following four major benefits of T-group experiences: (1) self-insight, or some increase in self-knowledge; (2) an understanding of the forces that inhibit or facilitate group functioning; (3) an understanding of the interpersonal operations in groups; and (4) an opportunity to develop skills for diagnosing individual, group, and organizational behavior.

In analyzing laboratory training, Michael Beer states:

> At the individual level participants may increase awareness of their own behavior, their sensitivity to the behavior of others, and they may change their own attitudes and behavior. More importantly, a laboratory training experience may increase a person's confidence and ability to analyze continually his own interpersonal behavior for the purpose of changing and improving its effectiveness. . . . Traditional values and assumptions underlying the management of organizational phenomena such as intergroup conflict, power, influence, status, leadership, and culture may also come into question in a T-group. A more realistic understanding of these organizational problems and the assumptions underlying them may increase organizational effectiveness. Increased effectiveness may come about through changes in individual attitudes and behavior, but may also result from increased individual skill in diagnosing these organizational problems and intervening successfully to eliminate them in the back-home organization.
> (Beer, 1976, pp. 440–441)

Organizational development provides a powerful set of tools when placed in the hands of an administrator who knows how to use them. Most important of these is its ability to help administrators create the organizational culture and group norms needed to support planned change. However, the tools and techniques are not easily pinpointed or summarily defined. Although some of these tools have been briefly discussed, their true power lies in the creative ability of the administrator or facilitator to breathe life into them through his or her own unique style and creativity. Although the techniques of OD provide the general form, the administrator must shape them to meet the unique needs of the organization.

GUIDELINES FOR PLANNING

1. One of the most basic OD intervention strategies is survey feedback. Survey data pertaining to behavioral aspects of the school system are collected, analyzed, and presented to members of the organization to corroborate beliefs about the organization, or to disconfirm beliefs, thereby unfreezing employee attitudes and encouraging inquiry concerning the reasons for the data.

2. Confrontation meetings are used when quick action is needed. The meetings are designed for the purpose of bringing together segments of an organization so that members are directly involved in problem identification and action planning for organizational improvement.

3. Team building uses various techniques to encourage individuals who work together to become involved in the process of examining how they function together, the way they communicate with each other, how various decisions are arrived at, the level of openness and trust established, the clearness and understanding of goals, the ways conflicts are handled, and especially their group norms, which more than anything else determine their ability to achieve planned objectives. This effort focuses on the process by which the team functions in developing and implementing plans.

4. Process consultation is used to help members of the organization to perceive, understand, and act upon observed and recorded process events that occur during planning and implementation. This method is often applied to analyze the effectiveness of group activities such as committee meetings.

5. The major emphasis of OD structural models is on altering the environment of the individual as a means of changing his or her behavior—the underlying assumption is that structural conditions in the environment shape individual behavior. The model is concerned with environmental pressures and constraints as they influence the behavior of the individual within the organization and the consequences of changes in the environmental configuration of these variables.

6. Job enrichment is used to enrich one's work through the deliberate upgrading of responsibility, scope, and challenge so as to provide greater opportunity for personal growth and meaningful work experience. The core dimensions of job enrichment are skill variety, task identification, task significance, autonomy, and feedback.

7. T-groups are one of the most common forms of OD laboratory techniques. In T-groups, individuals attend training sessions with no more than twelve other individuals in which they experiment with behavior and, based upon responses received, choose to accept or modify that behavior. The main mechanism to unfreeze inappropriate behavior and refreeze more appropriate behavior is nonevaluative feedback received by each individual from other group members.

13

Computer Information Systems

To err is human; to really foul things up requires a computer!

We have entered the computer age and yet little is known about the computer and its potential in the educational community. To adapt a Mark Twain quip: "Computers are something like the weather; everybody talks about it but nobody does very much about it." However, even if educational computer applications have not reached the level of sophistication that has been achieved in industry and government, there have been some significant strides toward greater use of computer technology in education.

A HISTORICAL PERSPECTIVE

The prototype of many of today's computers was developed in the mid-1940s by John von Neumann, the great mathematician and formulator of game theory. After World War II the computer industry developed rapidly throughout the United States and other parts of the world. In less than four decades, computers have progressed from experimental laboratory equipment to machines whose capabilities are exceeded only by the range of applications to which they can be put.

229

The 1950s was a period of rapid innovation in the capabilities of data processing systems and expansion in their opportunities for application. These innovations included changes in storage devices used to hold data, in input/output devices, and other related hardware. However, by the early 1960s it was realized that there was a practical limit to the size and capacity of machines operated on vacuum tubes. A major breakthrough came when tiny transistors were introduced to replace the vacuum tubes. Not only could the transistors be packed into a smaller space, not only did they demand less power and give off less heat, but they were more reliable.

The changeover to transistors is frequently referred to as the "second generation" of computers. The next technological advance, called the "third generation," further miniaturized and refined components of the second generation by means of a technology called "solid logic." In the second generation maybe three to four transistors and contacts could fit into a sewing thimble, but by the third generation fifty thousand transistors and contacts could fit into the same thimble.

Today, research is being developed on how to transfer data on laser beams at speeds greater than that of light, which will increase even further the speeds of computers that already work in nano-seconds.

Computer hardware

Each user or purchaser of a computer can buy a set of equipment that will outfit the computer in a different manner depending on the user's own needs. In fact, few computers are configured in exactly the same way. The one device that all computers share in common is a central processing unit (CPU), where all processing occurs. There are various ways in which auxiliary cores (storage and work areas) can be added to the CPU to expand its capabilities. However, this has its limits and if the user outgrows one machine, a larger CPU will have to be obtained. Larger CPU's allow for processing of larger jobs and more work, usually at a higher rate of speed. As a rough guide to computer size, a medium-sized CPU has two million bits or locations to store information.

The computer must have some form of input/output (I/O) device to get information in and out of the CPU. At first glance this might seem to be a relatively simple problem, but it is not. First of all, most CPU's are I/O bound. This means that the CPU can operate much faster than the I/O devices and so it may operate at much less than peak capacity because it cannot get instructions and data in and out of the CPU fast enough. However, if the I/O devices are configured properly for the CPU, it should run at close to 94 percent of its peak rate. Second, I/O devices depend on the specific needs of the user for speed, storage area, communication capabilities, remote job entry (data entries at points relatively far away from the location of the CPU), and the like. Third,

I/O capabilities depend on whether jobs will be handled in a batch mode, one after the other, or in an on-line time-share basis. On-line means programs and data can be coming in from many different locations at any time and, or even, all at the same time. In this mode the peripheral I/O devices are in direct communication with the CPU over an extended period of time. This process is usually called time-sharing.

Figure 13-1 provides an example of one common configuration of the components making up a computer system. I/O devices are attached to a single control unit, which relays the data to the primary storage unit and to the CPU.

Computer software

Computers are made up of what is called hardware and software. The hardware is the actual equipment. Software is the programs or sets of instructions that tell the machine what to do. The hardware by itself is totally incapable of doing anything except drawing electricity. Human beings must tell the computer exactly what to do from start to finish, using instructions that the computer can understand—this requires knowledge of one of the many computer programming languages. The programmed instructions are called software.

There are two types of software systems. One is described as the operating system; it is usually programmed by the computer manufacturer and is purchased or rented. The second type is user application systems; these can be programmed by the user or by purchasing canned programs similar to the ones needed but written by the manufacturer or a software house to meet the needs of all organizations sharing a similar function. The canned programs usually always have to be modified slightly to meet the user's specific needs.

The advances in user application software have paralleled, if not exceeded, the accomplishments in the technology itself. In the late 1940s and early 1950s, detailed instructions had to be wired in or read into the machine as the work progressed. This was changed so computers could store programs in a high-speed internal memory or storage unit. The early languages were very complex and required the programmer to detail information in a binary format, often adding the identification of computer storage addresses for locating all information and instructions. Programming languages have become increasingly less complicated. Today's languages are written in forms of the English language that are relatively easily understood. An operating-system software program, called the compiler, converts that easily understood language to a language the machine understands. In addition, locations in the computer no longer have to be addressed; this is all done automatically.

The early computers could only deal with one instruction at a time and had to be told where and how to handle every piece of information. Programs required immensely complicated sets of instructions to do the simplest of pro-

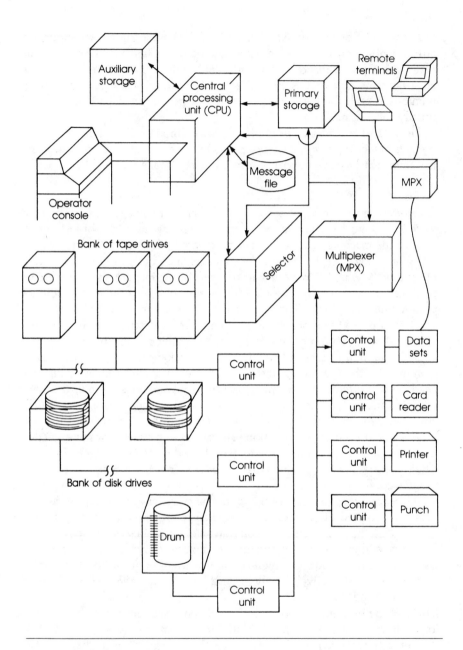

FIGURE 13-1

A Common Configuration of Computer
System Components

cedures. Today those complicated activities are handled by job control language (JCL) instructions that are placed around the user's program to activate the operating system. Sophisticated programs that do complicated activities can be called out of the operating system with the use of one instruction. The same technology has allowed the user to store his or her own user-written programs in a job file and to call them out and use them as needed. At one time the computer could only run one job at a time. Today fifty to seventy-five different jobs can be handled by the computer simultaneously. The end result has been the expansion of programming capabilities paralleled by a decrease in programming difficulty.

The operating system is loaded into the computer when it is installed at the user's location and is only modified or updated by the manufacturer as new innovations come along or as the user wishes to expand operating-system capabilities. This leaves the programming of the arithmetic and logic operations to the user. This can be done in one of two different ways. The programs can be developed and written in-house or they can be rented or purchased from a specialist in computer systems programming. In recent years, computer manufacturers, computer co-ops or consortiums, and software houses across the country have developed what are called "canned programs." These are programs that have been written to do the kinds of things that most school districts would want to do with their computers. The user buys these canned programs and has system analysts or programmers make the needed modifications to meet the user's unique requirements. The idea is that the cost of buying these canned programs, as well as modifying them to meet the school district's needs, is less than the cost required to have the user's system analysts design and computer programmers program and debug (that is, eliminate errors and problems) the software systems in-house. The "why reinvent the wheel" argument is used to defend using canned programs and the "need to tailor the program to meet the specific needs of the user" is given in defense of the in-house programming concept.

Economic dependency upon computers

The applications of computers in government, medicine, research, military, business, and industry are extensive. In industry the computer forecasts sales, maintains inventory records, places orders, schedules production, orders needed raw materials, prepares shipping orders, locates warehouse storage, maintains financial records, maintains payroll and personnel records, maintains capital inventories, and has many additional applications in research and other areas. In the railroad industry the colored stripes on the side of box cars are used to trace inventory all across the nation as the cars pass checkpoints. In medical services the computer is also used to control complex medical laboratory tests, such as sectional X-rays.

The police department uses computers to scan licenses, fingerprints, names, social security numbers, and the like to determine the records of individuals being stopped by the police. Department stores use computers to read price tags, compute customer bills including taxes, prepare financial statements, keep track of inventory, and place and keep track of orders. The use of the computer in the military is very broad, from keeping track of every part on every piece of military equipment to keeping track of the location of every military warhead, including those in motion, and every possible target; in addition, computers are prepared to guide those warheads to any target selected automatically. Could you imagine the airline industry today if it did not have computers to book passages and control air corridors? Bank transactions, the stock and future market, the bond markets—all require the computer to be up and running if the industry is to keep up with operational demands.

The list is endless and the information that can be provided cheaply and efficiently through such computer systems is limited only by imagination. Most large businesses now have an instantaneous status on all resources—human, financial, in-process inventory, finished goods, capital equipment, or whatever. Railroads now know exactly where every shipment is. Doctors have information that pinpoints the location of medical problems in such complex organs as the brain and the heart. In a matter of seconds, police know the descriptive characteristics of the individual they are dealing with. The military knows the exact location of the trillions of pieces of equipment needed in their operations. The airline industry knows the exact status of a plane, and the stock market knows the status of over fifty million different shares of stock traded each day. We are truly in the decade of what Alvin Toffler describes as "the information explosion."

Whether education can ever use the computer to such levels of sophistication is not clear. However, many successes to date suggest that the computer has an exciting and powerful potential providing information and assistance to educators.

COMPUTER APPLICATIONS IN EDUCATION

One of the keys to efficiency and quality improvements in every sector of our society has been through the augmentation of human efforts by technology. The potential in education is equally great. Initial efforts have resulted in systems that have greatly reduced the difficulty of planning and management efforts in educational administration. The application of computers in education provides a tool that can assist in a wide variety of administrative and instructional areas.

The American Institute of Research (Bukoski and Korotkin, 1976) reports that between 1970 and 1975 there was a 23.8 percent increase in the use of computers in secondary schools with a total of 58 percent of all school administrators surveyed stating they used the computer in some way or another. Over half of the schools using the computer reported that they used it for administrative purposes such as payroll and personnel, master scheduling, or student accounting. Of the 58 percent of the schools that used the computer in some way or another, 31.5 percent used the computer for administration only, 21.8 percent used the computer for both administration and instruction, and 4.7 percent used computers for instruction only.

A review of the educational administrative journals reveals that computers and computer-related matters take up a very small percentage of the concern of most educational administrators. In the February 1977 issue of the *Kappan*, which was devoted to educational computer technology, educational experts expressed a wide range of views about the potential of the computer in education. No real conclusions could be drawn other than the recognition of great potential and limited preparation to use that potential (Cunningham, 1977). One article suggested that "we should not awake the sleeping giant."

Recognizing the need for expanded communication regarding the application of computers in education, various societies for the development and expansion of computers in education have been established. For example, the Association for Educational Data Systems (AEDS) and the Society for Applied Learning Technology (SALT) were organized to help facilitate the application of computers in education and to help close what has been regarded as the "communication gap" between experts in education and specialists in the theory and practice of computer technology.

There have been many promising programming efforts by manufacturers (CDC/PLATO, IBM/EPIC, Honeywell/SCATT II), by local school districts and by state co-ops (Minnesota-TIES, Oregon-OTIS), which although moving at a slow pace are showing great promise. Most states now have chapters of AEDS, which meet on a semiannual or annual basis to share ideas. *Educational Technology, AEDS Journal, Technological Horizons in Education,* and others have reported successes in the implementation of computer technology.

Administrative systems

It would be impossible to detail the various software systems that have developed in each of the areas of education in which the computer has been applied; but a brief overview of the typical computer systems that supply information to educational planners is in order. The more advanced systems provide what is described as management information system (MIS) capabilities, which allow for integrating various computerized systems to obtain information that can answer all sorts of questions. For example, a computerized payroll and personnel system exists in almost all the larger school systems in the United States. Planners can use this system to obtain information regarding salaries, skills, positions, and the like, which can be used for planning purposes.

Beside the more obvious benefits of maintaining employee records, producing personnel reports, preparing payroll checks, and so on, the computer can produce summary statistics on all employees by race and sex for each of the EEO-1 codes or by job position. It can search the file from a skills inventory point of view and determine which employees presently on board meet the requirements established for a new job planned for in the school district.

The system can be used by planners to test different salary and benefit proposals to determine the exact cost impact of the proposal. The computer can prepare age or race profiles, salary–position profiles, and retirement lists; if tied to student files, it can rank teachers by performance of students as measured by standardized test grades or by academic and affective progress. For instance, it can determine in which teachers' classes students on the average show the greatest advancement in cognitive and affective development as measured by standardized tests.

The student accounting, scheduling, and report card system reduces clerical work, increases efficiency of operations, organizes information, and provides MIS capabilities. Attendance data can be handled and reported on a relatively routine basis, as well as report cards, honor roll lists, class lists, location data, class schedules, and the like. The system can develop class schedules on the basis of restricting class assignments by location, grade, ability, sex, or race criteria or by balancing classes according to ethnic group, semester workload, section, or sex. Such information can be used to simulate the effect of planned changes (that is, change in programs, class sizes, and so on) on the school district. When linked with census data and financial data, it can project enrollments and project future school expansion or closing, as well as future capital or operating costs. It can produce accountability records by school and classroom based on student attendance and performance. The system can be used to group students in many different ways and for many different purposes—academics, athletics, extracurricular activities, discipline, race, sex, and the like.

If appropriate data are maintained, the computer can assign students to teachers with whom they would have the highest probability of success in the future (teachers with whom similar students have shown the most progress in the past). This concept is described as aptitude/treatment interaction (Cunningham, 1975). Modular scheduling, phase electives, and individualized instruction become feasible because the computer can place people in appropriate classes, thus allowing greater administrative time to solve the difficult conflicts.

Computer manufacturers promote the benefits of using computerized simulations to forecast the impact of plans on the entire school district. In a manual for its EPIC/SOCRATES system, IBM claims that by "using simulation, you can vary the mix of students, teachers, and classrooms, and see in advance what impact will result from changes in facilities or educational policies, curriculum and personnel modifications, the design of new buildings, or the implementation of capital improvements."

Budget and finance computer systems allow the administrator quickly to determine cost savings (or increases) caused by the elimination, reduction, or expansion of an existing program. Costs can be broken out and reported for various line-item classifications; if program budgeting is used, the costs of various programs can be quickly detailed. The total expenditure year-to-date as a percentage of the budget and also the impact of any reduction in funding can be projected. The total per-pupil cost of one course can be compared to other courses. Costs can be projected into the future based on census and other forms of growth data with projected impact on salaries, equipment, and supplies. The computer can project year-end balances, develop three-year budget projections, and keep past budget records. Such systems provide for control of expenditures, year-end closing and carry-over balance, automatic cost distribution, budget adjustments, and check-writing capabilities.

Some have suggested that data at the local level should be made available to the state by linking school district computers to state computers so the state could abstract and provide up-to-date summary reports on a weekly or monthly basis (Pogrow, 1977). The state would specify data formats for all files maintained by the local school districts; the state computer could have a telephone line to each of the district computer files. The major rationale for such a centralized data base system is that it is a way to improve intra-organizational coordination.

Instructional systems

The potential for computer applications is as great in instruction as in administration. Testing programs that might fall under both categories can be scored and reported by the computer. The computer can assemble tests from a battery of questions related to each objective, give them to the student, score them, analyze them, provide diagnostic reports, and store results. Such information can be assembled in various ways for planning purposes. Student strengths and weaknesses could be diagnosed and the computer could group students by new objectives and recommend possible instructional programs. Planners could be provided reports on the performance of students regarding certain programs, basic skills, or behavioral objectives. Reports could also be maintained on how well students did while being taught by a particular teacher and/or particular text material. All these computerized activities greatly reduce clerical activities by both teachers and principals while improving data availability and analysis for school planning.

Functioning as a tutor, the computer can direct a student through a series of lessons and exercises, can go on to other lessons depending on the student's performance, can record areas of a student's strengths and weaknesses, and can branch out into other instructional programs to help the student understand difficult concepts or recommend that the student review audio-video tapes, books, or movies, or discuss the concept with his or her teacher before repeating the computer lesson. Some examples of computer-assisted instruction are math programs that help students work through each step of a math problem; language arts programs where students construct sentences and define words; decision-type simulations; algebra where students are taught to solve equations; and even spelling programs where the computer pronounces a list of words and gives immediate feedback on misspelled words.

In addition, the computer could be a major resource, allowing a student to browse and ramble through a vast variety of content-rich writings, three-dimensional moving pictures, manipulative figures, graphs, charts, and other simulations, as well as to freely manipulate these resources and to receive real-world responses. Such systems would not be controlled by student responses to programmed questions but would allow the student to discover answers by looking in obvious places. Student choice patterns might include "explain big picture," "more details," "go on," "don't understand," "disagree," "drill me," "test me," "draw me a diagram," "tell me a relevant joke," "change the subject," or "I'm bored."

The simulation and gaming function of the computer offers tremendous potential. For example, the Nelson Organization in New York City is working on a computerized system in which students can dissect a frog that appears on the cathode ray tube (CRT). The student places a slit down the frog using the light pen. The inside opens up and the student selects for viewing various systems, such as organs, cardiovascular, skeletal, muscular, or nervous. Based on the selection, the appropriate structures appear within the frog. If organs are selected, the student can simply point to organs for computer identification or the computer can request the child to dissect or remove various organs with the light pen. The child is typically told by the computer if he or she is removing the wrong organ. Greater detail can be provided by focusing on one organ, such as the heart, eye, ear, or brain.

The same concept can be used in geography. A CRT globe focuses on a country, then a city, and finally on living conditions within the city. Rivers, mountains, and so on can also be identified. The reading level can be set for each student, using a less sophisticated and shorter text for students with a less developed reading level and more detailed and complex words for students with a higher reading level. Nelson has dubbed this concept "stretchtext" (Nelson, 1970).

Control Data Corporation's PLATO system has an excellent graphic simulation of the operation of a retail business, which could be used as part of a business education course. During the simulation the student makes all the decisions regarding retail operations and the computer simulates the results of the decisions (PLATO, 1977). For history classes there is a simulation of the Civil War in which the student can pick either side as a general or the President and make key decisions, getting simulated results that are then compared to what actually happened. The main idea is to stimulate greater interest in actual events and an understanding of how difficult the decisions must have been. In genetics, there is a program of simulated experiments with the tsetse fly (Bork, 1976).

The computer has also been used in computer guidance systems. Sylvia Sharp and the computer staff from the Philadelphia School District have developed an excellent vocational guidance system. Students can use any number of computer terminals to browse through information related to their vocational interests. They can inquire by subjects of interest to determine job possibilities, by specific job, or for jobs related to the occupation they think they are interested in. Students can also complete a computerized questionnaire on interests, and the computer will recommend occupational areas based on their responses. They can inquire about the type of work performed at three or four various levels of detail. They can get information on future job outlook, salaries, educational and training requirements, good points and bad points, chances for advancement, what the job entails, interest factors, personality factors, physical factors, and the like, as well as salary, scholarships, and financial aid available, schools that have the best reputation for training in the field, and so forth. Local job opportunities are suggested for those students who already have the needed training.

In the computer management instructional system (CMI), the computer maintains information on each student. The computer is typically used to score standardized tests and to store the results for each student. In addition there are systems that allow the student to be tested by the computer when the child believes he or she is ready to demonstrate mastery of an objective. The computer knows what objective the child is working on and creates an exam based on a large bank of questions related to that objective; the computer calculates and records the student's performance; and, if the student has satisfied the requirements for the objective, the computer recommends and records a new objective. The student typically must get final objective approval from the teacher. The teacher approves the objective or enters a new objective through the computer before the student may be given a computer exam on the new objective. In addition, the teacher can select an objective and the computer will find the students who are prepared to tackle that objective and create an instructional group for the teacher.

There is an effort to convert CMI systems into diagnostic and prescriptive systems so that the computer can analyze results from computerized lessons, tests, and other data and make diagnostic recommendations on a daily, weekly, and yearly basis. When such a system includes demographic, attitudinal, and developmental data, it can be used to compare student profiles with previous students who are similar to the one being diagnosed in order to find instructional approaches that have been most successful with this type of student in the past. Such knowledge might decrease the length of time required to identify an effective instructional approach and improve the probability that the student will have a successful learning experience (Cunningham, 1975). The same type of logic can be used to identify teachers who probably will be most effective with a student on the basis that the teacher has been most effective with that type of student in the past (Cunningham, 1975, 1976). Such information can be used to plan for future needs.

CONCLUSIONS ABOUT USING COMPUTERS IN SCHOOLS

Certainly the potential for the computer is quite significant if we can find a cost-effective way in which it might be used. One of the keys to efficiency and quality improvements in every sector of our society is the augmentation of human efforts by technology. There are strong reasons to believe that this pattern is also true for education. The computer has proven to be an essential tool in the areas of payroll and personnel accounting, student accounting (class lists, attendance reports, and so on), master scheduling, report card systems, month-to-date and year-to-date financial accounting, and testing and research. In instruction, the computer has been used mainly in math and/or computer science courses and in the area of vocational and educational guidance.

Probably one of the most comprehensive studies of the effectiveness of computer applications was completed by the Minnesota Educational Computer Consortium under the sponsorship of the National Institute of Education (Hansen, Klassen, and Lindsay, 1978). They concluded that some of the major benefits of computer systems were the following:

1. For many people, a significant amount of time has been freed from clerical tasks. While for some, this "freed" time is absorbed by computer related duties, for others the time is truly available to perform other tasks.

2. More accurate personnel, student, and financial records can be kept. Records can be accessed more easily and the stored data can be sorted in a multitude of ways, thus facilitating flexible reporting to school personnel and external agencies.

3. More accurate projections of student enrollments can be produced, thus greatly aiding in planning for facilities and personnel needs, and in communication with constituents.

4. Decentralization of budgetary development and control is made more feasible because personnel receive accurate, detailed, and relevant budget information. Many more line items can be included in the chart of accounts.

5. More frequent and flexible scheduling of classes can be performed. More electives and more classes of varying lengths can be offered. In schools with less complicated, traditional schedules, this benefit is not realized, and the impact of computer use in scheduling is perceived as unfavorable by a few persons.

6. In most schools, a longer period of time now elapses between the end of a term and the distribution of student progress reports. Some teachers and administrators view this as an unfavorable impact of computer use.

7. Districts can more easily conduct research studies of their activities, such as student follow-up studies that aid in curricular decisions and planning.

8. Significant cost savings can be realized through use of the computer to aid in developing bus routes. Although the computer program does not automatically determine routes, the data stored and processed by the computer greatly aid the building of efficient routes and the performance of day-to-day transportation tasks. (Hansen, Klassen, and Lindsay, 1979, p. 15)

The researchers also suggest a second level of benefits. These come from the ease in obtaining and analyzing data that formerly took weeks and months to prepare, if done at all. This convenience results in better decision making, better planning, more effective resource management, and more time to work with people. Ultimately, such information improves the entire planning process.

Those who have experienced the vast amount of information the computer can provide in a matter of minutes and hours rather than weeks and months have an appreciation of its value in planning and management and are demanding more from their computers. Such users are beginning to reach a higher level of sophistication and are actively seeking ways to enhance current applications and develop new applications that will facilitate and support all planning efforts. This sophistication typically comes from an understanding of what their computers can do and how it has been applied in their system. This combination allows the creative administrator to know what information he or she can obtain from the computer.

GUIDELINES FOR PLANNING

1. Computers are made up of two major and equally important components—hardware and software.

2. One of the keys to efficiency and quality improvements in every sector of our society has been through the augmentation of human efforts by technology. Although much has been done in education, many opportunities still remain in both the administrative and instructional areas.

3. Some of the many applications of computers in providing administrative information to planners include payroll/personnel; student accounting, master scheduling, and reporting; attendance; budget/finance/accounting; and inventory control systems.

4. Some of the diverse applications of computers in providing instructional information to planners include testing and scoring; performance reporting; tutoring, simulation, and gaming; guidance and counseling; and student analysis/diagnosis/prescription systems.

5. We have only begun to scratch the surface for using computers as an administrative and instructional tool in education. The challenge will be to develop cost-efficient ways in which to provide the data needed for effective planning efforts.

Part 3

The Future

Our World of Tomorrow
Scenarios

14

Planning for Educational Futures

I am interested in the future because that is where I am going to spend the rest of my life.

–CHARLES KETTERING

The study of "educational futures" has prompted an upsurge of interest in planning. Planning is necessary since administrators have no choice but to anticipate the future, to attempt to both create and adjust to it, and to balance present operating goals with longer-range goals. Peter Drucker states:

> Unless the long range is built into, and based on, short-range plans and decisions, the most elaborate long-range plan will be an exercise in futility, and conversely, unless the short-range plans, that is, the decisions on the here and now, are integrated into one unified plan of action, they will be expedient, guesses, and misdirection. (Drucker, 1974, p. 122)

The essence of planning is to make present decisions based on knowledge of their future impact. Thus the old adage "Forewarned is forearmed" is especially true in planning.

Educational administrators must be able to anticipate the future; that is, be able to visualize how choices made today will influence tomorrow's educational practice. This requires that administrators be prepared to look beyond the traditional firing line to the future alternatives that will be available to their educational systems. The dizzying work pace and concern with economic survival does not encourage such a future focus. However, its absence in educational systems will betray our youth and put our schools at the mercy of the future. Those who cannot project themselves into the future can only respond to the immediacy of the present, unable to envision and assess possible futures. Those who cannot visualize the future are destined to regret the past and fear the future.

Educators are very conscious of the increasing rate at which social change is occurring. This increased pace of change has caused their plans to have a shorter and shorter operational life. Writers such as Herman Kahn and Alvin Toffler have addressed the causes of the increasing rate of change in society. Gradually, people are coming to see that they cannot expect the future to be the same as the past.

The United States came out of a deep depression to some dazzling heights in population and riches. We walked on the moon, industry became computerized, superhighways criss-crossed the nation, education was expanded to cover a broader set of human needs, and our standard of living improved. Industry grew at a rate unparalleled in human history, and then leveled off as other nations began to outproduce us. As cheap petroleum products became more expensive, we learned about our global dependence on others.

We have seen difficulties unfold at a rate many have been unable to absorb—Vietnam, youth and racial uprisings, the drug cult, the Arab oil embargo, detente, the renewal of the cold war, the Watergate scandal, hostages in Iran, soaring joblessness and inflation, loss of pride in workmanship, loss of productivity, changes in the roles of women, government control and subsidies, increase in the average age of Americans (from 24 to 37), increases in urban decay, pollution, suicide, divorce, and so on. The changes we have seen are dizzying but, as Barnum and Bailey might say, "You ain't seen nothin' yet."

The experience of race car drivers can be used to illustrate the importance of the future during increasing rates of change. The faster a racing car travels over a cross-country course to its destination, the farther ahead the driver must look if he or she is to avoid collision and manage the obstacles in front. This image should appear very accurately to the educational administrator who is faced with the fast pace of our present times. Educational administrators must have a view of the future—even if a blurred view—if they wish to stay in the race.

The fast pace of present society can be represented more specifically by broadening our race-car example to the transportation industry in general. The carriage used in the late 1800s was the same kind of vehicle as a pharaoh's chariot, and it traveled at about the same rate of speed. But in the last seventy-five years, rapid strides in transportation have occurred with the refinement of the piston engine, the jet, and the rocket engine. In little more than a half century, technology has enabled us to advance from speeds of a few miles per hour to seven times the speed of sound; and nothing indicates that there is an end in sight. Although the examples in education are not as dramatic, there have been significant changes from America's one-room school houses at the end of the 17th century to the large complicated school system that exists at the end of the 20th century. It is already clear that the 21st century will be quite different from any our history has recorded.

The administrator cannot just decide whether or not to make decisions with futurity in mind; he or she must make them by the definition of the role. All that is within an administrator's power is to decide whether to make decisions responsibly or irresponsibly, with an improved chance of effectiveness and success, or as a blind gamble against unforeseen odds. Lacking divine guidance, administrators must face the difficult responsibility of forecasting and planning for the future.

PLANNING FOR THE FUTURE

What will happen in the next twenty years and beyond? Few dare make public pronouncements of prophesy because of the role of the prophet down through the ages. In mythology there was Cassandra, the Trojan princess who was endowed with a gift of prophesy but fated by Apollo never to be believed. Then, of course, there were the Old Testament prophets whose very lives depended on the accuracy of their predictions. If they were wrong, their fate was death by stoning. Today when we need some image of the future we turn to a whole new species of intellectual: the professional futurist or futurologist. Unlike the old-fashioned prophet or seer, this new breed of thinker considers himself or herself to be a rigorous analyst, studying the laws that govern social, political, economic, technological, and educational trends and their effects on one another (Hoyle, 1980a).

The educational division of the World Future Society (WFS) has made a definite impact on the educational leadership in the American school system. The WFS defines modern futuristics as primarily an attempt to examine systematically the factors that can influence the future, and then project possible futures based on the interaction of these factors. But futuristics also involves imagining and exploring desirable futures in hopes of discovering new ideas, new alternatives, and new goals to aim for.

Futurists explicitly point out that we face a variety of futures, not one single future. These alternative futures are dependent on several factors: history, that is, past events and trends that have an influence on the future; chance, the occurrences we are unable to plan for; and human choice, the decisions we make that affect the future. It is important to understand that futurists do not claim to predict the future; rather they attempt to heighten our awareness of the range of alternatives rather than what is certain or inevitable. These perspectives can be best illustrated by two metaphors. One can view life as a long roller-coaster ride and the future as the track upon which we ride. We are unable to see all the twists and turns of the track in advance and can only see each part as we come to it. We cannot change the course of the ride or even get off when we want. We are a captive to this experience and can do little about a future that is fixed. Another view characterizes the future as a great ocean on which we are navigating a ship. There are many destinations that we may sail toward. While navigating, we take into consideration such factors as the currents, weather conditions, and unfamiliar waters in order to reach our destination safely. The first metaphor views the future as determined by our circumstances; there is not much we can do to change or alter it. Futurists reject this notion and instead choose the second metaphor, which claims that by using foresight, one is able to determine, to some extent, one's future (Allain, 1979). This is the same notion upon which planning must be based.

The alternative-futures approach requires the use of skills that can be developed through "futuristics" techniques. First, we must learn to think more imaginatively about the future in order to avoid the single-future trap. This often necessitates scrutinizing previous notions of likelihood and the impact of the future and reconstructing them to fit more flexible perspectives of the future as something to be created or invented. Second, one must evaluate the impact of possible futures. Reflecting upon the effects of certain actions is essential when considering future possibilities. We must not only be aware of alternative courses of action that are open to us, but we must also choose wisely among them. This process raises basic questions of what is possible, what is probable, and above all, what is preferable. Alvin Toffler (1970, p. 475) notes:

> Every society faces not merely a succession of probable futures, but an array of possible futures, and a conflict over preferable futures. The management of change is the effort to convert certain possibles into probables, in pursuit of agreed-on preferables.

So we can look ahead to an array of possible futures, of which some are more likely to occur than others. With this in mind, we can choose the most desirable future and then take steps to reach it. It is from this perspective that we disclaim the inevitability of a single future.

Futurists see the challenge now confronting educational planners as a shift in the mode of thinking from conscious adaptation to conscious anticipation. They see this as a conversion from maintenance and shock learning to innovative learning. "Maintenance" is defined here as the tendency to fall back on, to rely on, old formulas to meet new problems. Innovative learning occurs when new forms of actions are considered on the basis of the understanding that occurs when one learns that a rather large set of conditions has changed.

Anticipation is the ability to deal with the future, to foresee coming events as well as to evaluate the medium-term and long-range consequences of current decisions and actions. It requires not only learning from experience but also envisioning future situations. Conscious anticipation is not limited to encouraging desirable trends and averting potentially catastrophic ones, but must include "inventing" or creating new alternatives where none existed, and "preferred" alternatives where the possibilities were undesirable. It is directed at warding off the increasingly more traumatic and costly lessons of shock during the reactive or crisis-planning process. We have learned that shock can be fatal or very costly to the human species. Botkin, Elmandjra, and Malitya (1979, p. 26) state:

> In non-anticipatory, adaptive learning all we do is "react" and search for answers when it might be too late to implement solutions. We exhibit great insensitivity to small but critical signals. Under the influence of maintenance learning, those who should be alarmed are often not moved by gradual deterioration. Then when shock occurs and events roll like thunder, people finally stand up only to look for the lightning that has already struck.
>
> Since innovation emphasizes preparedness to act in new situations, the exploration of what may happen or is likely to occur necessarily becomes one of the main pillars of the learning enterprise. At the present time, however, anticipation does not play a sufficiently important role. As individuals, we do not speak enough in the future tense; and as societies, we tend to speak only in the past tense.

"Societal anticipation" will be one of the most important characteristics that a society of the 21st century can display. Botkin, Elmandjra, and Malitya (1979) end their comments in this section by stating, "Thus a key aim of innovative learning is to enlarge the range of options within sufficient time for sound decision-making processes. Without such innovative learning, humanity is likely to rely solely on reactive learning, making new shocks inevitable" (p. 44).

SCENARIOS

One of the better methods to plan probable, possible, or preferable futures is by developing scenarios of the future. A scenario is a "future history," a narrative that describes a possible series of events that might lead to some future state of affairs. This fictionalized forecast is written from the point of view of a specific future date, such as five to ten years hence. It describes the events that will occur from the present up to that date. In writing a scenario one attempts to construct a logical sequence of events leading from the present, or any other given time, to a future condition (Hoyle, 1980a).

A scenario is nothing more than a narrative in which the author strings together a series of probable events (planned and unplanned) that might occur over some given period of time. By weaving realistic data into a narrative, the planner can often build a powerful and convincing case for the probability of occurrence. The planner can also use the scenario as a strong argument for the desirability for strategic and/or operational plans needed to support, in Toffler's terms, a set of "agreed-on preferables." In this and other ways scenarios can be dramatic calls to action providing motivation and purposefulness to present actions. The works of Herman Kahn, Anthony Weiner, and Paul Ehrlich have been especially adept at motivating action through rather dramatic scenarios. Ehrlich's 1969 essay "Eco-Catastrophe"—in which he states that "the end of the ocean came late in the summer of 1979, and it came even more rapidly than the biologists had expected"—was given considerable credit for motivating bans on DDT and for leading to significant reductions in the ways in which DDT can get into the oceans. In this essay Ehrlich did not really forecast what would happen, but what could happen if nothing were done. Ehrlich's scenario was also projectable on the basis of scientific discovery that DDT slows down photosynthesis in marine plant life, which all life in the sea depends upon.

There are some basic rules in developing scenarios. For example, scenarios should be based on projectable events that are forecasted from data at hand. Certainly projection involves imagination, but it is not to be confused with it. Prediction has a taste of foretelling or prophecy that futurists find unpalatable. They deplore statements made without all available data in hand to support the probable developments. One must also guard against myopia caused by a tendency to assume that the future will be merely an analogic extension of past or present. One must be able to creatively put together knowns and unknowns to visualize a new future.

This requires one to keep an "open and unprejudiced mind" and be able to see interrelationships among presently occurring technological, biological, social, and human events. Paradoxically, those who are not limited by the bounds of some specialized expertise are free to discover more probabilities than those who are committed to verifying estimates permitted by whichever closed system of knowledge they are expert in.

Scenarios are not intended to be the future; they are future possibilities or desirabilities. They may or may not occur, depending in part on what people choose to do or not do. However, the future will be guided by people's actions or lack of actions and their effects on what happens in the future. For example, Seif (1979) suggests that a devastating nuclear war or a major energy crisis is not inevitable, but is in fact dependent on the actions of individuals and nations:

> If, for example, the Soviet Union and United States agree on a nuclear arms treaty that greatly reduces arms spending and the arms race, then this would have a profound effect on the potential for war and on the economy of the world. If during the next ten years there are serious efforts in the United States to reduce oil and other energy consumption and begin instituting sunpower or other simpler forms of energy, then our energy problems could be very different in the future. Individual and collective decisions will influence and help determine how we will live in the future." (Seif, 1979, p. 84)

This suggests that planners have a responsibility to use time, energy, and money to seek to create and shape an improved tomorrow. Planners must answer the question, "What can we do now to make tomorrow better?"

POSSIBLE ISSUES FOR AN EDUCATIONAL SCENARIO

Planners interested in developing anticipated (and/or preferable) scenarios confront a taxonomical problem. What systematic classification should be used to describe the future? We must be able to look to the future of schooling in some systematic fashion if our efforts are to be helpful in the planning process. Developing a classification system begins with a checklist of aspects of education that require delineation. The education section of the World Future Society and the Old Dominion University were involved in 1979 in a major research project using scenarios for strategic planning in education. Part of the project was to develop a classification system of issues that were believed to be central to education's future. Each of the issues identified needs to be anticipated and addressed in present planning efforts.

The issues are grouped under six headings: responsibilities of different agents, content, process, improvement of the profession, interaction with the individual, and interface with society. Planners in each school district can project future developments in each issue area, based on present initiatives, and these predictions can then be synthesized into an overall picture of how education within the district is evolving and improving. The following section outlines the twenty-three issue areas that can be used to classify the future (Allen and Dede, 1979, pp. 37-56).

I. *Responsibilities of Different Agents*

A. *Schooling.* In the next thirty years, rapid technological innovations and unstable financial and social conditions will require great sophistication and flexibility in the education of children . . . and the continuing education of adults. Do schools, as now defined and operated, provide the best delivery system for educating children and adults?

B. *Families.* In recent history, both the extended and the nuclear family structure have come under considerable strain because of changes in social values, and many educational tasks once the responsibility of the family are now seen as the function of the schooling system. How can alternatives and changing family structures be accommodated within the educational framework? Regardless of the allocation of responsibility, how can the schooling system work toward a position of educational partnership with the family?

C. *Communities.* Should communities, with their broad but localized range of skills and knowledge, assume major educational responsibilities? If so, which? What mix of local/national/global tradition and culture should communities convey?

D. *Media.* In the next thirty years, drastic alterations in existing media delivery systems seem probable, including increased popular access to prerecorded materials, computerized libraries, and interactive systems. To what extent will schools increase their reliance on media and shape its concepts, programming, and delivery?

E. *Industries/Professions.* How can training best be structured to foresee and address short- and long-term variations in career goals? How should counseling be done to maximize the fit between individual abilities and interests and the types of work society needs? How should society coordinate training agents so as to minimize total cost?

II. *Content*

A. *Social Responsibility.* What are the values and attitudes vital for successful cultural evolution into the twenty-first century, and by which educational agent is each best conveyed? How can and should instruction be individualized to respond to the diverse array of attitudes and values held by learners?

B. *Basic Cognitive Skills.* What cognitive skills are needed by all citizens, and by which educational agent is each best conveyed? How can the expression of creativity be encouraged?

C. *Basic Affective Skills.* Recent rapid and unexpected changes in cultural values have caused many people to feel stressed, overwhelmed, and unable to control their future. How can affective skills be coordinated and integrated to build higher-order constructs such as self-awareness, personal esteem, and ability to resist adversity? How should the affective domain be interfaced with social responsibility?

D. *Values.* Should the educational system deliberately communicate values and attitudes beyond those necessary for socialization? By what means can the values of individuals best be changed, and to what extent is this desirable if at all possible? How should values education (if any) be integrated with instruction for social responsibility?

E. *Future Thinking.* Forecasting is difficult because events, trends, and values of society are interdependent; the next thirty years are perilous because world support systems have become interdependent before world cultural systems have recognized this shift. This means that people of the world who now depend upon each other for their survival have not learned to get along with one another—nor to understand their cultural differences. How can education best convey an understanding of ecological, cultural, and social interdependence? In what ways should education build toward a "global consciousness"? To what extent can education prepare citizens for issues that may first become important in five years? a decade? a generation?

III. *Process*

A. *Diversity of Learning.* Each learner has different needs, expectations, capacities, life experiences, and readiness—and all these attributes vary with time. To what extent and in which areas of instruction should individualized learning packages be developed? What needs to be done toward further understanding of the development and cultural basis of learning styles?

B. *Educational Technology.* How major a role can technology legitimately play in the educative process? What effect will large-scale uniform instructional programming have on diversity of human resources, and to what extent is the specialization and individualization of technological instruction possible, given high software production costs? What new types of training for educators will be required to utilize these developing tools for instruction?

C. *Evaluation.* Evaluation in education, as distinct from credentialing, is concerned with providing feedback on performance: to learners on their mastery of instruction, to educators on their achievement of goals, and to organizations on their accomplishment of purposes. For each type of educational agent, which evaluation techniques are most accurate and in what manner should these be incorporated? How can evaluation validity be maximized? What are the best strategies for communicating evaluation results in a constructive manner? By what methods can evaluation results of "work in progress" be incorporated into decision structures?

IV. *Improvement of the Profession*

A. *Professionalism.* How can the scope of education be more clearly delineated so that a more detailed analysis of the nature of the profession can be made? By what means can the most effective practitioner techniques be identified? What role differentiations are appropriate within the field, and what standards of technical and ethical training should each role meet? How can the degree of expertise required to be a competent educator be made apparent to the society, so that recognition of the importance and difficulty of education can be increased?

B. *Staff Development.* Regardless of the educational agent—schooling system, family, community, media, industry—our cultural roles are presently structured such that the educational function is relatively nonrewarding. How can the image of the profession be improved so that educating is seen to be as challenging and difficult as being a surgeon, a basketball player, or an executive? Given unionization, how can procedures be developed for removal of practitioners who have ceased to be effective? How can the "burnout" of educators be prevented? For each educational agent, how might professional development take place?

C. *Professional Governance.* In the next thirty years, a lack of professional cohesion may sorely damage education. Leadership and cooperation are needed to meet the tremendous responsibilities and financial challenges society will place on education. How can the different educational agents (schooling system, family, community, media, industry) develop a framework for collaboration on common issues? What types of authority and power distribution systems will function most effectively in education?

V. *Interaction with the Individual*

A. *Lifelong Learning.* What types of educational experiences are important during infancy and early childhood, and by which educational agents would these best be delivered? What instructional systems can most effectively serve the needs of people and society for retraining, more sophisticated citizenship, and social interaction? How can instruction facilitate the fusion of work and leisure styles? By what means can this expansion in traditional instructional services best be staffed and financed?

B. *Credentialing.* Credentialing—of learners, instructors, and educational institutions—is a means of certifying future performance. How can educational credentialing systems be made a more effective means of determining quality, without eliminating the diversity and individual uniqueness valued in a free society?

C. *Special Needs.* Education is primarily provided for the middle-range-of-talent, physically and emotionally healthy individual in the majority culture. In as diverse a society as ours, this assumption means that many people are ill-served by educational institutions. How can instructional settings be structured to incorporate the maximum range of learner needs, so that through direct experience our culture will lose its fear of physical, sexual, intellectual, behavioral, emotional, linguistic, racial, cultural, and chronologic differences? How can learners with special needs best be given a sense of personal worth and a positive self-image? At what point does the responsibility of educational systems cease for learners for whom no instructional strategy seems to function?

D. *Equity.* No highly technological, complex society can survive either the loss of talent resultant from discrimination or the dissatisfaction and defiance that bias generates. What biases in each type of educational agent need to be removed, and how can these agents act to promote equity of access, outcome, and staffing? What are the limits (if any) to the pluralism for which eduction is responsible? How can equality of outcome be best interpreted so as to still allow for maximization of individual potential?

VI. *Interface with Society*

A. *Relation to Other Human Services.* The field of human services is split into numerous specialties, each having its own delivery system (e.g., education, health, welfare, etc.). Such specialization encourages a kind of parochialism in which a person is viewed only from certain perspectives (e.g., health) rather than as a total human being. How can educational and social services best be coordinated and under what overall authority? How can administrative governance systems be evolved that will transcend the problems of hierarchical authority and allow human services to view the individual holistically?

B. *Funding.* Without both a strong campaign to inform the public on the costs of *not* educating in a complex society and an equally strong drive to improve the efficiency of educational expenditure, schooling systems as currently constituted may well collapse. What is the best mixture of educational funding sources: individual, local, state, national, international? Can new sources of funding be generated (e.g., international taxes on deep sea mining)? How should resources be allocated among the various educational agents? What should be the relationship between funding and policy control? How can the costs/benefits of education be delineated to society so that informed expenditure decisions can be made? What economies of scale in education are significant? What is the most likely means for improving educational productivity?

C. *External Controls.* A fundamental task for educators is to apprise diverse external groups of what an instructional system can and cannot do within given funding limits, then ask for collective and coordinated goals and support. How can a coherent picture of the accomplishments and limits of the educational system, and the tradeoffs between its duties and costs, be communicated to the public? What mix of governmental, community, family, and individual input should shape educational policy? Can these different groups be organized to coordinate demands and evaluation procedures, and what types of assessment can best be made from outside the profession?

Each school district must develop scenarios to aid their individual planning regarding issues that are relevant to them. Dwight Allen and Christopher Dede are editing a volume entitled *Creating Better Futures for Education,* which will address each of these twenty-three issues with solutions from across the nation.

CONCLUSION

Educational futurists suggest that to develop the needed planning perspective, school systems must emphasize problem detecting, problem perceiving, problem formulating, and common understanding. This perceptual base, along with the solid planning process outlined in this book, plus vision and wisdom, will go a long way toward creating a bright future for educational systems.

Planning involves making some futuristic projections about a desired state of affairs given expected conditions. These are followed up by some strategic plans on how this desired state can best be achieved and how it will be funded. Next the projections are refined, which provides greater detail and fits all of the pieces together into an operational plan. In this way, planning provides a commonly understood, structured process by which all interested parties can communicate; ultimately, this will facilitate reasonable agreement and commitment. It is a collaborative process in which interested parties come to a mutual agreement as to future expectations and commit themselves to specific levels of accomplishment. Planning is a way of managing that must go on continually—a way of managing that guides present actions through anticipatory learning regarding probable future consequences. Planning seeks consistency of purpose and flexibility of action.

A certain mystique has grown up around planning because it is so often viewed as some kind of arcane futuristic wisdom and exotic technique to which one cannot hope to aspire. This book encourages educational administrators to incorporate the full potential of planning into their repertoire of management techniques. The key demand for the twenty-first century is planned action:

> This is perhaps the most important knowledge that futuristics brings—that
> the future is not some predetermined drama in which human beings can only act
> out their assigned parts, but rather the sum total of all the individual choices,
> actions, and aspirations of people everywhere. (Richardson, 1980)

GUIDELINES FOR PLANNING

1. The essence of planning is to make present decisions with some idea of their impact on future performance. Planning requires educators to visualize how choices made today will influence tomorrow's educational practice. This requires administrators to look beyond the traditional firing line into our educational future.

2. Our educational future is dependent upon three factors: history, that is, past events and trends that have an influence on the future; chance, the occur-

rences we are unable to plan for; and human choice, the decisions we make that affect the future. Because of this last factor, educational planners are automatically educational futurists. The only choice they have is whether they recognize and prepare for this role.

3. Educational planners need to develop the skills that come through futures techniques. All futures techniques are based on a shift in the mode of thinking from conscious adaptation to conscious anticipation. Anticipating educational futures requires the planner to encourage desirable trends, to avert potentially catastrophic ones, and to invent or create new alternatives where none or only undesirable ones exist.

4. One of the better futures techniques is scenario writing. A scenario is a narrative that describes a possible series of events which might lead to some future state of affairs. By weaving realistic data into a narrative, the planner can often build a powerful and convincing case for the probability of occurrence of future events or a strong argument for the desirability of a suggested strategic and/or operational plan. In this way, scenarios add dramatic calls to action to the planning process.

5. Establishing educational futures requires planners to look to the future of schooling in some systematic fashion. This is best done by developing a checklist of aspects of education that need to be anticipated and addressed in our current planning efforts. The education section of the World Future Society and Old Dominion University has come up with the following six major areas of concern: responsibilities of different agents, content, process, improvements of the profession, interaction with the individual, and interface with society.

Appendix A

A Line-Item Budget with Object Detail for the Functional Category of Instruction

(12020) INSTRUCTION—REGULAR DAY SCHOOL

Code	Program—Activity
108	Compensation other professional personnel: Deputy Superintendent, Assistant Superintendent Instructional Services, three (3) Directors, four (4) Staff Assistants, two (2) Special Assistants for Program Development.
120	Forty-three (43) elementary principals, including White Oaks and Indian Lakes Elementary Schools.
121	Thirty-one (31) elementary assistant principals, including two (2) for White Oaks Elementary School.
125	Sixteen (16) secondary school principals, including Career Development Annex and Brandon Junior High School.
126	Forty-one (41) secondary school assistant principals.
135	Provides for 2,881 full-time teachers. This number includes 1,338 elementary, 574 junior high, 684 senior high, 89 resource and special programs, 184 for Special Education; the remainder to be assigned when enrollment and program needs have been determined.
150	Thirty-three (33) supervisory positions.
151	Eight (8) positions.
170	Provides funds for employment of substitute teachers at a rate of $21 per day.
178	Provides for the employment of instructors for homebound students.

VIRGINIA BEACH CITY SCHOOL BOARD
ESTIMATE OF EXPENDITURES
1980-81

(12020) INSTRUCTION—REGULAR DAY SCHOOL (17 bl)

Code Number	Item of Expenditure	Expenditures 1978-79	Budget 1979-80	Budget 1980-81
108	Comp. Other Professional Personnel	—0—	—0—	$ 298,055.00
120	Comp. Elementary Principals	$ 861,767.08	$ 962,875.00	1,033,398.00
121	Comp. Assistant Elementary Principals	386,928.72	463,880.00	545,284.00
125	Comp. Secondary Principals	333,116.64	377,032.00	443,222.00
126	Comp. Assistant Secondary Principals	703,744.64	749,410.00	834,636.00
135	Comp. Teachers	30,947,699.24	34,363,591.00	37,663,703.00
150	Comp. Supervisors	717,001.05	903,683.00	810,801.00
151	Comp. Visiting Teachers	150,026.52	150,095.00	149,425.00
170	Comp. Substitute Teachers	515,694.42	450,000.00	546,000.00
178	Comp. Other Instructional Staff	74,180.50	71,500.00	71,500.00
	TOTAL INSTRUCTION— REGULAR DAY SCHOOL	$34,690,158.81	$38,492,066.00	$42,396,024.00

(12022) OTHER INSTRUCTIONAL COSTS—REGULAR DAY SCHOOL

Code	Program—Activity
110	Provides for 210 secretarial and clerical positions, including nine (9) new positions for new schools. Also provides for part-time and substitute clerical services. These are persons assigned to individual schools.
111	Salary for teachers selected to participate in special in-service workshops.
136	Provides for 220 full-time and part-time positions including eleven (11) new positions for Special Education and other programs.
199	Salary of photographer and deliveryman assigned to Educational Media Center.
218	Costs for Instruction and General Administration central offices. The increase is due to combining several budget items of previous years for detailed accounting.
220	In-city travel for all eligible Instructional personnel, such as supervisor, vocational teachers and teachers of special programs.
221	Local share based on per pupil cost for the operation of Norfolk Cerebral Palsy Center and Regional Diagnostic Center.
222	Costs to meet state statutes for pupils who need instruction not offered in the local system.
236	Costs for teacher instructional conferences, workshops and college courses.
299	Costs related to accreditation, printing of records and forms, curriculum development, Student Leadership Workshop, student activities and forensics.
305	Instructional supplies for classrooms, laboratories, shops. Examples are: maps, globes, charts, models, collections, preserved specimens, consumables, and special instructional supplies needed by homebound students, kindergarten and Special Education students.
314	Required to maintain accreditation standards.
319	Funds allocated on a $2.00 per pupil rate to provide office supplies for the operation of the school and office supplies for the Instructional Department.
320	Estimated cost to provide textbooks to indigent pupils.

VIRGINIA BEACH CITY SCHOOL BOARD
ESTIMATE OF EXPENDITURES
1980-81

(12022) OTHER INSTRUCTIONAL COSTS—REGULAR DAY SCHOOL

Code Number	Item of Expenditure	Expenditures 1978-79	Budget 1979-80	Budget 1980-81
110	Comp. Clerical Services	$1,248,122.76	$1,398,384.00	$1,583,594.00
111	Comp. Teacher Workshop	75,338.50	110,000.00	140,000.00
136	Comp. Instructional Aides	745,553.34	856,921.00	978,000.00
199	Comp. Other Personnel	—0—	—0—	23,982.00
	TOTAL PERSONNEL SERVICES	$2,069,014.60	$2,365,305.00	$2,725,576.00
218	Postage, Phone	30,158.75	9,750.00	45,112.00
220	Travel Instructional Personnel	89,154.89	139,516.00	146,525.00
221	Tuition Paid Other Divisions	155,617.27	177,193.00	190,000.00
222	Scholarship Grants	296,822.07	500,000.00	800,000.00
236	Professional Improvement	220,394.35	247,030.00	289,955.00
299	Other Instructional Costs	313,102.90	483,574.00	400,845.00
305	Instructional Supplies	568,689.85	461,482.00	1,093,590.00
314	Library Books, Supplies, Periodicals	592,829.67	351,932.00	340,215.00

Code Number	Item of Expenditure	Expenditures 1978-79	Budget 1979-80	Budget 1980-81
319	Office Supplies	115,264.78	135,260.00	152,000.00
320	Textbooks Furnished Free	21,569.31	37,700.00	38,500.00
	TOTAL OTHER SERVICES	$2,403,603.84	$2,543,437.00	$3,496,742.00
	TOTAL OTHER INSTRUCTIONAL COSTS	$4,472,618.44	$4,908,742.00	$6,222,318.00

Used with permission of the Virginia Beach City School Board with personal acknowledgment to Dr. E. E. Brickell, Superintendent of Schools, and H. S. Abernathy, Director of the Budget.

Appendix B

Sample Questionnaires for Organizational Development Analysis

---

BLOCKAGE QUESTIONNAIRE

INSTRUCTIONS

Use the Blockage Questionnaire Answer Sheet (p. 270) to respond to the statements. (If other people are also going to complete the questionnaire, it is best to photocopy the answer sheet.)

Work through the statements, in numerical order, marking an "X" on the appropriate square of the grid if you think a statement about your organization is broadly true. If you think a statement is not broadly true, leave the square blank.

Do not spend a great deal of time considering each statement; a few seconds should be long enough.

Remember that the results will be worthwhile only if you are truthful.

1. The company seems to recruit as many dullards as efficient people.
2. Lines of responsibility are unclear.
3. No one seems to have a clear understanding of what causes the company's problems.
4. The organization is not short of skills, but they seem to be of the wrong kind.
5. It would help if people showed more interest in their jobs.
6. Good suggestions are not taken seriously.
7. Each department acts like a separate empire.
8. The managers believe that people come to work only for money.
9. There are no clear successors to key people.
10. People do not spend adequate time planning for the future.
11. There is much disagreement about wage rates.
12. It takes too long for people to reach an acceptable standard of performance.
13. Jobs are not clearly defined.
14. There is not enough delegation.
15. Managers do not seem to have enough time to take training seriously.
16. There are no real incentives to improve performance, so people do not bother.

17. Unconventional ideas never get a hearing.
18. Groups do not get together and work on common problems.
19. Managers believe that tighter supervision produces increased results.
20. The organization often needs to hire new managers from the outside.
21. One of my major problems is that I do not know what is expected of me.
22. People often leave for higher wages.
23. Applicants' qualifications seem to get lower each year.
24. The organization reflects outdated standards and needs to be brought up to date.
25. Only top management participates in important decisions.
26. Departments have different attitudes on training—some take it seriously, others do not.
27. Punishments seem to be handed out more frequently than rewards.
28. The organization would be more successful if more risks were taken.
29. People are not prepared to say what they really think.
30. Managers believe that people are basically lazy.
31. The company does not try to develop people for future positions.
32. Employees are told one thing and judged on another.
33. It seems that conformity brings the best reward.
34. Too many newcomers leave quickly.
35. Different parts of the organization pull in different directions.
36. The company does not really know what talent is available.
37. Skills are picked up rather than learned systematically.
38. People are exploited—they are not rewarded adequately for the large amount of effort they exert.
39. Frequently, innovation is not rewarded.
40. In this organization it is every man for himself when the pressure is applied.
41. Managers would like to revert to the days when discipline reigned supreme.
42. Management does not identify and develop those who are potential high achievers.
43. Personal objectives have little in common with the firm's aims.
44. The payment system prevents work from being organized in the best way.
45. Many employees are only barely efficient.
46. The chief executive has so much to do that it is impossible for him to keep in touch with everything.
47. The right information needed to make decisions is not readily available.
48. The managers had to learn the hard way and think others should do the same.

49. People in the organization do not really get a thorough explanation of how their performance is valued.
50. Competing organizations seem to have brighter ideas.
51. Each manager is responsible for his own department and does not welcome interference.
52. The only reason this firm exists is to make money for the shareholders.
53. People do not know what the firm has in mind for them in the future.
54. People are judged on personal characteristics rather than on their contributions.
55. On the whole, there is no adequate method of rewarding exceptional effort.
56. There is resentment because new people seem to get the better jobs.
57. Some departments have more people than their contribution justifies.
58. The organization operates on old ideas rather than on new ones.
59. Managers are not capable of training others.
60. If the chips were down, managers would not be fully prepared to extend themselves for the firm.
61. Once something becomes an established practice it is rarely challenged.
62. Meetings are not popular because they are generally unproductive.
63. Management does not care whether people are happy in their work.
64. Management succession and development cannot be planned; there are too many variables.
65. The organization's future plans are of low quality.
66. The organization does not pay enough to attract sufficiently competent people.
67. There is really not much talent around.
68. All too often, important things either do not get done or get done twice.
69. Labor turnover figures are not calculated.
70. Production could be increased if the right skills were available.
71. I do not feel supported in what I am trying to do.
72. This is a dynamic age and the company is not moving fast enough.
73. Lessons learned in one department do not get transferred to others.
74. The firm does not try to make jobs interesting and meaningful.
75. Many people are trained who later join competitors.
76. Objectives are expressed in vague terms.
77. People have to work long hours to make an adequate living wage.
78. People with little or no talent and experience are hired.
79. Some managers are overloaded while others have it easy.
80. Employees do not know how competitive the wages are because comparative figures are not available.
81. People are not encouraged to update their skills.

82. People do not get the opportunity to contribute and, as a result, do not feel committed.
83. People do not like to "rock the boat."
84. Competition inside the organization is so fierce that it becomes destructive.
85. Managers do not think that people are interested in the quality of their working lives.
86. The experience of senior managers is not wide enough.
87. Priorities are not clear.
88. People feel as though they work in a "second-class" organization.
89. When recruiting, the firm finds it difficult to sort out the wheat from the chaff.
90. There is no use talking about reorganization; attitudes are fixed.
91. Management-control information is not generated where it is needed.
92. Quality would be improved if the staff were more skilled.
93. The firm pays below par and people are dissatisfied.
94. Managers are not sufficiently responsive to changes in the external environment.
95. People could help each other more, but they do not seem to care.
96. Managers are not addressed by their first names.
97. Managers do not believe that management education has much to offer them.
98. Plans seem unreal.
99. The firm's total "benefits package" compares unfavorably with that of similar organizations.
100. The organization does not have many recognized recruitment practices; individual managers do what they think best.
101. Departments do not respect the work of other groups.
102. Management does not recognize the cost of a dissatisfied employee.
103. It is not surprising that newcomers sometimes receive a poor impression of the organization, considering the way they are treated in the first few days.
104. People would welcome more challenge in their jobs.
105. Problems are not faced openly and frankly.
106. Teams do not consciously take steps to improve the way they work together.
107. There is a lot of under-the-surface fighting between managers.
108. Managers are not open about the future prospects of their people.
109. Decisions are made now that should have been made months ago.
110. I, personally, feel underpaid.

ANSWER SHEET
- Follow the instructions given at the beginning of the questionnaire.
- In the grid below there are 110 squares, each numbered to correspond to a question. Mark an "X" through the square if you think a statement about your organization is broadly true. If you think a statement is not broadly true, leave the square blank. Fill in the top line first, working from left to right; then fill in the second line, etc. Be careful not to miss a question.

Answer Sheet

A	B	C	D	E	F	G	H	I	J	K
1	2	3	4	5	6	7	8	9	10	11
12	13	14	15	16	17	18	19	20	21	22
23	24	25	26	27	28	29	30	31	32	33
34	35	36	37	38	39	40	41	42	43	44
45	46	47	48	49	50	51	52	53	54	55
56	57	58	59	60	61	62	63	64	65	66
67	68	69	70	71	72	73	74	75	76	77
78	79	80	81	82	83	84	85	86	87	88
89	90	91	92	93	94	95	96	97	98	99
100	101	102	103	104	105	106	107	108	109	110
Totals										

- When you have considered all 110 statements, total the number of "X's" in each vertical column.

INTERPRETING THE RESULTS
. . . The following are eleven blockages to the effective use of people.

1. Inadequate Recruitment and Selection
2. Confused Organizational Structure

3. Inadequate Control
4. Poor Training
5. Low Motivation
6. Low Creativity
7. Poor Teamwork
8. Inappropriate Management Philosophy
9. Lack of Succession Planning and Management Development
10. Unclear Aims
11. Unfair Rewards

In the Blockage Questionnaire, you have been considering statements relating to these blockages. You can now arrive at your score for each blockage as it relates to your own organization.

Let us stress that the questionnaire has been designed only to give you an indication of where to start looking for the roots of your people problems. As such, it is not scientifically accurate, and the results will need further confirmation.

Write below the totals from each vertical column on the answer sheet.

Totals

A		Blockage 1. Inadequate Recruitment
B		Blockage 2. Confused Organizational Structure
C		Blockage 3. Inadequate Control
D		Blockage 4. Poor Training
E		Blockage 5. Low Motivation
F		Blockage 6. Low Creativity
G		Blockage 7. Poor Teamwork
H		Blockage 8. Inappropriate Management Philosophy
I		Blockage 9. Lack of Succession Planning and Management Development
J		Blockage 10. Unclear Aims
K		Blockage 11. Unfair Rewards

The blockages with the highest scores are those that need to be explored further.

. . . As you read through the blockages, you should decide whether the state of affairs in your organization confirms or rejects the results of the questionnaire. Start with the two or three blockages for which you had the highest scores. As you read the details of each particular blockage, it will help to ask the following question: "Is this a real problem for us?" And, if your answer is positive, "Do we want to invest energy in solving the problem?"

Source: Dave Francis and Mike Woodcock, People at Work: A Practical Guide to Organizational Change (San Diego, Calif.: University Associates, 1975), pp. 26-34. Used with permission.

TEAM-BUILDING CHECKLIST

When a unit of human beings joined together to reach goals finds that it no longer has the capability to really solve its problems well or reach its goals at an acceptable level, it may need to look for a way to reshape itself.

Team development is one process for revitalizing a social system. When the diagnosis that results from adequate data gathering indicates that the work unit no longer is functioning productively, a team-development program may be advisable as a strategy to improve effectiveness. . . .

The underlying reason for starting a team-development program is an important factor to consider. A program should not begin unless there is clear evidence that a lack of effective teamwork is the fundamental problem. If the problem is an intergroup issue, a technical difficulty, or an administrative foul-up, team building would not be an appropriate change strategy.

I. Problem identification: To what extent is there evidence of the following problems in your work unit?

	Low evidence		Some evidence		High evidence
1. Loss of production or work-unit output.	1	2	3	4	5
2. Grievances or complaints within the work unit.	1	2	3	4	5
3. Conflicts or hostility between unit members.	1	2	3	4	5
4. Confusion about assignments or unclear relationships between people.	1	2	3	4	5
5. Lack of clear goals, or low commitment to goals.	1	2	3	4	5
6. Apathy or general lack of interest or involvement of unit members.	1	2	3	4	5
7. Lack of innovation, risk taking, imagination, or taking initiative.	1	2	3	4	5
8. Ineffective staff meetings.	1	2	3	4	5
9. Problems in working with the boss.	1	2	3	4	5
10. Poor communications: people afraid to speak up, not listening to each other, or not talking together.	1	2	3	4	5

11. Lack of trust between boss and member or
    between members.   1   2   3   4   5

12. Decisions made that people do not understand
    or agree with.   1   2   3   4   5

13. People feel that good work is not recognized
    or rewarded.   1   2   3   4   5

14. People are not encouraged to work together in
    better team effort.   1   2   3   4   5

Scoring: Add up the score for the fourteen items. If your score is between 14-28, there is little evidence your unit needs team building. If your score is between 29-42, there is some evidence, but no immediate pressure, unless two or three items are very high. If your score is between 43-56, you should seriously think about planning the team-building program. If your score is over 56, then building should be a top priority item for your work unit.

II. Are you (or your manager) prepared to start a team-building program? Consider the following statements. To what extent do they apply to you or your department?

	Low		*Medium*		*High*

1. You are comfortable in sharing organizational
   leadership and decision making with subordinates
   and prefer to work in a participative atmosphere.   1   2   3   4   5

2. You see a high degree of interdependence as
   necessary among functions and workers in order
   to achieve your goals.   1   2   3   4   5

3. The external environment is highly variable
   and/or changing rapidly and you need the best
   thinking of all your staff to plan against these
   conditions.   1   2   3   4   5

4. You feel you need the input of your staff to plan
   major changes or develop new operating policies
   and procedures.   1   2   3   4   5

5. You feel that broad consultation among your people as a group in goals, decisions, and problems is
   necessary on a continuing basis.   1   2   3   4   5

6. Members of your management team are (or can
   become) compatible with each other and are able
   to create a collaborative rather than a competitive
   environment.   1   2   3   4   5

7. Members of your team are located close enough
   to meet together as needed.   1   2   3   4   5

	Low		*Medium*		*High*

8. You feel you need to rely on the ability and willingness of subordinates to resolve critical operating problems directly and in the best interest of the company or organization.   1   2   3   4   5

9. Formal communication channels are not sufficient for the timely exchange of essential information, views, and decisions among your team members.   1   2   3   4   5

10. Organization adaptation requires the use of such devices as project management, task forces, and/or ad hoc problem-solving groups to augment conventional organization structure.   1   2   3   4   5

11. You feel it is important to surface and deal with critical, albeit sensitive, issues that exist in your team.   1   2   3   4   5

12. You are prepared to look at your own role and performance with your team.   1   2   3   4   5

13. You feel there are operating or interpersonal problems that have remained unsolved too long and need the input from all group members.   1   2   3   4   5

14. You need an opportunity to meet with your people and set goals and develop commitment to these goals.   1   2   3   4   5

Scoring: If your total score is between 50-70, you are probably ready to go ahead with the team-building program. If your score is between 35-49, you should probably talk the situation over with your team and others to see what would need to be done to get ready for team building. If your score is between 14-34, you are probably not prepared at the present time to start team building.

III. Should you use an outside consultant to help in team building? (Circle appropriate response.)

1. Does the manager feel comfortable in trying out something new and different with the staff?   Yes   No   ?

2. Is the staff used to spending time in an outside location working on different issues of concern to the work unit?   Yes   No   ?

3. Will group members speak up and give honest data?   Yes   No   ?

4. Does your group generally work together without a lot of conflict or apathy?   Yes   No   ?

5. Are you reasonably sure that the boss is not a major source of difficulty?   Yes   No   ?

6. Is there a high commitment by the boss and unit members to achieve more effective team functioning?   Yes   No   ?

7. Is the personal style of the boss and his or her management philosophy consistent with a team approach?   Yes   No   ?

8. Do you feel you know enough about team building to begin a program without help?   Yes   No   ?

9. Would your staff feel confident enough to begin a team-building program without outside help?   Yes   No   ?

Scoring: If you have circled six or more "yes" responses, you probably do not need an outside consultant. If you have four or more "no" responses, you probably do need a consultant. If you have a mixture of "yes," "no," and "?" responses, you should probably invite in a consultant to talk over the situation and make a joint decision.

Source: William G. Dyer, *Team Building: Issues and Alternatives,* copyright © 1977, Addison-Wesley, Reading, Mass., pp. 36-40. Reprinted with permission.

LIKERT'S LEADERSHIP PROFILE

Likert's System 4 for Participative Management

Rensis Likert, former director of the University of Michigan's prestigious Institute for Social Research, has been called "the father of participative management." Participative management is generally defined as inviting people who will be affected by a decision to share in the decision-making process. They are given a real voice; they are not merely consulted.

Likert feels not only that better decisions result from such participation, but also that people are more highly committed to carrying them out. Involvement in a decision or an action that affects them gives employees a sense that they have some power over their destiny, that they can develop ways to realize their personal goals while working for organizational objectives.

Most working people today would probably say that such extensive participation in decision making represents an ideal, that few organizations are structured to permit such involvement by people at all levels. Nonetheless, Likert maintains that most managers view this participation system as the one in which they believe they can operate more effectively. To demonstrate this, managers in a number of organizations were asked to complete what has become known as the Likert instrument, which describes four different kinds of organizational systems. These managers were asked to review the characteristics of each of the four systems and indicate which represents "the *most* productive department, division, or organization you have known well."

These are the general descriptions of the four systems as Likert formulates them in his book *The Human Organization* (McGraw-Hill, 1967).

System 1 (Exploitative authoritative):

Management does not trust subordinates, who are not free to discuss matters with supervisors and whose opinions are not sought in solving problems. Motivation comes from fears, threats, occasional rewards. Communication comes down from higher management. The information that goes up from lower levels tends to be inaccurate. Goals are ordered from on high, where all decisions are made.

System 2 (Benevolent authoritative):

Management and employees exist in a master-servant relationship. There is some involvement of employees; more rewards than in System 1; slightly better communications up. This is a paternalistic organization, not unfriendly (as System 1 is) but not giving much latitude to employees to "do their thing."

System 3 (Consultative):

Management controls things, but employees are consulted before solutions to problems and decisions are made by management. Communication upward is better, but is still cautious. Unpleasant or unfavorable information is not offered freely. Employees feel they will perform some roles in preliminary stages of decision making and policy setting but that their contributions may not always be taken seriously.

System 4 (Participative group):

Management trusts employees, regards them as working willingly toward the achievement of organizational objectives. People are motivated by rewards, and are involved at all levels in discussing and deciding issues that are important to them. Communication is quite accurate and goes up, down, and across. Goals are not ordered from on high, but are established with the participation of the people who will have to work to achieve them.

Decisions are better because the people who know the most about the issues join together in deciding. This differs from an organization in which, say, marketing decisions are made not by marketers but chiefly by top executives trained in law and/or finance.

Likert discovered that the majority of managers surveyed consider a System 4 organization the most effective of the four, even though the leadership style it demands involves group decision making: Everyone in a work group affected by the outcome of a decision shares in making it.

The unusual organization structure proposed by Likert for System 4 is a series of linking pins. Each work group is linked to the rest of the organization by persons who are members of more than one group. For example, supervisors at the first level are members of groups headed by, say, second-level managers, who, in turn, represent their groups in those at a higher level. This structure is maintained all the way to the top, where the highest-echelon executives have their own group.

Communications throughout are more effective in transmitting what the organization needs to know in order to function, Likert says, because the flow of information is up, down, and across. Not only are the lines and the transmission more complete than in the hierarchy where the lines are mainly vertical, but the information is more accurate. Management trusts those down the line and does not feel that releasing data is tantamount to surrendering power and status. People on lower levels know how important it is to management to be apprised of what is going on, and they feel less hesitant to let management know *all* the facts, not just the agreeable ones.

BUILDING ON HAWTHORNE

Obviously, this kind of free-flowing information system would help most organizations. Likert suggests that motivation would be stronger because the rewards for which people strive are based on the quantity and quality of their participation. Morale would certainly be higher, because relationships would, as Likert says, be "supportive" and thus ego building. By interacting with others, the employee would experience the kind of exchange that, in the light of his or her background, values, and expectations, increases and maintains a sense of personal worth. Bosses and peers seek the employee's expertise, listen to him or her, and value the contribution.

System 4 demands considerable organizational flexibility and some surrender of what many would see as managerial prerogatives to groups of subordinates. Perhaps that explains why many organizations fall somewhere between Systems 2 and 3.

Students of management theory and organizational behavior will recognize the extent to which Rensis Likert has built upon the conclusions of the Hawthorne researchers of the 1920s and 1930s and parallels the more recent theories of Abraham Maslow and Douglas McGregor.

Source: Thomas L. Quick, "Likert's System 4 for Participative Management," p. 51. Reprinted with permission from the July 1978 issue of *Training*, The Magazine of Human Resources Development.

Likert's Leadership Development Questionnaire

Organizational variables	Exploitative authoritative (System 1)	Benevolent authoritative (System 2)	Consultative (System 3)	Participative group (System 4)	Item Number	
How much confidence and trust is shown in subordinates?	Virtually none	Some	Substantial amount	A great deal	1	*Leadership*
How free do they feel to talk to superiors about job?	Not very free	Somewhat free	Quite free	Very free	2	
How often are subordinate's ideas sought and used constructively?	Seldom	Sometimes	Often	Very frequently	3	
Is predominant use made of 1 fear, 2 threats, 3 punishment, 4 rewards, 5 involvement?	1, 2, 3, occasionally 4	4, some 3	4, some 3 and 5	5, 4, based on group	4	
Where is responsibility felt for achieving organization's goals?	Mostly at top	Top and middle	Fairly general	At all levels	5	*Motivation*
How much cooperative teamwork exists?	Very little	Relatively little	Moderate amount	Great deal	6	

7 What is the usual direction of information flow?	Downward	Mostly downward	Down and up	Down, up, and sideways
8 How is downward communication accepted?	With suspicion	Possibly with suspicion	With caution	With a receptive mind
9 How accurate is upward communication?	Usually inaccurate	Often inaccurate	Often accurate	Almost always accurate
10 How well do superiors know problems faced by subordinates?	Not very well	Rather well	Quite well	Very well
11 At what level are decisions made?	Mostly at top	Policy at top, some delegation	Broad policy at top, more delegation	Throughout but well integrated
12 Are subordinates involved in decisions related to their work?	Almost never	Occasionally consulted	Generally consulted	Fully involved
13 What does decision-making process contribute to motivation?	Not very much	Relatively little	Some contribution	Substantial contribution

Organizational variables	Exploitative authoritative (System 1)	Benevolent authoritative (System 2)	Consultative (System 3)	Participative group (System 4)	Item Number	
How are organizational goals established?	Orders issued	Others, some comments invited	After discussion, by orders	By group action (except in crisis)	14	Goals
How much covert resistance to goals is present?	Strong resistance	Moderate resistance	Some resistance at times	Little or none	15	
How concentrated are review and control functions?	Very highly at top	Quite highly at top	Moderate delegation to lower levels	Widely shared	16	Control
Is there an informal organization resisting the formal one?	Yes	Usually	Sometimes	No—same goals as formal	17	
What are cost, productivity, and other control data used for?	Policing, punishment	Reward and punishment	Reward, some self-guidance	Self-guidance problem-solving	18	

Source: Copyright © 1967 by McGraw-Hill, Inc. Used by permission of McGraw-Hill Book Company. Modified from Appendix II in *The Human Organization: Its Management and Value* by Rensis Likert. No further reproduction or distribution authorized.

Interpreting Likert's Leadership Profile

1. *Limitations of the profile.* It should be emphasized that the instrument is not a completely accurate measuring instrument. It is a forced-choice instrument and the language may not reflect the exact feelings of the respondent. It gives a general picture of the manager's style and its best use is as a basis for planning and not as a final judgment or evaluation of management performance.

2. *The deviant respondent.* Frequently the profile will show a clustering of responses in one style area but there will be a rather consistent checking of one or two persons in a different style area. The most usual reason for this is that there are one or two people who see the manager differently. It is possible that these people have a different relationship to the manager than do others; it is also possible that the manager deals differently with these people.

3. *Split cluster responses.* At times a profile will show a clustering of responses in two different style areas. This often indicates a situation where a manager deals differently with one group of associates than with the others. This sometimes represents an in-group (those who are close to the manager and are dealt with in a more personal way) and an out-group (those who are not exposed to the more personal aspects of the manager's style).

4. *Use data for planning—not guessing.* A common occurrence, after receiving his profile, is a manager's trying to guess which of his associates said what. This usually is a rather fruitless process. It can lead to bad guesses and inappropriate feelings and reactions. A more productive stance is for the manager to say to himself, "I am not as effective as I would like to be in this area. What do I need to start doing, or do differently, to get more effective results?"

This position allows the manager to use the profile data as a basis for planning. The end result of the profile is to arrive at a point where each manager with a profile has a clear, specific program for his own management improvement.

Source: Adapted from William G. Dyer, "Management Profiling: A Disparity Model for Developing Motivation for Change," in W. W. Burke (ed.), *Current Issues and Strategies in Organizational Development* (New York: Human Sciences Press, 1977), pp. 437-438.

TEAM DEVELOPMENT SCALE

1. To what extent do I feel a real part of the team?

1	2	3	4	5
Completely a part all the time	A part most of the time	On the edge, sometimes in, sometimes out	Generally outside, except for one or two short periods	On the outside, not really a part of the team

2. How safe is it in this team to be at ease, relaxed, and myself?

1	2	3	4	5
I feel perfectly safe to be myself, they won't hold mistakes against me.	I feel most people would accept me if I were completely myself, but there are some I am not sure about.	Generally, you have to be careful what you say or do in this team.	I am quite fearful about being completely myself in this team.	A person would be a fool to be himself in this team.

3. To what extent do I feel "under wraps," that is, have private thoughts, unspoken reservations, or unexpressed feelings and opinions that I have not felt comfortable bringing out into the open?

1	2	3	4	5
Almost completely under wraps.	Under wraps many times.	Slightly more free and expressive than under wraps.	Quite free and expressive much of the time.	Almost completely free and expressive.

4. How effective are we, in our team, in getting out and using the ideas, opinions, and information of all team members in making decisions?

1	2	3	4	5
We don't really encourage everyone to share their ideas, opinions, and information with the team in making decisions.	Only the ideas, opinions, and information of a few members are really known and used in making decisions.	Sometimes we hear the views of most members before making decisions and sometimes we disregard most members.	A few are sometimes hesitant about sharing their opinions, but we generally have good participation in making decisions.	Everyone feels his or her ideas, opinions, and information are given a fair hearing before decisions are made.

5. To what extent are the goals the team is working toward understood and to what extent do they have meaning for you?

1	2	3	4	5
I feel extremely good about the goals of our team.	I feel fairly good, but some things are not too clear or meaningful.	A few things we are doing are clear and meaningful.	Much of the activity is not clear or meaningful to me.	I really do not understand or feel involved in the goals of the team.

6. How well does the team work at its tasks?

1	2	3	4	5
Coasts, loafs, makes no progress.	Makes a little progress, most members loaf.	Progress is slow, spurts of effective work.	Above average in progress and pace of work.	Works well, achieves definite progress.

7. Our planning and the way we operate as a team is largely influenced by:

1	2	3	4	5
One or two team members.	A clique.	Shifts from one person or clique to another.	Shared by most of the members, some left out.	Shared by all members of the team.

284

8. What is the level of responsibility for work in our team?

1	2	3	4	5
Each person assumes personal responsibility for getting work done.	A majority of the members assume responsibility for getting work done.	About half assume responsibility, about half do not.	Only a few assume responsibility for getting work done.	Nobody (except perhaps one) really assumes responsibility for getting work done.

9. How are differences or conflicts handled in our team?

1	2	3	4	5
Differences or conflicts are denied, suppressed, or avoided at all cost.	Differences or conflicts are recognized, but remain unresolved mostly.	Differences or conflicts are recognized and some attempts are made to work them through by some members, often outside the team meetings.	Differences and conflicts are recognized and some attempts are made to deal with them in our team.	Differences and conflicts are recognized and the team usually is working them through satisfactorily.

10. How do people relate to the team leader, chairman, or "boss"?

1	2	3	4	5
The leader dominates the team and people are often fearful or passive.	The leader tends to control the team, although people generally agree with the leader's direction.	There is some give and take between the leader and the team members.	Team members relate easily to the leader and usually are able to influence leader decisions.	Team members respect the leader, but they work together as a unified team with everyone participating and no one dominant.

11. What suggestions do you have for improving our team functioning?

Source: William G. Dyer, *Team Building: Issues and Alternatives,* copyright ©1977, Addison-Wesley, Reading. Mass.. pp. 68-70. Reprinted with permission.

LEAD QUESTIONNAIRE

This is a survey of your attitudes toward different methods of leadership. In each of the sixty items below there are two statements of things a leader can do or ways he can act. For each item, mark your answer sheet either (1) or (2) for the statement that *you* feel is the *more important* way for him to behave. If you feel that both alternatives are unimportant for a leader, choose the statement you think is *more* important.

There are no right or wrong answers; we are interested only in your opinions. Work rapidly; your first impressions are usually best.

It is more important for a leader:

1. (1) To assign workers to specific tasks.
   (2) To allow workers to do the job the way they want to, as long as they accomplish the objectives.
2. (1) To treat all workers equally and according to the rules.
   (2) To be aware of the feelings of his workers.
3. (1) To be accepted by his workers.
   (2) To point out the rules and policies in situations where complaints arise.
4. (1) To be an authority in the type of work the group does.
   (2) To explain the reasons for changes.
5. (1) To call the group together to discuss work.
   (2) To work right alongside the workers.
6. (1) To make decisions independently of the group.
   (2) To be a real part of his work group.
7. (1) To pitch right in with the workers.
   (2) To plan the work.
8. (1) To authorize his workers to exercise a high degree of authority and responsibility in making decisions.
   (2) To supervise his workers closely.
9. (1) To maintain an open, informal relationship with his workers.
   (2) To have a well-regulated department.
10. (1) To be the most technically skilled member of the work group.
    (2) To meet with the workers to consider proposed changes.
11. (1) To teach his workers new things.
    (2) To attempt to vary his job only slightly from the jobs of his workers.
12. (1) To spend over half his time in supervisory activities, such as planning.
    (2) To make prompt, firm decisions.
13. (1) To have a complete knowledge of the technical aspects of his job.
    (2) To attempt to place workers in jobs they deserve whenever possible.
14. (1) To take an interest in the worker as a person.
    (2) To maintain definite standards of performance.
15. (1) To explain each worker's duties and responsibilities to him.
    (2) To spend some of his time helping get the work done.

16. (1) To allow his workers to do their work the way they think is best.
    (2) To rule with a firm hand.
17. (1) To speak with unquestioned authority.
    (2) To get along well with his workers.
18. (1) To decide in detail how the work shall be done by the workers.
    (2) To let workers make decisions in areas where they feel competent to do so.
19. (1) To spend considerable time in planning.
    (2) To be respected as a man of superior technical skill in the field.
20. (1) To be proud of the work record of his group.
    (2) To create friendly competition among his workers.
21. (1) To have the loyalty of his workers.
    (2) To maintain definite standards of performance.
22. (1) To work hard at all times.
    (2) To schedule the work to be done.
23. (1) To put the group's welfare above any individual's welfare.
    (2) To organize the work individually rather than by groups whenever possible.
24. (1) To be an authority in the type of work the group does.
    (2) To tell poor workers when their work isn't measuring up to what it should be.
25. (1) To let the workers set their own pace, as long as they finish the job on time.
    (2) To divide the work load into separate and clearly defined job duties for each worker.
26. (1) To urge his group to meet together to set group goals.
    (2) To prefer workers who work well alone.
27. (1) To perform the same functions as the workers whenever possible.
    (2) To plan the work.
28. (1) To prefer workers who do not need much supervision.
    (2) To give exact, detailed instructions for each job.
29. (1) To stand up for his workers when they make a mistake.
    (2) To submit his reports on time.
30. (1) To call the group together to discuss the work.
    (2) To attempt to vary his job only slightly from the jobs of the workers.
31. (1) To be respected as a man of superior technical skill in the field.
    (2) To spend over half his time in supervisory activities, such as planning.
32. (1) To be the most technically skilled member of the work group.
    (2) To explain the reasons for changes.
33. (1) To let his workers know how well they are doing their jobs.
    (2) To spend some of his time helping to complete the work.
34. (1) To make prompt, firm decisions.
    (2) To spend considerable time in planning.
35. (1) To make decisions independently of the group.
    (2) To urge his men to work together.
36. (1) To pass along to his workers information from higher management.
    (2) To help complete the work.

37. (1) To be respected as a man of superior technical skill in the field.
    (2) To schedule the work to be done.
38. (1) To foster his workers' pride in their work group's accomplishments.
    (2) To discourage talking between workers on the job.
39. (1) To reward the good worker.
    (2) To encourage the workers to assist each other on the job.
40. (1) To feel he belongs in the group.
    (2) To accomplish tasks on the basis of his own initiative.
41. (1) To teach his workers new things.
    (2) To help get the work done.
42. (1) To do the important jobs himself.
    (2) To allow workers to take their rest periods when they wish.
43. (1) To organize new practices and procedures.
    (2) To encourage one worker in the group to speak up for the rest.
44. (1) To set up all projects himself.
    (2) To let his workers make all routine daily decisions.
45. (1) To be trained in the basic technical knowledge needed in his department.
    (2) To keep his workers happy.
46. (1) To meet with the workers to consider proposed changes.
    (2) To pitch right in with the workers.
47. (1) To discourage strong friendships from forming within the group.
    (2) To foster his workers' pride in their work group's accomplishments.
48. (1) To complete the work on time.
    (2) To be friendly toward his workers.
49. (1) To realize that a worker knows when he is a slacker without being told.
    (2) To explain each worker's duties and responsibilities to him.
50. (1) To set an example by working hard.
    (2) To spend considerable time in planning.
51. (1) To encourage his workers to check with him frequently about the work.
    (2) To let the workers decide how to do each task.
52. (1) To allow workers to make decisions concerning their work.
    (2) To prefer workers who are agreeable and willing to follow rules.
53. (1) To be an authority in the type of work the group does.
    (2) To pass along to his workers information from higher management.
54. (1) To encourage his workers to discover the best job methods by experience.
    (2) To meet with his workers to consider proposed changes.
55. (1) To explain each worker's duties and responsibilities to him.
    (2) To pitch right in with the workers.
56. (1) To plan his day's activities in considerable detail.
    (2) To perform the same functions as the workers whenever possible.
57. (1) To create friendly competition among his workers.
    (2) To urge his group to meet together to set group goals.
58. (1) To organize new practices and procedures.
    (2) To make his job similar to the jobs of his workers.

59. (1) To be skilled in training.
    (2) To set an example by working hard.
60. (1) To work right alongside his workers.
    (2) To try out new ideas in the work group.

SCORING INSTRUCTIONS

To score the LEAD questionnaire, the five steps below should be followed.

1. Set up a scoring template, using an answer sheet. For the E scale, punch out response one on the answer sheet for questions 3, 8, 9, 14, 16, 20, 21, 23, 25, 26, 28, 29, 38, 40, and 52. Punch out response two on the answer sheet for questions 1, 2, 6, 13, 17, 18, 35, 39, 42, 44, 45, 47, 48, 51, and 57.
2. Make a similar scoring template for the D scale. Using a second answer sheet punch out response one for questions 5, 11, 12, 15, 19, 30, 33, 36, 41, 43, 46, 55, 56, 58, and 59. Punch out response two for questions 4, 7, 10, 22, 24, 27, 31, 32, 34, 37, 49, 50, 53, 54, and 60.
3. Lay the E-scale template over the completed answer sheet, and count the number of X's showing. Write this number on the top line of the box on the answer sheet (E score).
4. Do the same with the D template, writing the number of X's showing on the second line of the box (D score). Add the numbers, and write the total under the other two scores (Total score).
5. Transfer the scores to the LEAD Questionnaire Result form (p. 290). Hand back the forms to the individuals who completed them. Have them mark an X on the E and D scale lines to show where their scores fall. You can also give them a *group* average based on the group with whom they were administered the questionnaire.

This questionnaire has been used successfully in management seminars in an aircraft plant and in an insurance company. The managers completed the questionnaire, and in the following session, a presentation was made on the University of Michigan study. The managers were then given their own results, and this served to bring the discussion of leadership methods to a meaningful personal basis. The group averages also served to facilitate discussions of the leadership climate in each organization. By using the LEAD Questionnaire Results form, groups can compare their results with results from the aircraft and insurance managers. In both groups, managers from several levels were included. The number of managers in the aircraft company sample was 26, and in the insurance sample the data are based on 151 managers.

ANSWER SHEET

1. _____	13. _____	30. _____	47. _____
2. _____	14. _____	31. _____	48. _____
3. _____	15. _____	32. _____	49. _____
4. _____	16. _____	33. _____	50. _____
5. _____	17. _____	34. _____	51. _____
6. _____	18. _____	35. _____	52. _____
7. _____	19. _____	36. _____	53. _____
8. _____	20. _____	37. _____	54. _____
9. _____	21. _____	38. _____	55. _____
10. _____	22. _____	39. _____	56. _____
11. _____	23. _____	40. _____	57. _____
12. _____	24. _____	41. _____	58. _____
	25. _____	42. _____	59. _____
	26. _____	43. _____	60. _____
	27. _____	44. _____	E _____
	28. _____	45. _____	D _____
	29. _____	46. _____	Totals _____

NORMS AND INTERPRETATION SUGGESTIONS

The result form on the next page provides you with some information to better help you understand the meaning of your scores on the Employee-orientation scale, the Differentiation scale, and the total LEAD score.

If you score *high* on the Employee-orientation scale, it means you tend to agree with the following leadership techniques: being oriented toward your employees as people rather than as a means of production, delegating authority and responsibility for decisions to the employees where possible, and creating an atmosphere of teamwork and cooperation. If you score *low* on this scale, you agree with these methods: assigning all tasks to employees rather than let-

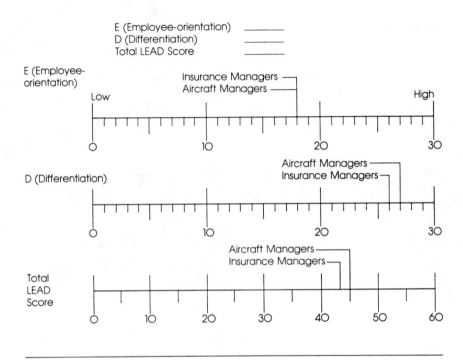

ting them help decide assignments, making most decisions yourself, supervising closely, stressing rules and work standards, and focusing on individual performance and competition rather than cooperation.

On the Differentiation scale, a *high* score means that you tend to agree that a leader's activities are different from those of his employees, and include: explaining and discussing changes in the work, planning and scheduling the overall group's activity, training employees, explaining their job responsibilities, giving them feedback on good and poor performance, and trying out new ideas. If you score *low* on this scale, you tend to feel that a leader should stress: doing the same kind of activities as the employees, being a high individual performer himself, being an outstanding technical expert in his field, and working hard personally to get a big share of the work done.

The Total Score is just used for summarizing your position on the two separate scales. If you are high on both scales, you will be high on the Total Score, and vice versa. A high score on one scale and a low one on the other will result in a middle score on the Total.

Research studies conducted by the Survey Research Center at the University of Michigan showed that a sample of successful supervisors in several different industries used methods which are reflected on the high end of these scales, and less successful supervisors used methods reflected on the low end of the scales. You can compare your scores on the Results Sheet with those of a group of 26 aircraft company managers, and a group of 151 insurance company managers, from another study. These are group averages, and you should remember that individual scores may vary according to the situation; for example, a supervisor who only supervises one employee may not feel strongly about the importance of Differentiation, since he may have to do a great deal of the actual work himself. It should also be remembered that this questionnaire measures attitudes toward leadership methods, not whether an individual is actually using the methods.

Source: Russell Dore, in J. W. Pheiffer and John E. Jones (eds.), *The 1973 Annual Handbook for Group Facilitators* (San Diego, Calif.: University Associates, 1973), pp. 95-102. Used with permission.

GROUP EXPECTATION SURVEY

The Group Expectation Survey enables group members to discover what kinds of information they want from others in the group and what kinds of information they are willing to give to others. Protocols collected from a wide range of groups show . . . that group members usually say they are receptive to interpersonal feedback but perceive others as unwilling to give it, and . . . that group members usually say they would report their feelings candidly but doubt that others would do so. . . . The survey is useful not only for measuring and reporting data for discussion but for showing group members that attempts at openness might be safer than they had formerly believed.

DIRECTIONS

Before each of the items below, put a number from the rating scale that best expresses your opinion.

RATING SCALE

5 = all members of this group
4 = all members except one or two
3 = a slight majority of the members of this group
2 = slightly less than half the members of this group
1 = one or two members of this group
0 = none of this group

How many members of this group do you expect will candidly report the following information during future group sessions?

_____ 1. When he does not understand something you said?
_____ 2. When he likes something you said or did?
_____ 3. When he disagrees with something you said?
_____ 4. When he thinks you have changed the subject or become irrelevant?
_____ 5. When he feels impatient or irritated with something you said or did?
_____ 6. When he feels hurt—rejected, embarrassed, or put down—by something you said or did?

To how many members will *you* candidly report the following information in future group sessions?

_____ 7. When you do not understand something he said?
_____ 8. When you like something he said or did?
_____ 9. When you disagree with something he said?
_____ 10. When you think he has changed the subject or become irrelevant?
_____ 11. When you feel impatient or irritated with something he said or did?
_____ 12. When you feel hurt—rejected, embarrassed, or put down—by something he said or did?

In your opinion, how many in this group are interested in knowing . . .

_____ 13. When you do not understand something he said?
_____ 14. When you like something he said or did?
_____ 15. When you disagree with something he said?
_____ 16. When you think he has changed the subject or become irrelevant?
_____ 17. When you feel impatient or irritated with something he said or did?
_____ 18. When you feel hurt—rejected, embarrassed, or put down—by something he said or did?

From how many members of this group are *you* interested in knowing . . .

_____ 19. When he does not understand something you said?
_____ 20. When he likes something you said or did?
_____ 21. When he disagrees with something you said?
_____ 22. When he thinks you have changed the subject or become irrelevant?
_____ 23. When he feels impatient or irritated with something you said or did?
_____ 24. When he feels hurt—rejected, embarrassed, or put down—by something you said or did?

Source: John Wallen, in R. A. Schmuck, P. J. Runkel, J. H. Arends, and R. I. Arends, *The Second Handbook of Organization Development in Schools* (Palo Alto, Calif.: Mayfield Publishing, 1977), pp. 240-242. Copyright © 1977 by The Center for Educational Policy and Management.

TALLYING LEADERSHIP FUNCTIONS IN GROUPS

While observing each member of the group, make a tally mark every time you hear or see behavior (verbal or nonverbal) that approximates in your estimation the following categories:

CATEGORIES	1	2	3	4	5	.	.	.	N
1. Setting goals									
2. Proposing problems									
3. Asking for information									
4. Giving information									
5. Proposing solutions									
6. Asking clarification									
7. Giving clarification									
8. Testing for consensus									
9. Supporting									
10. Asking about group progress									
11. Summarizing									
12. Evaluating									

Source: R. A. Schmuck, P. J. Runkel, J. H. Arends, and R. I. Arends, *The Second Handbook of Organization Development in Schools* (Palo Alto, Calif.: Mayfield Publishing, 1977), p. 244. Copyright © 1977 by The Center for Educational Policy and Management.

MEASURING ORGANIZATIONAL CLIMATE

In determining a school's readiness to deal with conflict it is important to know whether the organizational climate supports open confrontation of differences, receiving and giving feedback, and generally fosters an atmosphere of two-way interaction and discussion. The following questionnaire helps to ascertain informal norms or an organizational climate that can help or hinder staff members in uncovering and working with conflict.

1. Suppose Teacher X feels hurt and "put down" by something another teacher has said to him. In Teacher X's place, would most of the teachers you know in your school be likely to . . .

1a.   . . . tell the other teacher that they felt hurt and put down?

     (   ) Yes, I think most would.
     (   ) Maybe about half would.
     (   ) No, most would *not*.
     (   ) I don't know.

1b.   . . . tell their friends that the other teacher is hard to get along with?

     (   ) Yes, I think most would do this.
     (   ) Maybe about half would do this.
     (   ) No, most would *not*.
     (   ) I don't know.

2.   Suppose Teacher X strongly disagrees with something B says at a staff meeting. In Teacher X's place, would most of the teachers you know in your school . . .

2a.   . . . seek out B to discuss the disagreement?

     (   ) Yes, I think most would do this.
     (   ) Maybe about half would do this.
     (   ) No, most would *not*.
     (   ) I don't know.

2b.   . . . keep it to themselves and say nothing about it?

     (   ) Yes, I think most would do this.
     (   ) Maybe about half would do this.
     (   ) No, most would *not*.
     (   ) I don't know.

3.   Suppose Teacher X were present when two others got into a hot argument about how the school is run. Suppose Teacher X tried to help each one understand the view of the other. How would you feel about the behavior of Teacher X?

     (   ) I would approve strongly.
     (   ) I would approve mildly or some.
     (   ) I wouldn't care one way or the other.
     (   ) I would disapprove mildly or some.
     (   ) I would disapprove strongly.

4.   Suppose Teacher X were present when two others got into a hot argument about how the school is run. And suppose Teacher X tried to get them to quiet down and stop arguing. How would you feel about the behavior of Teacher X?

     (   ) I would approve strongly.
     (   ) I would approve mildly or some.
     (   ) I wouldn't care one way or the other.
     (   ) I would disapprove mildly or some.
     (   ) I would disapprove strongly.

5. Suppose you are in a committee meeting with Teacher X and the other members begin to describe their personal feelings about what goes on in the school. Teacher X quickly suggests that the committee get back to the topic and keep the discussion objective and impersonal. How would you feel toward Teacher X?

    (   ) I would approve strongly.
    (   ) I would approve mildly or some.
    (   ) I wouldn't care one way or the other.
    (   ) I would disapprove mildly or some.
    (   ) I would disapprove strongly.

6. Suppose you are in a committee meeting with Teacher X and the other members begin to describe their personal feelings about what goes on in the school. Teacher X listens to them but does not describe his own feelings. How would you feel toward Teacher X?

    (   ) I would approve strongly.
    (   ) I would approve mildly or some.
    (   ) I wouldn't care one way or the other.
    (   ) I would disapprove mildly or some.
    (   ) I would disapprove strongly.

Source: R. A. Schmuck, P. J. Runkel, J. H. Arends, and R. I. Arends, *The Second Handbook of Organization Development in Schools* (Palo Alto, Calif.: Mayfield Publishing, 1977), pp. 206-208. Copyright © 1977 by The Center for Educational Policy and Management.

ACCURACY ABOUT COMMUNICATION

■ Perhaps there are some people in your organization with whom you talk rather frequently about matters important to you. Please think of people with whom you talk *seriously about things important to you,* inside or outside formal meetings, *once a week or more* on the average. Write their names below:

1. _____   4. _____

2. _____   5. _____

3. _____   6. _____

■ Now look back at the above question. Each name is numbered. Listed below are all the pairs that can be made among six numbers. Perhaps you know whether some of the six people talk to *each other* about matters important to them. Please look at each pair of numbers below, look back to see what names they represent, and *circle* the pair of numbers if you have good reason to believe that the two people talk to each other *once a week or more* about matters important to them.

```
1-2   1-3   1-4   1-5   1-6
      2-3   2-4   2-5   2-6
            3-4   3-5   3-6
                  4-5   4-6
                        5-6
```

Runkel, Wyant, and Bell scored each respondent on the accuracy with which he or she indicated pairs who did or did not talk once a week, then examined the questionnaires of all the persons mentioned by any one respondent. If both members of a pair named each other in answer to the first item, and if the first respondent said that those two talked in answer to the second question, then that respondent was credited with one point of accuracy. If only one of a pair, or neither, named the other in answer to the first item and the first respondent refrained from circling that pair, (i.e., did *not* say they talked at least once a week), he or she was again credited with one point of accuracy. Points were cumulated for each respondent, and the mean was calculated for each school.

Source: R. A. Schmuck, R. J. Runkel, J. H. Arends, and R. I. Arends, *The Second Handbook of Organization Development in Schools* (Palo Alto, Calif.: Mayfield Publishing, 1977), p. 58. Copyright © 1977 by The Center for Educational Policy and Management.

Bibliography

Ackoff, R. L. 1970. *A Concept of Corporate Planning.* New York: Wiley Interscience.

_____. 1974. *Redesigning the Future.* New York: John Wiley & Sons.

_____. 1978. *The Art of Problem Solving.* New York: John Wiley & Sons.

Adams, James L. 1979. *Conceptual Blockbusting.* New York: W. W. Norton.

Adelson, Marvin. 1967. "Planning Education for the Future: Comments on a Pilot Study." *American Behavioral Scientist,* March.

Alderfer, C. P. 1974. "Change Process in Organizations." In M. D. Dunnette (ed.), *Handbook of Industrial and Organizational Psychology.* Chicago: Rand McNally.

Alioto, Robert F., and Jungherr, J. A. 1971. *Operational PPBS for Education.* New York: Harper and Row.

Allain, Violet A. 1979. *Futuristics and Education.* Bloomington, Ind.: Phi Delta Kappa Educational Foundation, Fastback.

Allen, Dwight. 1978. Paper presented at a Phi Delta Kappa meeting, October 12, Old Dominion University, Norfolk, Va.

Allen, Dwight, and Dede, C. 1979. *An Invitation to Participate in Creating Better Futures for Education.* Norfolk, Va.: Old Dominion University Press.

_____. 1981a. "Education in the 21st Century: Scenarios as a Tool for Strategic Planning." *Phi Delta Kappan,* January.

_____. 1981b. *Creating Better Futures for Education.* Pending publication.

Allison, Graham T. 1969. "Conceptual Models and the Cuban Missile Crisis." *The American Political Science Review*, Vol. 63, No. 3, September, pp. 689-718.

_____. 1971. *The Essence of Decision*. Boston: Little, Brown.

Anderson, D. P. 1970. "Clarifying and Setting Objectives on an Intermediate School District's Objective: Utilizing the Delphi Technique." Paper presented at the American Educational Research Association's symposium on Exploring the Potential of the Delphi Technique, Minneapolis, Minn., March 4.

Ansoff, H. Igor. 1965. *Corporate Strategy*. New York: McGraw-Hill.

Ansoff, H. Igor, et al. 1976. *Strategic Planning to Strategic Management*. New York: John Wiley & Sons.

Anthony, Robert N. 1965. *Planning and Control Systems: A Framework for Analysis*. Boston: Harvard University Press.

Argyris, Chris. 1964. *Integrating the Individual and the Organization*. New York: John Wiley & Sons.

_____. 1967. "On the Future of Laboratory Education." *The Journal of Applied Behavioral Science*, Vol. 3, No. 2.

_____. 1973. "Personality and Organization Theory Revisited." *Administrative Science Quarterly*, Vol. 18, June, pp. 141-167.

_____. 1978. *Management and Organizational Development: The Path from XA to YB*. New York: McGraw-Hill.

Argyris, Chris, and Schon, Donald. 1978. *Organizational Learning: A Theory of Action Perspective*. Reading, Mass.: Addison-Wesley.

Armstrong, Robert D. 1968. *A Systematic Approach to Developing and Writing Behavioral Objectives*. Tucson, Ariz.: Educational Innovation Press.

Ayers, R. U. 1969. *Technological Forecasting and Long-Range Planning*. New York: McGraw-Hill.

Baldridge, J. V., and Tierney, M. L. 1979. *New Approaches to Management*. San Francisco, Calif.: Jossey-Bass.

Banfield, Edward G. 1952. "Ends and Means in Planning." *International Social Science Journal*, Vol. 11, No. 3.

Batten, J. D. 1966. *Beyond Management by Objectives*. New York: American Management Association.

_____. 1980. *Beyond Management by Objectives: A Management Classic*. New York: American Management Association.

Beckhard, R. 1967. "The Confrontation Meeting." *Harvard Business Review*, Vol. 45, No. 2, pp. 149-155.

Beer, Michael. 1976. "The Technology of Organizational Development." In M. D. Dunnette (ed.), *Handbook of Industrial and Organizational Psychology*. Chicago: Rand McNally.

Bell, Terrel H. 1974. *A Performance Accountability System for School Administrators*. Englewood Cliffs, N.J.: Parker Publishing.

Bennis, Warren G. 1969. *Organizational Development: Its Nature, Origins, and Prospects*. Reading, Mass.: Addison-Wesley.

Benson, Charles S. 1968. *The Economics of Public Education*. Boston: Houghton Mifflin.

Blake, Robert R., and Mouton, Jane S. 1964. *The Managerial Grid*. Houston, Tex.: Gulf Publishing.

_____. 1968. *Corporate Excellence Diagnosis*. Austin, Tex.: Scientific Methods.

_____. 1978a. *The New Managerial Grid*. Houston, Tex.: Gulf Publishing.

_____. 1978b. "Should You Teach There's Only One Best Way To Manage?" *Training*, April.

Bolan, Richard S. 1969. "Community Decision Behavior: The Culture of Planning." *Journal of the American Institute of Planners*, Vol. 35, September.

Bork, Richard. 1976. "Computer Usage in Instruction." Paper presented at the Association of Educational Data Systems Convention, Virginia Beach, Va.

Bosch, Alfred M. 1976. "Graphics and Teaching Conversations with the XDS SIGMA 7." Presentation at the 1976 Association for Educational Data Systems Convention, Virginia Beach, Va.

Botkin, James W.; Elmandjra, Mahdi; and Malitya, Mircea. 1979. *No Limits to Learning: A Report to the Club of Rome*. Oxford, England: Pergamon Press.

Bowers, David G. 1977. "Organizational Development: Promises, Performance, Possibilities." *Organizational Dynamics*, Winter, pp. 50-62.

Brady, Rodney H. 1976. "MBO Goes to Work in the Public Sector." *Harvard Business Review*, March-April, pp. 65-74.

Braybrooke, D., and Lindblom, C. E. 1963. *A Strategy of Decision: Policy Evaluation as a Social Process*. New York: Free Press.

Bridges, Edwin M. 1964. "Teacher Participation in Decision-Making." *Administrator's Notebook*, May.

Brieve, Fred G.; Johnston, A. P.; and Young, Ken M. 1973. *Educational Planning*. Worthington, Ohio: Charles A. Jones Publishing.

Bruweningsen, A. F. 1976. "SCAT—A Process of Alternatives." *Management Accounting*, November.

Buchanan, P. C. 1969. "Laboratory Training and Organizational Development." *Administrative Science Quarterly*, Spring, pp. 446-480.

Bukoski, William J., and Korotkin, Arthur L. 1976. "Computing Activities in Secondary Education." *Educational Technology*, January.

Burkhart, Robert C. 1974. *The Assessment Revolution: New Viewpoints for Teacher Education*. Denver: National Symposium on Evaluation in Education.

Bushnell, David S. 1969. "A Systems Approach to Curriculum Change in Secondary Education." *Educational Technology*, Vol. 90, September.

Callahan, Raymond E. 1962. *Education and the Cult of Efficiency*. Chicago: University of Chicago Press.

Campbell, J. P. 1968. "Individual versus Group Problem Solving in an Industrial Sample." *Journal of Applied Psychology*, Vol. 52, No. 3, pp. 206-210.

Campbell, R. F.; Cunningham, L. L.; Nystrand, R. O.; and Usdan, M. D. 1980. *The Organization and Control of American Schools*. Columbus, Ohio: Charles E. Merrill.

Carroll, Stephen J., and Tosi, Henry L. 1973. *Management by Objectives: Applications and Research*. New York: Macmillan.

Chase, Francis S. 1952. "The Teacher and Policy Making." *Administrator's Notebook*, May.

Chase, P. A. 1968. "A Survey Feedback Approach to Organization Development." In Proceedings of the Executive Study Conference. Princeton: Educational Testing Service, November.

Chin, Robert, and Benne, Kenneth D. 1976. "General Strategies for Effective Changes in Human Systems." In Warren G. Bennis et al., *The Planning of Change*. New York: Holt, Rinehart and Winston.

Churchman, W. C. 1968. *The Systems Approach*. New York: Penguin Books.

Coch, Lester, and French, John R. P. 1948. "Overcoming Resistance to Change." *Human Relations*, Vol. 1, pp. 512-32.

Cohen, J., and March, J. G. 1977. "Almost Random Careers: The Wisconsin Superintendency, 1940-1972." *Administrative Science Quarterly*, Vol. 22, September.

Commonn, Cortlandt, and Nadler, David A. 1976. "Fit Control Systems to Your Managerial Style." *Harvard Business Review*, January-February, pp. 65-72.

Cook, Desmond L. 1966. *Program Evaluation and Review Technique: Applications in Education*. Washington, D.C.: U.S. Government Printing Office.

Crockett, William J. 1970. "Team Building: One Approach to Organizational Development." *The Journal of Applied Behavioral Science*, Vol. 6, No. 3.

Cunningham, William G. 1975. "The Impact of Student-Teacher Pairings on Teacher Effectiveness." *American Educational Research Journal*, Vol. 12, No. 2, Spring.

_____. 1976. "A Model for Matching Teacher Style with Learning Style in Elementary Schools." *Journal of Instructional Psychology*, Vol. 3, No. 2, Spring.

_____. 1977. "The Need for Dialogue between Educational Technologists." *Phi Delta Kappan*, February.

_____. 1981. "Reducing Purple Hearts." *The AASA Professor*, Vol. 4, No. 2, Fall.

Cyert, Richard M., and March, James G. 1965. *A Behavior Theory of the Firm*. Englewood Cliffs, N.J.: Prentice-Hall.

Cyphert, F. R., and Gant, W. L. 1971. "The Delphi Technique: A Case Study." *Phi Delta Kappan*, January.

Dalkey, N. C., and Helmer, O. 1963. "An Experimental Application of the Delphi Method to the Use of Experts." *Management Science*, Vol. 9.

Delbecq, Andre L. 1968. "The World Within the 'Span of Control': Managerial Behavior in Groups of Varied Size." *Business Horizon*, August.

Delbecq, Andre L.; Van De Ven, A. H.; and Gustafson, D. H. 1975. *Group Techniques for Program Planning*. Dallas, Tex.: Scott, Foresman.

Devons, Ely. 1968. "The Problem of Co-ordination in Aircraft Production." In E. Devons (ed.), *Planning and Economic Management*. Manchester: Manchester University Press.

Dowling, William. 1978. *Effective Management and the Behavioral Sciences*. New York: American Management Association.

Doyle, Michael. 1976. *How to Make Meetings Work*. New York: Wyden Books.

Dror, Yehezkel. 1968. *Public Policymaking Reexamined*. Scranton, Penn.: Chandley Publishing.

Drucker, Peter F. 1954. *The Practice of Management*. New York: Harper & Row.

_____. 1959. "Long-Range Planning." *Management Science*, April.

_____. 1974. *Management: Tasks, Responsibilities, and Practices*. New York: Harper & Row.

_____. 1976. "What Results Should You Expect? A User's Guide to MBO." *Public Administration Review*, January/February, pp. 12-19.

Dunn, Piere. 1975. *School Leadership Digest: Management by Objectives*. Arlington, Va.: National Association of Elementary School Principals.

Dyer, William G. 1977. *Team Building: Issues and Alternatives*. Reading, Mass.: Addison-Wesley.

Earley, Leigh C., and Rutledge, Pearl B. 1980. "A Nine-Step Problem-Solving Model." In John E. Jones and William J. Pfeiffers (eds.), *1980 Annual Handbook of Group Facilitators*. San Diego, Calif.: University Associates.

Etzioni, Amitai. 1967. "Mixed Scanning: A Third Approach to Decision-Making." *Public Administration Review*. Vol. 27, December, pp. 385-392.

Faludi, Andreas (ed.). 1973a. *A Reader in Planning Theory*. Oxford, England: Pergamon Press.

_____. 1973b. *Planning Theory*. Oxford, England: Pergamon Press.

Fayol, Henri. 1949. "Administration industrielle et generale." In Constance Starrs (ed.), *General and Industrial Management*. London: Sir Isaac Pitman & Sons.

Feiffer, John P. 1968. *New Look at Education*. New York: Odyssey Press.

Fiedler, Fred E. 1967. *A Theory of Leadership Effectiveness*. New York: McGraw-Hill.

Fleishman, Edwin A. 1973. "Twenty Years of Consideration and Structure." In E. Fleishman and J. Hunt (eds.), *Current Developments in the Study of Leadership*. Carbondale, Ill.: Southern Illinois University Press.

Fleishman, Edwin A. (ed.). 1961. *Studies in Personnel and Industrial Psychology*. Homewood, Ill.: Dorsey.

Foley, W. J., and Harr, G. G. 1972. *Management Information System Project*. Iowa City: Iowa Center for Research in School Administration, University of Iowa, ED. 072 528.

Ford, Robert N. 1973. "Job Enrichment Lessons From AT&T." *Harvard Business Review*, January-February, pp. 96-106.

Frame, Robert M., and Luthans, Fred. 1978. "Merging Personnel and O.D.: Not-So-Odd Couple." *Personnel*, January-February, Vol. 54, No. 1, pp. 12-22.

French, J. R., and Lewin, K. 1950. "Changing Group Productivity." In J. G. Miller (ed.), *Experiments in Social Process: A Symposium on Social Psychology*. New York: McGraw-Hill.

French, Wendell L., and Bell, Cecil H. 1973. *Organizational Development*. Englewood Cliffs, N.J.: Prentice-Hall.

_____. 1978. *Organization Development: Behavioral Science Interventions for Organizational Improvement*. Englewood Cliffs, N.J.: Prentice-Hall.

Friedlander, Frank. 1976. "OD Reaches Adolescence: An Exploration of Its Underlying Values." *The Journal of Applied Behavioral Science*, March.

Friedlander, Frank, and Brown, P. 1974. "Organizational Development." *Annual Review of Psychology*, pp. 313-341.

Friedman, John. 1967. "A Conceptual Model for the Analysis of Planning Behavior." *Administrative Science Quarterly*, Vol. 12, No. 2, September.

Friedman, John, and Hudson, Barclay. 1974. "Knowledge and Action: A Guide to Planning Theory." *Journal of American Institute of Planning*, January, pp. 2-16.

Fromm, Erich. 1972. "Humanistic Planning." *Journal of the American Institute of Planning*, March, pp. 67-71.

Fullan, Michael; Miles, Matthew B.; and Taylor, Gib. 1980. "Organization Development in Schools: The State of the Art." *Review of Educational Research*, Vol. 50, No. 1, Spring, pp. 121-183.

Gant, W. L. 1969. *Consensus on Elementary School Goals*. Unpublished Ph.D. dissertation, University of Virginia.

_____. 1970. "Application of Delphi." Unpublished studies of the application of the Delphi technique.

Gibson, Cyrus F., and Nolan, Richard L. 1974. "Managing the Four Stages of EDP Growth." *Harvard Business Review*, Vol. 52, No. 1, January-Februrary, pp. 77-88.

Glaser, Edward M. 1976. *Productivity Gains Through Worklife Improvements*. New York: Harcourt Brace Jovanovich.

Goodlad, John I. 1966. *Computers and Information Systems in Education*. New York: Harcourt Brace Jovanovich.

Gordon, T. J., and Helmer, O. 1964. *Report on Long-Range Forecasting Study*. Rand Paper P-2982, September.

Granger, Charles H. 1972. "The Hierarchy of Objectives." *Harvard Business Review*, Vol. 50, No. 3, May-June, pp. 63-74.

Guba, Egon, and Stufflebeam, Daniel L. 1970. *Evaluation: The Process of Stimulating, Aiding, and Abetting Insightful Action*. Bloomington, Ind.: Indiana University Press, Monograph.

Gulick, Luther, and Urwich, L. 1937. *Papers on the Science of Administration*. New York: Institute of Public Administration.

Hackman, J. Richard. 1975. "Is Job Enrichment Just a Fad?" *Harvard Business Review*, September-October, pp. 129-138.

Hackman, J. Richard, and Aldham, G. 1975. "Development of the Job Diagnostic Survey." *Journal of Applied Psychology*, pp. 159-170.

Halprin, Andrew W. 1971. *Theory and Research in Administration*. New York: Macmillan.

Hammond, John S. III, 1974. "Do's and Don'ts of Computer Models for Planning." *Harvard Business Review*, March-April.

Handy, H. W., and Hussain, K. M. 1969. *Network Analysis for Educational Management*. Englewood Cliffs, N.J.: Prentice-Hall.

Hansen, Thomas; Klassen, Daniel; and Lindsay, James. 1978. *A Study of the Availability, Use and Impact of Computers in the Administration of Schools and School Districts*. St. Paul, Minn.: Minnesota Educational Computing Consortium.

Harris, Britton. 1972. Foreward in Ira M. Robinson (ed.), *Decision-Making in Urban Planning*. Beverly Hills, Calif.: Sage Publications.

Hartley, Harry J. 1968. *Educational Planning-Programming-Budgeting*. Englewood Cliffs, N.J.: Prentice-Hall.

Harvey, Donald F., and Brown, Donald R. 1976. *An Experiential Approach to Organizational Development*. Englewood Cliffs, N.J.: Prentice-Hall.

Havens, Harry S. 1976. "MBO and Program Evaluation, or Whatever Happened to PPBS?" *Public Administration Review*, Vol. 36, No. 1, January/February.

Helmer, Olaf. 1966a. "The Rise of the Delphi Technique in Problems of Educational Innovation." *Rand Corporation P-3499*, December.

_____. 1966b. *Social Technology*. New York: Basic Books.

_____. 1975. Foreward in H. A. Linstone and M. Turoff (eds.), *The Delphi Method*. Reading, Mass.: Addison-Wesley.

Hemphill, J. K. 1956. *Group Dimensions: A Manual for Their Measurement*. Bureau of Business Research Monograph, No. 87, Columbus, Ohio: Ohio State University.

Hemphill, J. K., and Coons, A. E. 1957. "Development of the Leader Behavior Description Questionnaire." In Ralph M. Stogdill and Alvin E. Coons (eds.), *Leader Behavior: Its Description and Measurement*. Columbus, Ohio: The Ohio State University Press.

Henry, Harold W. 1977. "Formal Planning in Major U.S. Corporations." *Long Range Planning*, Vol. 10, October.

Hersey, Paul, and Blanchard, Kenneth H. 1977. *Management of Organizational Behavior: Utilizing Human Resources*. Englewood Cliffs, N.J.: Prentice-Hall.

Herzberg, F. 1966. *Work and the Nature of Man*. Cleveland: World Publishing.

Heyle, Carl. 1973. *Encyclopedia of Management*. New York: Van Nostrand Reinhold.

Hostrop, Richard W. 1975. *Managing Education for Results*. Palm Springs, Calif.: ETC Publications.

Howard, Eugene R., and Brainard, Edward A. 1975. *How School Administrators Make Things Happen*. West Nyack, N.Y.: Parker Publishing.

Hoyle, John R. 1980a. "The Great Issue: Your Future." Delivered at Lee's Summit Public Schools, Lee's Summit, New Jersey, April 3.

_____. 1980b. "Administering Learning Environments in the 21st Century." Delivered at the University Council for Educational Administration Anticipatory Leadership Conference at Montclair Public Schools, Montclair, New Jersey, May 9.

Humble, John W. (ed.) 1970. *Management by Objectives in Action*. London: McGraw-Hill.

Immegart, Glen L., and Pilecki, Francis J. 1971. *An Introduction to Systems for the Educational Administrator*. Reading, Mass.: Addison-Wesley.

Institute for Advanced Technology. 1968. *Data Communication Systems*. Minneapolis, Minn.: Control Data Corporation.

Instructional Objectives Exchange. 1972. *IOX Taxonomies of Objectives: Books 1-16*. A Project of the Center for the Study of Evaluation. Los Angeles: UCLA University Press.

James, H. Thomas. 1964. "Modernizing State and Local Financing of Education." In J. H. Thomas (ed.), *A Financial Program for Today's Schools*. Washington, D.C.: National Education Association Committee on Educational Finance.

Jamison, Dean; Suppes, Patrick; and Wells, Stuart. 1975. "The Effectiveness of Alternative Instructional Media: A Survey." *Review of Educational Research*, Vol. 44, No. 1, Winter, pp. 1-67.

Janis, Irving. 1975. *Decision Making: A Psychological Analysis of Conflict, Choice, and Comment*. New York: Free Press.

Janson, Robert. 1974. "Job Design for Quality." *The Personnel Administrator*, October.

Jay, Antony. 1976. "How to Run a Meeting." *Harvard Business Review*, March-April, pp. 43-57.

Johns, Roe L., and Morphet, Edgar L. 1969. *The Economics and Financing of Education*. Englewood Cliffs, N.J.: Prentice-Hall.

Johnston, A. P. 1977. "Stabilizing the Policy Environment." *Educational Administration Quarterly*, Vol. 13, No. 3, Fall, pp. 70-86.

Kastens, Merritt L. 1976. *Long-Range Planning for Your Business: An Operating Manual*. New York: American Management Association.

Kent, R. 1979. "Tasks Planning in Educational Organizations." In R. E. Herriott and Neil Gross (eds.), *The Dynamics of Planned Educational Change*. Berkeley, Calif.: McCutchan Publishing.

Kirp, David L. 1980. "Do Judges Run The Schools?" An interview for the Institute for Research on Educational Finance and Governance, *IFG Policy Notes*, Vol. 1, No. 2.

Kirst, Michael W. 1975. "The Rise and Fall of PPBS in California." *Phi Delta Kappan*, April.

Knezevich, Stephen J. 1960. *Business Management of Local School Systems*. New York: Harper & Row.

_____. 1973a. *Administrative Technology and the School Executive*. Washington, D.C.: American Association of School Administrators.

_____. 1973b. *Management by Objectives and Results*. Washington, D.C.: American Association of School Administrators.

_____. 1973c. *Program Budgeting*. Berkeley, Calif.: McCutchan Publishing.

_____. 1975. *Administration of Public Education*. New York: Harper & Row.

Krathwohl, David R., et al. 1964. *Taxonomy of Educational Objectives: The Classification of Educational Goals, Handbook II*. New York: David McKay.

Larson, R. 1980. "Effectiveness of the PDK Planning Model Among a Select Group of School Districts." Research Report. Burlington: University of Vermont (mimeographed).

Lawler, E. E. 1969. "Job Design and Employee Motivation." *Personnel Psychology*, pp. 426-435.

Lawrence, L. C., and Smith, P. C. 1955. "Group Decision and Employee Participation." *Journal of Applied Psychology*, No. 39, pp. 334-337.

Lawrence, Paul, and Lorsch, Jay. 1961. *Organization and Environment: Managing Differentiation and Integration*. Boston: Harvard University Graduate School of Business Administration, Division of Research.

LeBreton, Preston P., and Henning, Dale A. 1961. *Planning Theory*. Englewood Cliffs, N.J.: Prentice-Hall.

Lehne, Richard. 1978. *The Quest for Justice: The Politics of School Finance Reform*. New York: Longham.

LeLoup, Lance T., and Moreland, William B. 1978. "Agency Strategies and Executive Review: The Hidden Politics of Budgeting." *Public Administration Review*, May/June.

Levine, J., and Butler, J. 1951. "Lecture Versus Group Discussion in Changing Behavior." *Journal of Applied Psychology*, No. 42, pp. 331-334.

Levinson, Harry. 1970. "Management by Whose Objective." *Harvard Business Review*, July-August, pp. 125-135.

_____. 1972. *Organizational Diagnosis*. Cambridge, Mass.: Harvard University Press.

Lewin, Kurt. 1947. "Frontiers in Group Dynamics." *Human Relations*, Vol. 1, pp. 5-41.

_____. 1948. "The Consequences of an Authoritarian and Democratic Leadership." In Gertrude Weiss (ed.), *Resolving Social Conflicts*. New York: Harper & Row.

Lewin, Kurt; Lippitt, R.; and White, R. K. 1939. "Patterns of Aggressive Behavior in Experimentally Created Social Climates." *Journal of Social Psychology*, No. 10, pp. 271-299.

Lewis, James Jr. 1976. *Appraising Teacher Performance*. West Nyack, N.Y.: Parker Publishing.

Likert, Rensis. 1961. *New Patterns of Management*. New York: McGraw-Hill.

_____. 1967. *The Human Organization: Its Management and Value*. New York: McGraw-Hill.

_____. 1973. "Human Resource Accounting: Building and Assessing Productive Organizations." *Personnel*, May-June.

Lindblom, Charles E. 1959. "The Science of 'Muddling Through.'" *Public Administration Review*, Vol. 19, Spring, pp. 79-88.

_____. 1965. *The Intelligence of Democracy*. New York: Free Press.

Linstone, H. A., and Turoff, Murray (eds.). 1975. *The Delphi Method: Techniques and Applications*. Reading, Mass.: Addison-Wesley.

Luce, R. D., and Raiffa, H. 1957. *Games and Decisions*. New York: Wiley.

Luthans, Fred. 1973. *Organizational Behavior*. New York: McGraw-Hill.

Luthans, Fred, and Reif, William E. 1978. "Job Enrichment: Long on Theory, Short on Practice." *Organizational Dynamics*, Fall, pp. 30-49.

Lyden, Fremont J. 1975. "Control, Management, and Planning: An Empirical Examination." *Public Administration Review*, November/December.

McCaffery, Jerry. 1976. "MBO and the Federal Budgetary Process." *Public Administration Review*, January/February, pp. 33-39.

McCann, Davis B. 1970. "Getting Ready." *Datamation*, August 1.

McConnell, J. Douglas. 1971. "Strategic Planning: One Workable Approach." *Long Range Planning*, December.

McGee, Victor E. 1971. *Principles of Statistics: Traditional & Bayesian*. New York: Appleton-Century-Crofts.

McGill, Michael E. 1977. *Organizational Development for Operating Managers*. New York: American Management Association.

McGregor, Douglas. 1957. "An Uneasy Look at Performance Appraisal." *Harvard Business Review*, May-June.

_____. 1960. *The Human Side of Enterprise*. New York: McGraw-Hill.

MacKenzie, R. Alec. 1975. *New Time Management Methods for You and Your Staff*. Chicago, Ill.: Dartnell Publishing.

McLaughlin, Milbrey W. 1975. *Evaluation and Reform: The Elementary and Secondary Education Act of 1965, Title I*. Cambridge, Mass.: Ballinger Publishing.

McLoone, Eugene P.; Lupco, Gabrielle C.; and Mushkin, Selma J. 1967. *Long-Range Revenue Estimation*. Washington, D.C.: George Washington University Press.

McNamarra, John. 1975. "Computer Applications in Wisconsin's IGE System." Paper presented at the 1975 Association for Educational Data Systems Conference, Virginia Beach, Va.

Magee, John F. 1964. "Decision Trees for Decision Making." *Harvard Business Review*, July-August, pp. 126-128.

Mager, Robert F. 1962. *Preparing Instructional Objectives*. Palo Alto, Calif.: Fearon.

Maier, N. R. F. 1950. "The Quality of Group Decisions as Influenced by the Discussion Leader." *Human Relations*, Vol. 3, pp. 155-174.

Mann, Dale. 1975a. *Policy Decision-Making in Education*. New York: Teachers College Press.

_____. 1975b. "What Peculiarities in Educational Administration Make It Difficult to Profess: An Essay." *The Journal of Educational Administration*, Vol. 13, No. 1, May.

_____. 1978. "Democracy, School Administration, and Semi-Decision Making." A paper presented at the Conference on Power Structures in American Society, San Francisco, November 11.

Mann, Floyd C., and Baumgartel, H. 1954. "Absences and Employee Attitudes in an Electric Power Company." *Institute for Social Research*, Ann Arbor: University of Michigan.

Mann, Floyd C., and Likert, Rensis. 1952. "The Need for Research on the Communication of Research Results." *Human Organization*, Winter, pp. 15-19.

March, James G. 1962. "Some Substantive and Methodological Developments in the Theory of Organizational Decision Making." In Austin Ramey (ed.), *Essays on the Behavioral Study of Politics*. Urbana: University of Illinois Press.

_____. 1973. "Model Bias in Social Action." *Review of Educational Research*, Vol. 42, No. 3.

_____. 1978. "American Public School Administration: A Short Analysis." *School Review*, February.

March, James G., and Simon, Herbert A. 1959. *Organization*. New York: John Wiley & Sons.

Margerison, Charles. 1974. *Managerial Problem Solving*. New York: McGraw-Hill.

Martin, Michael. 1972. *Concepts of Science Education*. Glenview, Ill.: Scott, Foresman.

Meglina, J. D., and Mobley, B. M. 1977. "Minimizing Risk in Organizational Development Interventions." *Personnel*, November/December.

Meyer, John W. 1979. "The Impact of the Centralization of Educational Funding and Control on State and Local Organizational Governance." Institute for Research on Educational Finance and Governance, Stanford: School of Education, IFG Policy Paper.

Meyerson, Martin, and Banfield, Edward C. 1955. *Politics, Planning and the Public Interest*. New York: The Free Press.

Miller, Donald R. 1969. "Policy Formulation and Policy Implementation in an Education System." In Richard H. K. Kraft (ed.), *Strategies of Educational Planning*. Tallahassee: Educational Systems Development Center, Florida State University.

Mills, Ted. 1978. *Quality of Work Life: What's In a Name?* A Report of General Motors Executive Conference on Quality of Work Life. Detroit, Mich.: General Motors Corporation.

Morphet, Edgar L.; Jesser, David L.; and Ludha, Arthur P. 1972. *Planning and Providing for Excellence in Education*. New York: Citation Press.

Morphet, Edgar L.; Johns, Roe L.; and Reller, Theodore L. 1977. *Educational Organization and Administration.* Englewood Cliffs, N.J.: Prentice-Hall.

Morrisey, George I. 1970. *Management by Objectives and Results.* Reading, Mass.: Addison-Wesley.

Mushkin, Selma J. 1969. *PPB Pilot Project Report (S-S-S).* Washington, D.C.: George Washington University Press.

Naylor, T. H. 1977. "Integrating Models into the Planning Process." *Long Range Planning,* Vol. 10, December.

Neddin, W. G. 1973. *Effective Management by Objectives.* New York: McGraw-Hill.

Nelson, Theodor H. 1970. "No More Teachers' Dirty Looks." *Computer Decisions,* September.

Nevstadt, Richard. 1979. "Regulatory Reform, The President's Program." A policy paper prepared for the White House Conference on State and Local Regulatory Reform.

Newland, Chester A. 1974. "Management by Objectives in the Federal Government." *The Bureaucrat.* Vol. 2, No. 4, Winter, pp. 351-361.

_____. 1976. "Policy/Program Objectives and Federal Management: The Search for Government Effectiveness." *Public Administration Review.* January/February.

Newman, Joseph W. 1971. *Management Applications of Decision Theory.* New York: Harper & Row.

Newman, William H.; Summer, Charles E.; and Warren, E. Kirby. 1967. *The Process of Management.* Englewood Cliffs, N.J.: Prentice-Hall.

Norris, William C. 1977. "Via Technology to a New Era in Education." *Phi Delta Kappan,* February, pp. 454-460.

Odiorne, George S. 1965. *Management by Objectives.* Belmont, Calif.: Pitman Learning.

_____. 1976. "MBO in State Government." *Public Administration Review,* January/February, pp. 28-33.

Oppenheimer, Robert. 1955. "Prospects in the Arts and Sciences." *Perspective U.S.A.,* Vol. 2, Spring.

Owens, Robert G. 1970. *Organizational Behavior in Schools.* Englewood Cliffs, N.J.: Prentice-Hall.

Panush, Louis. 1974. "One Day in the Life of an Urban High School Principal." *Phi Delta Kappan,* September, pp. 46-49.

Patten, T. H., and Vail, P. B. 1976. "Organizational Development." In Robert L. Craig, *Training and Development Handbook.* New York: McGraw-Hill.

PLATO. 1977. *Control Data PLATO Services.* Minneapolis, Minn.; Control Data Corporation.

Pogrow, Stanley. 1977. "Implications of a Resource Approach to Data Management for Improving Intergovernmental Data Flow in Education." Paper presented at the 1977 American Educational Research Association Convention, New York.

Porras, Jerry I., and Olafberg, Per. 1978. "Evaluation Methodology in Organizational Development: An Analysis and Critique." *The Journal of Applied Behavioral Science,* Vol. 14, No. 2.

Prather, Hugh. 1976. "Corollary Regard Perceptions as Universals." In Robert Maidment (ed.), *Robert's Rules of Disorder.* Gretna, La.: Pelican Publishing.

Project Administrative Techniques. Undated. Dayton, Ohio: National Cash Register Educational Publication.

Pyhrr, Peter A. 1970. "Zero-Base Budgeting." *Harvard Business Review,* November/December.

_____. 1973. *Zero-Base Budgeting: A Practical Management Tool for Evaluating Expenses.* New York: John Wiley & Sons.

_____. 1976. "Zero-Base Budgeting: Where to Use It and How to Begin." *S.A.M. Advanced Management Journal,* Summer.

Raia, Anthony P. 1974. *Managing by Objectives.* Glenview, Ill.: Scott, Foresman.

Raiffa, Howard. 1970. *Decision-tree Analysis: Introductory Lectures on Choices Under Uncertainty.* Reading, Mass.: Addison-Wesley.

Rathe, Alex W. (ed.). 1961. *Gantt on Management.* Cambridge, Mass.: American Management Association.

Reddin, W. J. 1971. *Effective Management by Objective.* New York: McGraw-Hill.

Rice, Charlton, R. 1975. "Conferencing Via Computer: Cost Efficient Communication for the Era of Forced Choice." In Harold Linstone and Murray Turoff (eds.), *The Delphi Method.* Reading, Mass.: Addison-Wesley.

Rice, George H. 1977. "Structural Limits on Organizational Development." *Human Resource Management,* Winter, pp. 9-13.

Richardson, Jerey. 1980. *World Future Society Catalog.* Washington, D.C.: World Future Society.

Robinson, I. M. (ed.). 1972. *Decision Making in Urban Planning.* Beverly Hills, Calif.: Sage Publications.

Roe, William H. 1961. *School Business Management.* New York: McGraw-Hill.

Rose, Richard. 1977. "Implementation and Evaporation: The Record for MBO." *Public Administration Review,* January/February.

Rosenthal, Lawrence E. 1976. "A Model for Implementation of Computer Based Instructional Systems." *Educational Technology,* February.

Sadler, Philip G. 1970. "Leadership Style, Confidence in Management, and Job Satisfaction." *The Journal of Applied Behavioral Science,* Vol. 6, No. 1.

Schein, Edgar H. 1969. *Process Consultation: Its Role in Organizational Development.* Reading, Mass.: Addison-Wesley.

Schick, Allen. 1973. "A Death in Bureaucracy: The Demise of Federal PPB." *Public Administration Review,* Vol. 33, March/April.

Schlaifer, Robert. 1959. *Probability and Statistics for Business Decisions.* New York: McGraw-Hill.

_____. 1969. *Anaysis of Decisions Under Uncertainty.* New York: McGraw-Hill.

Schleh, Edward C. 1961. Management by Results. New York: McGraw-Hill.

Schmuck, Richard, A.; Runkel, Philip J.; Arends, Jane H.; and Arends, Richard I. 1977. *The Second Handbook of Organizational Development in Schools.* Palo Alto, Calif.: Mayfield Publishing.

Schoderbek, Peter P., and Digman, Lester A. 1967. "Third Generation PERT/LOB." *Harvard Business Review,* September-October.

Scurrah, Martin J., and Shani, Moske. 1974. "PPBS versus Conventional Budgeting in a Simulated Education Organization." *Educational Administration Quarterly*, Vol. 10, Autumn.

Seif, Elliott. 1979. "Planning Schooling for the Future." In Kierstead, Fred; Bowman, Jim; and Dede, Christopher (eds.), *Educational Futures: Sourcebook I.* Washington, D.C.: World Future Society.

Sergiovanni, Thomas J., and Carver, Fred. 1975. *The New School Executive: A Theory of Administration.* New York: Dodd, Mead.

Shane, Harold G. 1973. "The Educational Significance of the Future." *Phi Delta Kappan.*

Sharkansky, Ira. 1968. "Agency Requests, Gubernatorial Support, and Budget Success in State Legislatures." *American Political Science Review*, Vol. 62, December.

Shaw, Malcolm E. 1977. "The Behavioral Sciences: A New Image." *Training and Development Journal*, February.

Simon, Herbert A. 1960. *The New Science of Management Decision.* New York: Harper & Row.

_____. 1976. *Administrative Behavior.* 4th ed. New York: Macmillan (1st ed., 1947).

Stein, Barry A., and Kanter, Rosabeth M. 1980. "Building Parallel Organizations: Creating Mechanisms for Permanent Quality of Work Life." *The Journal of Applied Behavioral Science*, Vol. 16, No. 3.

Steiner, George A. 1970. "Purpose of the Corporate Planner." *Harvard Business Review*, September-October, pp. 133-139.

Steiss, Alan W. 1972. *Public Budgeting and Management.* Lexington, Mass.: Lexington Books.

Steles, B., and Bernardi, R. 1969. *Writing and Using Behavioral Objectives.* Tuscaloosa, Ala.: University Supply Store, University of Alabama.

Stoner, Floyd E. 1978. "Federal Auditors as Regulators, The Case of Title I of ESEA." In Judith V. May and Aaron Wildavsky (eds.), *The Policy Cycle.* Beverly Hills, Calif.: Sage Publications.

Stonich, Paul J. 1977. *Zero-Base Planning and Budgeting.* Homewood, Ill.: Dow Jones-Irwin.

Stuart, Darwin G. 1976. *Systematic Urban Planning.* New York: Praeger.

Strauss, George. 1973. "Organizational Development: Credits and Debits." *Organizational Dynamics*, Winter, pp. 2-19.

_____. 1976. "Organizational Development." In Robert Dubin (ed.), *Handbook of Work Organization and Society.* Chicago, Ill.: Rand McNally.

Suver, James D., and Brown, Ray L. 1977. "Where Does Zero-Base Budgeting Work?" *Harvard Business Review*, November/December.

Tannebaum, Robert, and Schmidt, Warren H. 1958. "How to Choose a Leadership Pattern." *Harvard Business Review*, March-April.

_____. 1973. "How to Choose a Leadership Pattern—A Perspective." *Harvard Business Review*, May-June.

Taylor, Frederick W. 1923. *The Principles of Scientific Management.* New York: Harper & Row.

Tersine, Richard G., and Riggs, Walter E. 1976. "The Delphi Technique: A Long Range Planning Tool." *Business Horizons*, Vol. 19, No. 2, April.

Thomas, Kenneth. 1976. "Conflict and Conflict Management." In Marvin D. Dunnette (ed.), *Handbook of Industrial and Organizational Psychology.* Chicago: Rand McNally.

Toffler, Alvin. 1970. *Future Shock.* New York: Random House.

Trump, J. L. 1979. *Secondary School Curriculum Improvements: Meeting Challenges of the Times.* Boston: Allyn and Bacon.

Turoff, Murray. 1970. "The Decision of a Policy Delphi." *Technological Forecasting and Social Change,* No. 2, pp. 149-171.

Twente, John W. 1922. *Budgetary Procedure for a Local School System.* Montpelier, Vt.: Capital City Press.

Urwich, Lyndall R. 1952. *Notes on the Theory of Organization.* New York: American Management Association.

U.S. Department of Health, Education and Welfare. 1973. *Financial Accounting for Local and State School Systems,* 3rd ed. Washington, D.C.: Government Printing Office (1st ed., 1957; 2nd ed., 1966).

U.S. Government Accounting Office. 1979. "Protecting the Public from Unnecessary Federal Paperwork: Does the Control Process Work?" Washington, D.C.: Government Accounting Office.

Van De Ven, Andrew H. 1974. *Group Decision Making and Effectiveness.* Kent, Ohio: Kent State University Press.

Vicker, Geoffrey. 1980. "The Assumptions of Policy Analysis." *Policy Studies Journal,* Vol. 9, No. 4, pp. 552-558.

Von Neumann, John, and Morgenstern, O. 1947. *Theory of Games and Economic Behavior.* Princeton: Princeton University Press.

Vroom, Victor. 1964. *Work and Motivation.* New York: Wiley.

_____. 1965. *Motivation in Management.* New York: American Foundation for Management Research.

Vroom, Victor, and Yetton, P. 1973. "A New Look at Managerial Decision-Making." *Organizational Dynamics,* Vol. 1, No. 4, Spring.

Wacaster, C. T. 1979. "Jackson County: Local Norms, Federal Initiatives, and Administrator Performance." In Robert E. Herriett and Neil Gross (eds.), *The Dynamics of Planned Educational Change.* Berkeley, Calif.: McCutchan Publishing.

Watson, G. S. (trans.). 1956. "Plato and Zenophon." In Ernest Rhys (ed.), *Socratic Discourses.* New York: Dutton Publishing.

Weatherly, Richard A. 1979. *Reforming Special Education: Policy Implementation From State Level to Street Level.* Cambridge, Mass.: M.I.T. Press.

Weber, Max. 1947. *The Theory of Social and Economic Organizations.* A. M. Henderson, trans.; Talcott Parsons, ed. New York: Free Press.

Weick, Karl E. 1976. "Educational Organizations as Loosely Coupled Systems." *Administrative Science Quarterly,* Vol. 21, March, pp. 1-19.

_____. Undated. "Loosely Coupled Systems: Relaxed Meanings and Thick Interpretations." Mimeographed.

Wickert, F. R., and McFarland, D. E. (eds.). 1967. *Measuring Executive Effectiveness.* New York: Appleton-Century-Crofts.

Wildavsky, Aaron. 1974. *The Politics of the Budgeting Process.* Boston: Little, Brown.

Wildavsky, Aaron, and Hamman, Arthur. 1968. "Comprehensive Versus Incremental Budgeting in the Department of Agriculture." In Fremont J. Lyden and Ernest G. Miller (eds.), *Planning Programming Budgeting: A Systems Approach to Management.* Chicago: Markham.

Wilson, Charles, and Alexis, Marcus. 1964. "Basic Frameworks for Decisions." In William J. Gore and J. W. Dyson (eds.), *The Making of Decisions.* New York: Free Press.

Winkler, Robert L. 1972. *An Introduction to Bayesian Inference and Decision.* New York: Holt, Rinehart & Winston.

Wise, Arthur E. 1979. *Legislated Learning, the Bureaucratization of the American Classroom.* Berkeley, Calif.: University of California Press.

Worthen, Blaine R., and Sanders, James R. (eds.). 1973. *Educational Evaluation: Theory and Practice.* Worthington, Ohio: Charles A. Jones Publishing.

Young, Robert C. 1966. "Goals and Goal Setting." *Journal of the American Institute of Planning,* March, pp. 76-85.

Index